THE COOK'S ENCYCLOPEDIA OF

FRENCH COOKING

THE COOK'S ENCYCLOPEDIA OF

FRENCH COOKING

CAROLE CLEMENTS
ELIZABETH WOLF-COHEN

HERMES HOUSE

This edition published in 2003 by Hermes House

Hermes House is an imprint of
Anness Publishing Limited
Hermes House
88–89 Blackfriars Road
London SE1 8HA

A CIP catalogue record for this book is available from the British Library.

PUBLISHER: Joanna Lorenz
MANAGING EDITOR: Linda Fraser
COPY EDITOR: Christine Ingram
DESIGNER: Sheila Volpe
PHOTOGRAPHY AND STYLING: Amanda Heywood
FOOD FOR PHOTOGRAPHY: Elizabeth Wolf-Cohen assisted by Janet Brinkworth
PRODUCTION CONTROLLER: Don Campaniello

Previously published as *The French Recipe Cookbook & The Cook's Encyclopedia of French Cooking*

Printed and bound in China

1 3 5 7 9 10 8 6 4 2

NOTES

For all recipes, quantities are given in both metric and imperial measures and, where appropriate, measures are also given in standard cups and spoons. Follow one set, but not a mixture, because they are not interchangeable.

Standard spoon and cup measures are level.
1 tsp = 5ml, 1 tbsp = 15ml, 1 cup = 250ml/8fl oz

Australian standard tablespoons are 20ml. Australian readers should use 3 tsp in place of 1 tbsp for measuring small quantities of gelatine, cornflour, salt, etc.

Medium eggs are used unless otherwise stated.

The publishers would like to thank Sopexa UK for the Photographs appearing on pages 1, 6, 7, 8, 9, 11, 37, 65, 87, 117, 151, 187, 215.

Contents

The French and Their Food

The joys of the table are everything to the French and fundamental to their way of life. Food is a constant source of conversation, talked about everywhere, on the Metro, in shops, in the office and at the school gate. Mealtimes are sacrosanct – why do you think it is that at one o'clock, the traffic suddenly becomes much lighter? The French have their feet under the table.

In France, family meals are an occasion. An everyday event becomes a celebration of one of life's most basic pleasures, and special occasions, birthdays and holidays are lavishly enjoyed with food and wine.

It is therefore not surprising to learn that a French family spends a greater proportion of its budget on food than do many families elsewhere in the world. And money spent is rarely for convenience foods, but for top quality meat and poultry, fresh fish and shellfish and fine cheeses.

French cuisine is universally revered and is often seen as a benchmark for the cooking of other countries. But what makes it so special? Part of what distinguishes French cuisine is simply the attitude of the French towards food.

One element is the pride that the French have in their country, craftsmen and products. Chefs, cheesemakers, winemakers, pastry chefs and bakers are respected and even revered in a way unheard of elsewhere. At the foundation is a reverence for the raw material – the basic ingredient.

France is and always has been primarily an agricultural economy and fresh seasonal ingredients are widely available. In the past, the French housewife would shop twice a day for the two main meals. The constraints of modern life have brought change but it is characteristic that the French are

still prepared to spend time seeking out fine fresh products, rather than stocking up on processed food.

Similarly, the classic techniques of French cooking have been developed with a high regard for the ingredients, from the preparation of an onion to the cooking of exotic shellfish. The repertoire of techniques that forms the foundation of French cooking is not as extensive as you might think. Perhaps surprisingly, its variety and finesse rest on a relatively small number of basic techniques. For example, sautéed chicken breasts with a wine and cream sauce require essentially the same cooking method as pan-fried trout with a lemon and butter sauce. This book will help you

The French pride themselves on cooking with the freshest and best ingredients, like these eggs on a Breton stall (above). Shrimps netted by a fisherman (right) are likely to be eaten within a day.

gain a basic knowledge of these techniques, so you too can cook "the French way".

French cuisine is not just one style of cooking. In restaurants particularly, it covers a wide spectrum of food. At the top, *haute cuisine* restaurants have several chefs, a large staff and well-equipped professional kitchens to make the elaborate recipes and complex sauces that are beyond the capabilities of untrained cooks. Traditional home cooking, which is centred on hearty stews, quick sautés and comforting desserts, can also be found in small, family restaurants. Many visitors to France are as delighted with the food in these simple restaurants as in their more sophisticated counterparts. The common factor is the use of fresh ingredients and the pride and pleasure in making the most of them.

France is a land of variety and contrast, with a rich array of home-grown produce. Every region has its own specialities which reflect the local products and traditions. This regional food, *cuisine regionale*, has its roots in the home – cooking characterized by simple techniques and few ingredients – quite different from *haute cuisine*. Regional cuisine really came into its own after the First World War when popular French food writers such as Curnonsky began to document it, going miles in search of the best *cassoulet* or *choucroute*.

The basic respect for the ingredients which characterizes French cooking was behind the *nouvelle cuisine* movement. The term was coined by the journalists Henri Gault and Christian Millau in the 1970s, to describe the dramatic changes taking place in the preparation of restaurant food, including simplified procedures, reduced cooking times, constantly changing menus offering the best of the marketplace, an emphasis on creativity and a rejection of marinating and flour-based sauces, so that the essential characteristics of the ingredients could be fully appreciated. Since then, the excesses of the movement, like over-decorated plates and minute portions, have thankfully all but disappeared, but the benefits of emphasizing the natural ingredients have remained an important part of a more heart-warming style of cooking. Escoffier's watchword, "*faites simple*", "keep it simple", may be surprising to those who think of French food as complicated and elaborate, but the essence of French cooking is simplicity – bringing out the best in the ingredients.

The French style of serving a meal differs from many other countries and for foreigners part of the enjoyment of French food is in eating "the French way" – in separate courses. Whether it is simply a fresh egg perfectly fried in butter or an extravagantly rich layered meringue cake, each part of a meal is savoured separately.

Today, as in the past, most French people consider the midday meal the main one, although the demands of modern urban life make it more difficult to realize.

An informal family meal is likely to be two courses, a starter and main course, plus cheese and perhaps fresh fruit. If a dessert is served, the starter will be very light, but it is rarely omitted.

The starter sets the tone for the rest of the meal. Cooked vegetables, such as asparagus or artichokes with a flavourful dressing, or a slice of ham or pâté from the local *charcuterie*, are popular starters, as are composed salads or *crudités*. Soup has always been a traditional starter at supper, supper followed, perhaps, by a vegetable gratin or quiche. Egg

Geese wandering through a farmyard (above), a rustic weathered barn (right) and enthusiastic shoppers at a market (left) all capture the essence of country life in France.

and cheese dishes make more substantial starters and may also be served as a light lunch or as a main course for supper.

A rich or filling starter should be followed by a more spartan main course, such as steamed or poached fish. A plain green salad is often served with or after the main course, followed by a cheese course. Desserts are reserved for special meals and celebrations, and with the superb creations available in *pâtisseries*, a special dessert is more often bought than home-made.

Formal menus are more elaborate and offer five or sometimes more courses, each served with a wine to complement it. The meal might start with, for instance, a shellfish *hors d'oeuvre*, followed by a fish course, then a roast of meat or poultry, cheese and finally a dessert. *Petits fours*, small cakes and sweetmeats, might be offered with the coffee. Restaurants often feature a *menu de dégustation*, a sort of sampler meal with multiple small courses highlighting the chef's specialities.

Sauces are perhaps the best known elements of French cuisine. The union of good ingredients and a skilfully made sauce elevates the simplest of dishes. A sauce can be as quick and easy as deglazing a pan with a few tablespoons of wine, or more elaborate like Béarnaise. Either way, the point is to make the food taste even better.

A good sauce should enhance food and not disguise it and some thought must be given, as well, to balancing the courses. A starter of asparagus with a rich hollandaise should not be followed by chicken breasts with a creamy sauce – a simple pan-fried sole or grilled lamb chop would be more appropriate.

For the French, wine is an integral part of the meal. Just as a sauce is designed to complement the meat or vegetable it accompanies, so the wines are chosen to complement the whole meal. Many of the world's great wines come from France and French wine, like French cuisine, remains the standard for all others. In wine-producing regions people drink the wines of that area, and these wines almost invariably enhance the regional foods. In areas where wine is not produced, as in Normandy and Brittany, the local products – apples and pears – are made into other drinks, such as sparkling dry cider or Calvados.

You don't have to live in France to cook and eat "the French way". This book offers a tempting range of recipes from all over the country and these provide the key to unlocking the secrets of French cooking and enjoying it in your own home.

HUILE D'OLIVE

Soups and Salads

Soups and salads form two of the cornerstones of French cooking. Soup is the traditional evening meal – in fact, supper comes from the word *souper*, which means 'to take soup'. However, soups are also eaten at lunch and even at breakfast in some rural homes! Once merely a slice of bread with hot liquid, now the choice is immense and there are soups of every kind, from delicate consommés to hearty regional recipes. French salads are equally diverse, varying according to the seasons and regions. They range from the classic green salad to heartier combinations of vegetables, salad leaves, meat, poultry and fish.

FRENCH ONION SOUP

Soupe à l'Oignon Gratinée

In France, this standard bistro fare is served so frequently, it is simply referred to as gratinée.

SERVES 6–8

15g/½oz/1 tbsp butter
30ml/2 tbsp olive oil
4 large onions (about 675g/1½lb), thinly sliced
2–4 garlic cloves, finely chopped
5ml/1 tsp sugar
2.5ml/½ tsp dried thyme
30ml/2 tbsp plain flour
125ml/4fl oz/½ cup dry white wine
2 litres/3⅓ pints/8 cups chicken or beef stock
30ml/2 tbsp brandy (optional)
6–8 thick slices French bread, toasted
1 garlic clove
340g/12oz Gruyère or Emmenthal cheese, grated

1 ▼ In a large heavy saucepan or flameproof casserole, heat the butter and oil over a medium-high heat. Add the onions and cook for 10–12 minutes until they are softened and beginning to brown. Add the garlic, sugar and thyme and continue cooking over a medium heat for 30–35 minutes until the onions are well browned, stirring frequently.

2 ▲ Sprinkle over the flour and stir until well blended. Stir in the white wine and stock and bring to the boil. Skim off any foam that rises to the surface, then reduce the heat and simmer gently for 45 minutes. Stir in the brandy, if using.

3 ▲ Preheat the grill. Rub each slice of toasted French bread with the garlic clove. Place six or eight ovenproof soup bowls on a baking sheet and fill about three-quarters full with the onion soup.

4 ▲ Float a piece of toast in each bowl. Top with grated cheese, dividing it evenly, and grill about 15cm/6in from the heat for about 3–4 minutes until the cheese begins to melt and bubble.

Oriental Duck Consommé

Consommé de Canard Orientale

The Vietnamese community in France has had a profound influence on French cooking, as in this soup – light and rich at the same time, with its intriguing flavours of Southeast Asia.

Serves 4

1 duck carcass (raw or cooked), plus 2 legs or any giblets, trimmed of as much fat as possible
1 large onion, unpeeled, with root end trimmed
2 carrots, cut into 5cm/2in pieces
1 parsnip, cut into 5cm/2in pieces
1 leek, cut into 5cm/2in pieces
2–4 garlic cloves, crushed
2.5cm/1in piece fresh root ginger, peeled and sliced
15ml/1 tbsp black peppercorns
4–6 thyme sprigs, or 5ml/1 tsp dried thyme
1 small bunch coriander (6–8 sprigs), leaves and stems separated

For the garnish

1 small carrot
1 small leek, halved lengthways
4–6 shiitake mushrooms, thinly sliced
soy sauce
2 spring onions, thinly sliced
watercress or finely shredded Chinese leaves
freshly ground black pepper

1 ▲ Put the duck carcass, the legs or giblets, the onion, carrots, parsnip, leek and garlic in a large heavy saucepan or flameproof casserole. Add the ginger, peppercorns, thyme and coriander stems, cover with cold water and bring to the boil over a medium-high heat, skimming any foam that rises to the surface.

2 Reduce the heat and simmer gently for 1½–2 hours, then strain through a muslin-lined sieve into a bowl, discarding the bones and vegetables. Cool the stock and chill for several hours or overnight. Skim off any congealed fat and blot the surface with kitchen paper to remove any traces of fat.

3 ▲ To make the garnish, cut the carrot and leek into 5cm/2in pieces. Cut each piece lengthways in thin slices, then stack and slice into thin julienne strips. Place in a large saucepan with the mushrooms.

4 ▲ Pour over the stock and add a few dashes of soy sauce and some pepper. Bring to the boil over a medium-high heat, skimming any foam that rises to the surface. Adjust the seasoning. Stir in the spring onions and watercress or Chinese leaves. Ladle the consommé into warmed bowls and sprinkle with the coriander leaves.

Provençal vegetable soup

Soupe au Pistou

This satisfying soup captures all the flavours of a summer in Provence. The basil and garlic purée, pistou, *gives it extra colour and a wonderful aroma – so don't omit it.*

Serves 6–8

275g/10oz/1½ cups fresh broad beans, shelled, or 175g/6oz/¾ cup dried haricot beans, soaked overnight
2.5ml/½ tsp dried herbes de Provence
2 garlic cloves, finely chopped
15ml/1 tbsp olive oil
1 onion, finely chopped
2 small or 1 large leek, finely sliced
1 celery stick, finely sliced
2 carrots, finely diced
2 small potatoes, finely diced
120g/4oz French beans
1.2 litres/2 pints/5 cups water
120g/4oz/1 cup shelled garden peas, fresh or frozen
2 small courgettes, finely chopped
3 medium tomatoes, peeled, seeded and finely chopped
handful of spinach leaves, cut into thin ribbons
salt and freshly ground black pepper
sprigs of fresh basil, to garnish

For the pistou

1 or 2 garlic cloves, finely chopped
15g/½oz/½ cup (packed) basil leaves
60ml/4 tbsp grated Parmesan cheese
60ml/4 tbsp extra virgin olive oil

1 ▲ To make the *pistou*, put the garlic, basil and Parmesan cheese in a food processor and process until smooth, scraping down the sides once. With the machine running, slowly add the olive oil through the feed tube. Or, alternatively, pound the garlic, basil and cheese in a mortar and pestle and stir in the oil.

2 ▲ To make the soup, if using dried haricot beans, place them in a saucepan and cover with water. Boil vigorously for 10 minutes and drain. Place the par-boiled beans, or fresh beans if using, in a saucepan with the herbes de Provence and one of the garlic cloves. Add water to cover by 2.5cm/1in. Bring to the boil, reduce the heat and simmer over a medium-low heat until tender, about 10 minutes for fresh beans and about 1 hour for dried beans. Set aside in the cooking liquid.

3 ▲ In a large saucepan or flameproof casserole heat the oil. Add the onion and leeks, and cook for 5 minutes, stirring occasionally, until the onion just softens.

Cook's tip

Both the *pistou* and the soup can be made one or two days in advance and chilled. To serve, reheat gently, stirring occasionally.

4 ▲ Add the celery, carrots and the other garlic clove and cook, covered, for 10 minutes, stirring.

5 ▲ Add the potatoes, French beans and water, then season lightly with salt and pepper. Bring to the boil, skimming any foam that rises to the surface, then reduce the heat, cover and simmer gently for 10 minutes.

6 ▲ Add the courgettes, tomatoes and peas together with the reserved beans and their cooking liquid and simmer for 25–30 minutes, or until all the vegetables are tender. Add the spinach and simmer for 5 minutes. Season the soup and swirl a spoonful of *pistou* into each bowl. Garnish with basil and serve.

Cold Leek and Potato Soup

Vichyssoise

Serve this flavourful soup with a dollop of crème fraîche or soured cream and sprinkle with a few snipped fresh chives – or, on very special occasions, garnish with a small spoonful of caviar.

Serves 6–8

450g/1lb potatoes (about 3 large), peeled and cubed
1.5 litres/2½ pints/6 cups chicken stock
350g/12oz/4 medium leeks, trimmed
150ml/¼ pint/⅔ cup crème fraîche or soured cream
salt and freshly ground black pepper
45ml/3 tbsp snipped fresh chives, to garnish

1 Put the potatoes and stock in a saucepan or flameproof casserole and bring to the boil. Reduce the heat and simmer for 15–20 minutes.

2 ▼ Make a slit along the length of each leek and rinse well under cold running water. Slice thinly.

3 ▲ When the potatoes are barely tender, stir in the leeks. Season with salt and pepper and simmer for 10–15 minutes until the vegetables are soft, stirring occasionally. If the soup appears too thick, thin it down with a little more stock or water.

4 ▲ Purée the soup in a blender or food processor, in batches if necessary. If you would prefer a very smooth soup, pass it through a food mill or press through a coarse sieve. Stir in most of the cream, cool and then chill. To serve, ladle into chilled bowls and garnish with a swirl of cream and snipped chives.

Variation

To make a low-fat soup, use low-fat fromage frais instead of crème fraîche or soured cream. Alternatively, leave out the cream altogether and thin the soup with a little skimmed milk.

FRESH PEA SOUP

Potage Saint-Germain

This soup takes its name from a suburb of Paris where peas used to be cultivated in market gardens. If fresh peas are not available, use frozen peas, but thaw and rinse them before use.

SERVES 2–3

small knob of butter
2 or 3 shallots, finely chopped
400g/14oz/3 cups shelled fresh peas (from about 1.3kg/3lb garden peas) or thawed frozen peas
500ml/16fl oz/2 cups water
45–60ml/3–4 tbsp whipping cream (optional)
salt and freshly ground black pepper
croûtons or crumbled crisp bacon, to garnish

1 ▲ Melt the butter in a heavy saucepan or flameproof casserole. Add the shallots and cook for about 3 minutes, stirring occasionally.

2 ▲ Add the peas and water and season with salt and a little pepper. Cover and simmer for about 12 minutes for young or frozen peas and up to 18 minutes for large or older peas, stirring occasionally.

3 ▲ When the peas are tender, ladle them into a food processor or blender with a little of the cooking liquid and process until smooth.

4 ▼ Strain the soup into the saucepan or casserole, stir in the cream, if using, and heat through without boiling. Add seasoning and serve hot, garnished with croûtons or bacon.

Asparagus Soup with Crab *Crème d'Argenteuil au Crabe*

The word Argenteuil *in any French recipe almost always indicates asparagus, being the town in north central France famed for this superb seasonal delicacy.*

Serves 6–8

1.3kg/3lb fresh asparagus
30g/1oz/2 tbsp butter
1.5 litres/2½ pints/6 cups chicken stock
30ml/2 tbsp cornflour
125ml/4fl oz/½ cup whipping cream
salt and freshly ground black pepper
175–200g/6–7oz white crab meat, to garnish

1 Trim the woody ends from the bottom of the asparagus spears and cut the spears into 2.5cm/1in pieces.

2 ▼ Melt the butter in a heavy saucepan or flameproof casserole over a medium-high heat. Add the asparagus and cook for 5–6 minutes, stirring frequently, until they are bright green, but not browned.

3 ▲ Add the stock and bring to the boil over a high heat, skimming off any foam that rises to the surface. Simmer over a medium heat for 3–5 minutes until the asparagus is tender, yet crisp. Reserve 12–16 of the asparagus tips for garnishing. Season with salt and pepper, cover and continue cooking for about 15–20 minutes until very tender.

4 ▲ Purée the soup in a blender or food processor and pass the mixture through the fine blade of a food mill back into the saucepan. Bring the soup back to the boil over a medium-high heat. Blend the cornflour with 30–45ml/2–3 tbsp cold water and whisk into the boiling soup to thicken, then stir in the cream. Adjust the seasoning.

5 To serve, ladle the soup into bowls and top each with a spoonful of the crab meat and a few of the reserved asparagus tips.

Wild Mushroom Soup *Velouté de Champignons Sauvages*

In France, many people pick their own wild mushrooms, taking them to a chemist to be checked before using them in all sorts of delicious dishes. The dried mushrooms bring an earthy flavour to this soup, but use 175g/6oz fresh wild mushrooms instead when available.

Serves 6–8

30g/1oz dried wild mushrooms, such as morels, ceps or porcini
1.5 litres/2½ pints/6 cups chicken stock
30g/1oz/2 tbsp butter
2 onions, coarsely chopped
2 garlic cloves, chopped
900g/2lb button or other cultivated mushrooms, trimmed and sliced
2.5ml/½ tsp dried thyme
1.5ml/¼ tsp freshly grated nutmeg
30–45ml/2–3 tbsp plain flour
125ml/4fl oz/½ cup Madeira or dry sherry
125ml/4fl oz/½ cup crème fraîche or soured cream
salt and freshly ground black pepper
snipped fresh chives, to garnish

1 ▲ Put the dried mushrooms in a sieve and rinse well under cold running water, shaking to remove as much sand as possible. Place them in a saucepan with 250ml/8fl oz/1 cup of the stock and bring to the boil over a medium-high heat. Remove the pan from the heat and set aside for 30–40 minutes to soak.

2 Meanwhile, in a large heavy saucepan or flameproof casserole, melt the butter over a medium-high heat. Add the onions and cook for 5–7 minutes until they are well softened and just golden.

3 ▲ Stir in the garlic and fresh mushrooms and cook for 4–5 minutes until they begin to soften, then add the salt and pepper, thyme and nutmeg and sprinkle over the flour. Cook for 3–5 minutes, stirring frequently, until well blended.

4 ▲ Add the Madeira or sherry, the remaining chicken stock, the dried mushrooms and their soaking liquid and cook, covered, over a medium heat for 30–40 minutes until the mushrooms are very tender.

5 Purée the soup in batches in a blender or food processor. Strain it back into the saucepan, pressing firmly to force the purée through the sieve. Stir in the crème fraîche or soured cream and sprinkle with the snipped chives just before serving.

Cook's Tip

Serve the soup with a little extra cream swirled on top, if you like.

Summer Tomato Soup

Soupe de Tomates Fraîches

The success of this soup depends on having ripe, full-flavoured tomatoes, such as the oval plum variety, so make it when the tomato season is at its peak. It is equally delicious served cold.

Serves 4

15ml/1 tbsp olive oil
1 large onion, chopped
1 carrot, chopped
1kg/2¼lb ripe tomatoes, cored and quartered
2 garlic cloves, chopped
5 thyme sprigs, or 1.5ml/¼ tsp dried thyme
4 or 5 marjoram sprigs, or 1.5ml/¼ tsp dried marjoram
1 bay leaf
45ml/3 tbsp crème fraîche, soured cream or yogurt, plus a little extra to garnish
salt and freshly ground black pepper

1 Heat the olive oil in a large preferably stainless steel saucepan or flameproof casserole.

2 ▼ Add the onion and carrot and cook over a medium heat for 3–4 minutes, until just softened, stirring occasionally.

Variation

To serve the soup cold, omit the cream or yogurt and leave to cool, then chill.

3 ▲ Add the tomatoes, garlic and herbs. Reduce the heat and simmer, covered, for 30 minutes.

4 Pass the soup through a food mill or press through a sieve into the pan. Stir in the cream or yogurt and season. Reheat gently and serve garnished with a spoonful of cream or yogurt and a sprig of marjoram.

Pumpkin Soup

Crème de Citrouille

When the first frosts of autumn chill the air, large bright orange pumpkins are a vivid sight at local markets all over France and provide the basis for some warm and comforting soups.

Serves 6–8

30g/1oz/2 tbsp butter
1 large onion, chopped
2 shallots, chopped
2 medium potatoes, peeled and cubed
900g/2lb/6 cups cubed pumpkin
2 litres/3⅓ pints/8 cups chicken or vegetable stock
2.5ml/½ tsp ground cumin
pinch of freshly grated nutmeg
salt and freshly ground black pepper
fresh parsley or chives, to garnish

1 Melt the butter in a large saucepan. Add the onion and shallots to the pan and cook for 4–5 minutes until just softened.

2 ▲ Add the potatoes, pumpkin, stock and spices to the pan, and season with a little salt and black pepper. Reduce the heat to low and simmer, covered, for about 1 hour, stirring occasionally.

3 ▼ With a slotted spoon, transfer the cooked vegetables to a food processor and process until smooth, adding a little of the cooking liquid if needed. Return the purée to the pan and stir into the cooking liquid. Adjust the seasoning and reheat gently. Garnish with the fresh herbs.

Saffron Mussel Soup

Soupe de Moules Safranée

This is one of France's most delicious seafood soups – for day-to-day eating, the French would normally serve all the mussels in their shells. Serve with plenty of French bread.

Serves 4–6

40g/1½oz/3 tbsp unsalted butter
8 shallots, finely chopped
1 bouquet garni
5ml/1 tsp black peppercorns
350ml/12fl oz/1½ cups dry white wine
1kg/2¼lb mussels, scrubbed and debearded
2 medium leeks, trimmed and finely chopped
1 fennel bulb, finely chopped
1 carrot, finely chopped
several saffron strands
1 litre/1⅔ pints/4 cups fish or chicken stock
125ml/4fl oz/½ cup whipping cream
30–45ml/2–3 tbsp cornflour, blended with 45ml/3 tbsp cold water
125ml/4fl oz/½ cup whipping cream
1 medium tomato, peeled, seeded and finely chopped
30ml/2 tbsp Pernod (optional)
salt and freshly ground black pepper

1 ▲ In a large heavy pan, melt half the butter over a medium-high heat. Add half the shallots and cook for 1–2 minutes until softened but not coloured. Add the bouquet garni, peppercorns and white wine and bring to the boil. Add the mussels, cover tightly and cook over a high heat for 3–5 minutes, shaking the pan occasionally, until the mussels have opened.

2 With a slotted spoon, transfer the mussels to a bowl. Strain the cooking liquid through a muslin-lined sieve and reserve.

3 ▲ When the mussel shells are cool enough to handle, pull open and remove most of the mussels, adding any extra juices to the reserved liquid. Discard any closed mussels.

4 Rinse the saucepan and melt the remaining butter over a medium heat. Add the remaining shallots and cook for 1–2 minutes. Add the leeks, fennel, carrot and saffron and cook for 3–5 minutes until softened.

5 Stir in the reserved cooking liquid, bring to the boil and cook for 5 minutes until the vegetables are tender and the liquid is slightly reduced. Add the stock and bring to the boil, skimming any foam that rises to the surface. Season with salt, if needed, and black pepper and cook for a further 5 minutes.

6 ▲ Stir the blended cornflour into the soup. Simmer for 2–3 minutes until the soup is slightly thickened, then add the cream, mussels and chopped tomato. Stir in Pernod, if using, and cook for 1–2 minutes until hot, then serve at once.

Prawn Bisque

Bisque de Crevettes

The classic French method for making a bisque requires pushing the shellfish through a tamis, *or drum sieve. This is much simpler and the result is just as smooth.*

Serves 6–8

675g/1½lb small or medium cooked prawns in the shell
25ml/1½ tbsp vegetable oil
2 onions, halved and sliced
1 large carrot, sliced
2 celery sticks, sliced
2 litres/3⅓ pints/8 cups water
a few drops of lemon juice
30ml/2 tbsp tomato purée
bouquet garni
55g/2oz/4 tbsp butter
55g/2oz/⅓ cup plain flour
45–60ml/3–4 tbsp brandy
150ml/¼ pint/⅔ cup whipping cream
salt and white pepper

1 Remove the heads from the prawns and peel away the shells, reserving the heads and shells for the stock. Chill the peeled prawns.

2 ▲ Heat the oil in a large saucepan, add the prawn heads and shells and cook over a high heat, stirring frequently, until they start to brown. Reduce the heat to medium, add the onions, carrot and celery and fry gently, stirring occasionally, for about 5 minutes until the onions start to soften.

3 Add the water, lemon juice, tomato purée and bouquet garni. Bring the stock to the boil, then reduce the heat, cover and simmer gently for 25 minutes. Strain the stock through a sieve.

4 ▼ Melt the butter in a heavy saucepan over a medium heat. Stir in the flour and cook until just golden, stirring occasionally. Add the brandy and gradually pour in about half of the prawn stock, whisking vigorously until smooth, then whisk in the remaining liquid. Season with salt, if necessary, and white pepper. Reduce the heat, cover and simmer for 5 minutes, stirring frequently.

5 ▲ Strain the soup into a clean saucepan. Add the cream and a little extra lemon juice to taste, then stir in most of the reserved prawns and cook over a medium heat, stirring frequently, until hot. Serve at once, garnished with the reserved prawns.

Crudités

A colourful selection of raw vegetables, or crudités, *is often served in France as a quick and easy accompaniment to drinks or as small starters before lunch, especially in warm weather.*

The term *crudités* is used both for small pieces of vegetables served with a tasty dip and for a selection of vegetable salads presented in separate dishes. Country-style restaurants often feature a selection of *crudités* and sometimes a whole trolley of individual vegetables salads in small *raviers*, or shallow dishes, arrives. At a family lunch, at least two or three salads would be served. Their appeal lies in the use of fresh uncomplicated ingredients and a selection which offers visual and textural contrasts.

By choosing contrasting colours, any combination of vegetables, raw or lightly cooked, attractively arranged on a platter or in baskets and served with a tangy dip, such as *aïoli* or *tapenade*, can make a beautiful presentation. Allow 85–120g/3–4oz of each vegetable per person. Remember, leftovers can be used in soups or a stir-fry. Add fruits, cold meats or seafood and a pretty herb or flower garnish – anything goes as long as you like it.

Aïoli (Garlic mayonnaise)

Put 4 crushed garlic cloves (or more or less to taste) in a small bowl with a pinch of salt and crush with the back of a spoon. Add 2 egg yolks and beat for 30 seconds with an electric mixer until creamy. Beat in 250ml/8fl oz/1 cup extra virgin olive oil, by drops, until the mixture thickens. As it begins to thicken, the oil can be added in a thin stream until the mixture is thick. Thin the sauce with a little lemon juice and season to taste. Chill for up to 2 days; bring to room temperature and stir before serving.

Tapenade (Provençal olive paste)
Put 200g/7oz stoned black olives, 6 anchovy fillets, 30ml/2 tbsp capers, rinsed, 1 or 2 garlic cloves, 5ml/1 tsp fresh thyme leaves, 15ml/1 tbsp Dijon mustard, juice of half a lemon, freshly ground black pepper and, if you like, 15ml/1 tbsp brandy in a food processor fitted with the metal blade. Process for 15–30 seconds until smooth, scraping down the sides of the bowl. With the machine running, slowly pour in 60–90ml/4–6 tbsp extra virgin olive oil to make a smooth firm paste. Store in an airtight container.

Raw Vegetable Platter
Assiette de crudités

Serves 6–8

2 red and yellow peppers, sliced lengthways
225g/8oz fresh baby corn, blanched
1 chicory head (red or white), trimmed and leaves separated
175–225g/6–8oz thin asparagus, trimmed and blanched
small bunch radishes with small leaves attached, washed
175g/6oz cherry tomatoes, washed
12 quail's eggs, boiled for 3 minutes, drained, refreshed and peeled
aïoli *or* tapenade, *for dipping*

Arrange a selection of prepared vegetables, such as those above, on a serving plate. Cover with a damp tea towel until ready to serve.

Tomato and Cucumber Salad
Salade de tomates et concombre

Serves 4–6

1 medium cucumber, peeled and thinly sliced
30ml/2 tbsp white wine vinegar
90ml/3fl oz/⅓ cup crème fraîche or soured cream
30ml/2 tbsp chopped fresh mint
4 or 5 ripe tomatoes, sliced
salt and freshly ground black pepper

Place the cucumber in a bowl, sprinkle with a little salt and 15ml/ 1 tbsp of the vinegar and toss with 5 or 6 ice cubes. Chill for 1 hour to crisp, then rinse, drain and pat dry. Return to the bowl, add the cream, pepper and mint and stir to mix well. Arrange the tomato slices on a serving plate, sprinkle with the remaining vinegar, and spoon the cucumber slices into the centre.

Carrot and Orange Salad

Carottes rapées à l'orange

Serves 4–6

1 garlic clove, crushed
grated rind and juice of 1 unwaxed orange
30–45ml/2–3 tbsp groundnut oil
450g/1lb carrots, cut into very fine julienne strips
30–45ml/2–3 tbsp chopped fresh parsley
salt and freshly ground black pepper

Rub a bowl with the garlic and leave in the bowl. Add the orange rind and juice and salt and pepper. Whisk in the oil until blended then remove the garlic. Add the carrots, half of the parsley and toss well. Garnish with the remaining parsley.

MIXED GREEN SALAD *Salade de Mesclun*

Mesclun *is a ready-mixed Provençal green salad composed of several kinds of salad leaves and herbs. A typical combination might include rocket, radicchio, lamb's lettuce and curly endive with herbs such as chervil, basil, parsley and tarragon.*

SERVES 4–6

1 garlic clove, peeled
30ml/2 tbsp red wine or sherry vinegar
5ml/1 tsp Dijon mustard (optional)
75–120ml/5–8 tbsp extra virgin olive oil
200–225g/7–8oz mixed salad leaves and herbs
salt and freshly ground black pepper

VARIATION

Mesclun always contains some pungent leaves. When dandelion leaves are in season, they are usually found in the mixture, so use them when available.

1 Rub a large salad bowl with the garlic clove and leave in the bowl.

2 ▼ Add the vinegar, salt and pepper and mustard, if using. Stir to mix the ingredients and dissolve the salt, then whisk in the oil slowly.

3 ▲ Remove the garlic clove and stir the vinaigrette to combine. Add the salad leaves to the bowl and toss well. Serve the salad at once.

APPLE AND CELERIAC SALAD *Pomme et Céleri-rave Remoulade*

Celeriac, despite its coarse appearance, has a sweet and subtle flavour. Traditionally par-boiled in lemony water, in this salad it is served raw allowing its unique taste and texture come through.

SERVES 3–4

1 celeriac (about 675g/1½lb), peeled
10–15ml/2–3 tsp lemon juice
5ml/1 tsp walnut oil (optional)
1 apple,
45ml/3 tbsp mayonnaise
10ml/2 tsp Dijon mustard
15ml/1 tbsp chopped fresh parsley
salt and freshly ground black pepper

1 Using a food processor or coarse cheese grater, shred the celeriac. Alternatively, cut it very into thin julienne strips. Place the celeriac in a bowl and sprinkle with the lemon juice and the walnut oil, if using. Stir well to mix.

2 ▲ Peel the apple, if you like, cut into quarters and remove the core. Slice thinly crossways and toss with the celeriac.

3 ▼ Mix together the mayonnaise, mustard, parsley and salt and pepper to taste. Stir into the celeriac mixture and mix well. Chill for several hours until ready to serve.

PROVENÇAL SALAD *Salade Niçoise*

There are probably as many versions of this salad as there are cooks in Provence. With good French bread, this regional classic makes a wonderful summer lunch or light supper.

SERVES 4–6

225g/8oz French beans
450g/1lb new potatoes, peeled and cut into 2.5cm/1in pieces
white wine vinegar and olive oil, for sprinkling
1 small Cos or round lettuce, washed, dried and torn into bite-size pieces
4 ripe plum tomatoes, quartered
1 small cucumber, peeled, seeded and diced
1 green or red pepper, thinly sliced
4 hard-boiled eggs, peeled and quartered
24 Niçoise or black olives
225g/8oz can tuna in brine, drained
55g/2oz can anchovy fillets in olive oil, drained
basil leaves, to garnish
garlic croûtons, to serve

FOR THE ANCHOVY VINAIGRETTE
20ml/1 heaped tbsp Dijon mustard
55g/2oz can anchovy fillets in olive oil, drained
1 garlic clove, crushed
60ml/4 tbsp lemon juice or white wine vinegar
125ml/4fl oz/½ cup sunflower oil
125ml/4fl oz/½ cup extra virgin olive oil
freshly ground black pepper

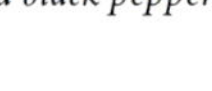

COOK'S TIP

To make garlic croûtons, thinly slice a French stick or cut larger loaves, such as rustic country bread, into 2.5cm/1in cubes. Place the bread in a single layer on a baking sheet and bake in a 180°C/350°F/Gas 4 oven for 7–10 minutes or until golden, turning once. Rub the toast with a garlic clove and serve hot, or cool then store in an airtight container to serve at room temperature.

1 ▲ First make the anchovy vinaigrette. Place the mustard, anchovies and garlic in a bowl and blend together by pressing the garlic and anchovies against the sides of the bowl. Season generously with pepper. Using a small whisk, blend in the lemon juice or wine vinegar. Slowly whisk in the sunflower oil in a thin stream and then the olive oil, whisking until the dressing is smooth and creamy.

2 Alternatively, put all the ingredients except the oil in a food processor fitted with the metal blade and process to combine. With the machine running, slowly add the oils in a thin stream until the vinaigrette is thick and creamy.

3 ▲ Drop the French beans into a large saucepan of boiling water and boil for 3 minutes until tender, yet crisp. Transfer the beans to a colander with a slotted spoon, then rinse under cold running water. Drain again and set aside.

4 ▲ Add the potatoes to the same boiling water, reduce the heat and simmer for 10–15 minutes until just tender, then drain. Sprinkle with a little vinegar and olive oil and a spoonful of the vinaigrette.

5 ▲ Arrange the lettuce on a platter, top with the tomatoes, cucumber and pepper, then add the French beans and potatoes.

6 ▲ Arrange the eggs, olives, tuna and anchovies on top and garnish with the basil leaves. Drizzle with the remaining vinaigrette and serve with garlic croûtons.

POTATO SALAD WITH SAUSAGE *Salade de Pommes de Terre*

This salad is often served in bistros and cafés as a starter. Sometimes the potatoes are served on their own, simply dressed with vinaigrette and perhaps accompanied by marinated herrings.

SERVES 4

450g/1lb small waxy potatoes
30–45ml/2–3 tbsp dry white wine
2 shallots, finely chopped
15ml/1 tbsp chopped fresh parsley
15ml/1 tbsp chopped fresh tarragon
175g/6oz cooked garlic sausage, such as saucisson à l'ail
a sprig of parsley, to garnish

FOR THE VINAIGRETTE
10ml/2 tsp Dijon mustard
15ml/1 tbsp tarragon vinegar or white wine vinegar
75ml/5 tbsp extra virgin olive oil
salt and freshly ground black pepper

1 ▼ In a medium saucepan, cover the potatoes with cold salted water and bring to the boil. Reduce the heat to medium and simmer for 10–12 minutes until tender. Drain the potatoes and refresh under cold running water.

2 Peel the potatoes if you like or leave in their skins and cut into 6mm/¼in slices. Sprinkle with the wine and shallots.

3 ▲ To make the vinaigrette, mix the mustard and vinegar in a small bowl, then whisk in the oil, 15ml/1 tbsp at a time. Season and pour over the potatoes.

4 ▲ Add the herbs to the potatoes and toss until well mixed.

5 ▲ Slice the sausage thinly and toss with the potatoes. Season with salt and pepper to taste and serve at room temperature, garnished with a parsley sprig.

Curly Endive Salad with Bacon *Frisée aux Lardons*

This country-style salad is popular all over France. When they are in season, dandelion leaves often replace the endive and the salad is sometimes sprinkled with chopped hard-boiled egg.

Serves 4

225g/8oz/6 cups curly endive or escarole leaves
75–90ml/5–6 tbsp extra virgin olive oil
175g/6oz piece of smoked bacon, diced, or 6 thick-cut smoked bacon rashers, cut crossways into thin strips
55g/2oz/1 cup white bread cubes
1 small garlic clove, finely chopped
15ml/1 tbsp red wine vinegar
10ml/2 tsp Dijon mustard
salt and freshly ground black pepper

1 ▲ Tear the lettuce into bite-size pieces and put in a salad bowl.

2 ▲ Heat 15ml/1 tbsp of the oil in a medium non-stick frying pan over a medium-low heat and add the bacon. Fry gently until well browned, stirring occasionally. Remove the bacon with a slotted spoon and drain on kitchen paper.

3 ▼ Add another 30ml/2 tbsp of oil to the pan and fry the bread cubes over a medium-high heat, turning frequently, until evenly browned. Remove the bread cubes with a slotted spoon and drain on kitchen paper. Discard any remaining fat.

4 ▲ Stir the garlic, vinegar and mustard into the pan with the remaining oil and heat until just warm, whisking to combine. Season to taste, then pour the dressing over the salad and sprinkle with the fried bacon and croûtons.

Mushroom Salad *Salade de Champignons à la Crème*

This simple refreshing salad is often served as part of a selection of vegetable salads, or crudités*. Leaving it to stand before serving brings out the inherent sweetness of the mushrooms.*

Serves 4

175g/6oz white mushrooms, trimmed
grated rind and juice of ½ lemon
about 30–45ml/2–3 tbsp crème fraîche or soured cream
salt and white pepper
15ml/1 tbsp snipped fresh chives, to garnish

Variation

If you prefer, toss the mushrooms in a little vinaigrette – made by whisking 60ml/4 tbsp walnut oil or extra virgin olive oil into the lemon juice.

1 ▼ Slice the mushrooms thinly and place in a bowl. Add the lemon rind and juice and the cream, adding a little more cream if needed. Stir gently to mix, then season with salt and pepper.

2 ▲ Leave the salad to stand for at least 1 hour, stirring occasionally.

3 Sprinkle the salad with snipped chives before serving.

Lamb's Lettuce and Beetroot *Salade de Mache aux Betteraves*

This salad makes a colourful and unusual starter – the delicate flavour of the lamb's lettuce is perfect with the tangy beetroot. If you like, sprinkle with chopped walnuts before serving.

Serves 4

150–175g/5–6 oz/3–4 cups lamb's lettuce, washed and roots trimmed
250g/½lb/3 or 4 small beetroot, cooked, peeled and diced
30ml/2 tbsp chopped fresh parsley

For the vinaigrette

30–45ml/2–3 tbsp white wine vinegar or lemon juice
20ml/1 heaped tbsp Dijon mustard
2 garlic cloves, finely chopped
2.5ml/½ tsp sugar
125ml/4fl oz/½ cup sunflower or grapeseed oil
125ml/4fl oz/½ cup crème fraîche or double cream
salt and freshly ground black pepper

1 First make the vinaigrette. Mix the vinegar or lemon juice, mustard, garlic, sugar, salt and pepper in a small bowl, then slowly whisk in the oil until the sauce thickens.

2 ▲ Lightly beat the crème fraîche or double cream to lighten it slightly, then whisk it into the dressing.

3 ▲ Toss the lettuce with a little of the vinaigrette and arrange on a serving plate or in a bowl.

4 Spoon the beetroot into the centre of the lettuce and drizzle over the remaining vinaigrette. Sprinkle with chopped parsley and serve at once.

Composed Salads

Salade Composée

Composed salads make perfect starters. They are light and colourful and lend themselves to endless variation – and the components can often be prepared ahead for quick assembly.

The French are masters of the composed salad. Any combination of ingredients can be used – let your imagination and your palate guide you. Arranged attractively on a plate or in a bowl, this type of salad offers contrasting flavours, textures and colours. Raw or cooked vegetables, fresh fruits, hard-boiled hen's or quail's eggs, smoked or cooked poultry, meat, fish or shellfish can all be used, but it is important that the dressing or other seasoning unite all the elements harmoniously.

Unlike a tossed salad such as *Salade de Mesclun*, in which the leaves are tossed together with a simple vinaigrette, the components of a composed salad are kept more separate. The ingredients might be arranged in groups, sometimes on a base of lettuce or other leaves, or simply arranged in circles on the plate. Composed salads, like *Salade Niçoise* or any of the following salads, are often served as a first course or a light main course, especially in warm weather. A tossed green salad is frequently eaten after the main course and is generally thought to cleanse the palate for the cheese course or dessert.

Prawn, Avocado and Citrus Salad
Salade de crevettes aux agrumes

SERVES 6
15ml/1 tbsp fresh lemon juice
15ml/1 tbsp fresh lime juice
15ml/1 tbsp clear honey
45ml/3 tbsp olive oil
30–45ml/2–3 tbsp walnut oil
30ml/2 tbsp snipped fresh chives
450g/1lb large cooked prawns, shelled and deveined
1 avocado, peeled, stoned and cut into tiny dice
1 pink grapefruit, peeled and segmented
1 large navel orange, peeled and segmented
30ml/2 tbsp toasted pine nuts (optional)
salt and freshly ground black pepper

Blend the lemon and lime juices, salt and pepper and honey in a small bowl. Slowly whisk in the olive oil, then the walnut oil to make a creamy sauce, then stir in the snipped chives. Arrange the prawns with the avocado pieces, grapefruit and orange segments on individual plates. Drizzle over the dressing and sprinkle with the toasted pine nuts, if using.

Smoked Salmon Salad with Dill
Salade de saumon fumé à l'aneth

SERVES 4
30ml/2 tbsp fresh lemon juice
125ml/4fl oz/½ cup extra virgin olive oil
30ml/2 tbsp fresh chopped dill, plus a few sprigs for garnishing
225g/8oz smoked salmon, thinly sliced
1 fennel bulb, thinly sliced
1 medium cucumber, seeded and cut into julienne strips
black pepper
caviar, to garnish (optional)

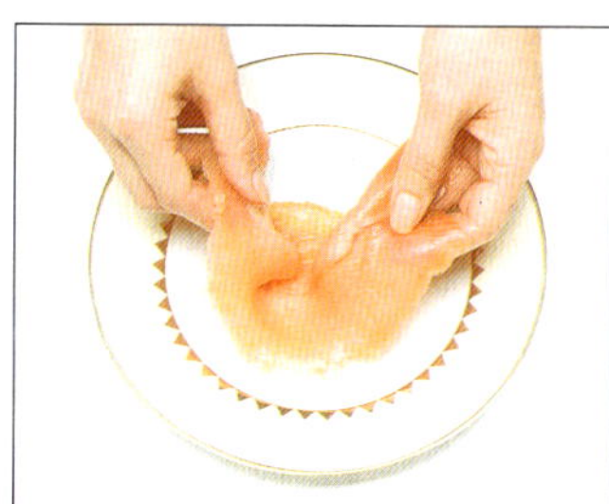

Arrange the salmon slices on four individual plates and arrange the slices of fennel on top, then scatter over the cucumber julienne strips. Mix together the lemon juice and pepper in a small bowl. Slowly whisk in the olive oil to make a creamy vinaigrette. Stir in the chopped dill. Spoon a little vinaigrette over the fennel and cucumber. Drizzle the remaining vinaigrette over the salmon and garnish with sprigs of dill. Top each salad with a spoonful of caviar, if you like.

Chicory Salad with Roquefort
Salade aux endives et au Roquefort

SERVES 4
30ml/2 tbsp red wine vinegar
5ml/1 tsp Dijon mustard
60ml/2fl oz/¼ cup walnut oil
15–30ml/1–2 tbsp sunflower oil
2 chicory heads, white or red
1 celery heart or 4 celery sticks, peeled and cut into julienne strips
85g/3oz/1 cup walnut halves, lightly toasted
30ml/2 tbsp chopped fresh parsley
125g/4oz Roquefort cheese, crumbled
salt and freshly ground black pepper
fresh parsley sprigs, to garnish

Whisk together the vinegar, mustard, salt and pepper to taste in a small bowl. Slowly whisk in the walnut oil, then the sunflower oil. Arrange the chicory on individual plates. Scatter over the celery, walnut halves and parsley. Crumble equal amounts of Roquefort cheese over each plate and drizzle a little vinaigrette over each.

VEGETABLES AND SIDE DISHES

If you visit any French market, you will be struck by the abundance of fresh vegetables. The selection will depend on the region and the time of year, but the French cook can always make the most of what's available. Vegetables are so highly regarded that, except for potatoes, they are very often served on a separate plate, or even as a separate course, so that they can be savoured and appreciated for their own sake. In many homes, a family lunch would also include vegetables as a starter – this might be in the form of *crudités*, as a colourful composed salad, or cooked and served with a sauce.

ARTICHOKES WITH VINAIGRETTE *Artichauts Vinaigrette*

The French enjoy artichokes prepared in many different ways. Simply cooked and eaten leaf by leaf is one of the best ways to savour the delicate flavour of the large Brittany artichokes.

SERVES 2

2 globe artichokes (about 250–350g/ 9–12oz each)
½ lemon
FOR THE VINAIGRETTE
1 shallot, very finely chopped
7.5ml/1½ tsp Dijon mustard
10ml/2 tsp lemon juice
30ml/2 tbsp extra virgin olive oil
30ml/2 tbsp vegetable oil
salt and freshly ground black pepper

1 Cut off about 4cm/1½in from the top of each artichoke. Using kitchen scissors, trim the tops of the remaining leaves to remove the sharp points and browned edges. Rub the cut surfaces with lemon juice to prevent discoloration, then cut the stem level with the base.

2 ▼ Wrap each artichoke in microwave clear film and stand on a large plate in the microwave or place directly on to the turntable. Microwave on High (full power) for about 10 minutes (7 minutes for one) until tender when the base is pressed; continue cooking at 1 minute intervals, if necessary. Leave to stand for 5 minutes, then prick the film to release the steam and unwrap.

3 ▲ Leave the artichokes to cool slightly, then, using a small sharp spoon, scrape out the "choke" (the prickly inner leaves and the fuzzy layer underneath).

4 ▲ To make the vinaigrette, place the shallot, mustard, lemon juice and salt and pepper in a small bowl and stir to mix. Gradually add the oil, 15ml/1 tbsp at a time, whisking until thickened.

5 Fill the centre of each artichoke with the vinaigrette and serve.

COOK'S TIP

Cooking artichokes in the microwave saves a lot of bother. Otherwise, cook them in a large pan of boiling water with a few tablespoons each of vinegar and flour, with a heat resistant plate resting on top of them to keep them submerged.

Stuffed Artichoke Bottoms *Fonds d'Artichauts aux Duxelles*

This recipe is a partnership of two favourites of classic French cuisine: duxelles *– the savoury chopped mushrooms used in the filling – and the artichoke with its distinctive flavour.*

Serves 4–6

225g/8oz button mushrooms
15g/½oz/1 tbsp butter
2 shallots, finely chopped
55g/2oz full- or medium-fat soft cheese
30ml/2 tbsp chopped walnuts
45ml/3 tbsp grated Gruyère cheese
4 large or 6 small artichoke bottoms (from cooked artichokes, leaves and choke removed, or cooked frozen or canned artichoke bottoms)
salt and freshly ground black pepper
fresh parsley sprigs, to garnish

1 ▲ Wipe or rinse the mushrooms and pat dry. Put them in a food processor fitted with the metal blade and pulse until finely chopped.

2 ▲ Melt the butter in a non-stick frying pan and cook the shallots over a medium heat for 2–3 minutes until just softened. Add the mushrooms, raise the heat slightly, and cook for 5–7 minutes until they have rendered and re-absorbed their liquid and are almost dry, stirring frequently. Season with salt and pepper.

3 Preheat the oven to 200°C/400°F/Gas 6. Lightly grease a shallow baking tin or dish.

4 ▼ In a small bowl, combine the soft cheese and mushrooms. Add the walnuts and half the grated cheese.

5 ▲ Divide the mushroom mixture among the artichokes bottoms and arrange them in the baking tin or dish. Sprinkle over the remaining cheese and bake for 12–15 minutes, or until bubbly and browned. Serve hot, garnished with parsley sprigs.

WARM LEEKS WITH VINAIGRETTE *Poireaux à la Vinaigrette*

In France, leeks are sometimes called "poor man's asparagus", as they are cooked in similar ways and, like asparagus, are very good to eat. Use tender baby leeks if you can find them.

SERVES 6

12 small leeks (about 1.3kg/3lb)
2 hard-boiled eggs
15ml/1 tbsp Dijon mustard
30ml/2 tbsp white wine vinegar or lemon juice
90ml/6 tbsp sunflower oil
90ml/6 tbsp extra virgin olive oil, plus more if needed
salt and freshly ground black pepper
15–30ml/1–2 tbsp snipped fresh chives, to garnish

1 ▼ Remove the dark tough outer leaves of the leeks, then cut the leeks to the same length, and trim the dark green tops. Trim the root end, leaving enough to hold the leek together, then split the top half of the leeks lengthways and rinse well under cold running water.

2 ▲ Lay the leeks flat in a large frying pan, pour over enough boiling water to just cover them and add a little salt. Cook the leeks over a medium-high heat for 7–10 minutes until just tender. Carefully transfer to a large colander to drain, then lay the leeks on a tea towel and press them gently to remove as much liquid as possible.

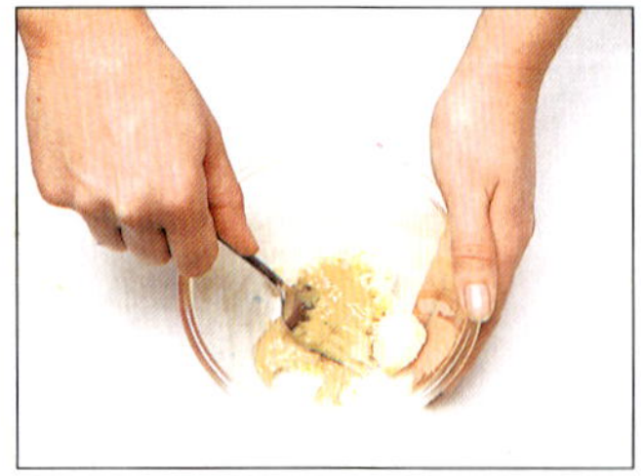

3 ▲ In a bowl, mash together the hard-boiled egg yolks and mustard to form a smooth paste. Season with salt and pepper and add the vinegar or lemon juice stirring until smooth. Slowly whisk in the sunflower oil, then the olive oil to make a thick creamy vinaigrette.

4 Arrange the leeks in a serving dish and pour over the vinaigrette while the leeks are still warm. Chop the egg whites and sprinkle them over the leeks, then scatter over the snipped chives and serve warm or at room temperature.

Asparagus with Orange Sauce

Asperges Sauce Maltaise

The white asparagus found in France is considered a delicacy by many, although it doesn't have the intense flavour of the green. White and large green spears are best peeled.

Serves 6

175g/6oz/¾ cup unsalted butter, diced
3 egg yolks
15ml/1 tbsp cold water
15ml/1 tbsp fresh lemon juice
grated rind and juice of 1 unwaxed orange
salt and cayenne pepper, to taste
30–36 thick asparagus spears
a few shreds of orange rind, to garnish

1 ▲ Melt the butter in a small saucepan over a low heat; do not boil. Skim off any foam and set aside.

2 ▲ In a heatproof bowl set over a saucepan of barely simmering water or in the top of a double boiler, whisk together the egg yolks, water, lemon juice, 15ml/1 tbsp of the orange juice and season with salt. Place the saucepan or double boiler over a very low heat and whisk constantly until the mixture begins to thicken and the whisk begins to leave tracks on the base of the pan. Remove the pan from the heat.

3 Whisk in the melted butter, drop by drop until the sauce begins to thicken, then pour it in a little more quickly, leaving behind the milky solids at the base of the pan. Whisk in the orange rind and 30–60ml/2–4 tbsp of the orange juice. Season with salt and cayenne pepper and keep warm, stirring occasionally.

4 ▲ Cut off the tough ends from the asparagus spears and trim to the same length. If peeling, hold each spear gently by the tip, then using a vegetable peeler, strip off the peel and scales from just below the tip to the end. Rinse in cold water.

5 Fill a large deep frying pan or wok with 5cm/2in of water and bring to the boil over a medium-high heat. Add the asparagus and bring back to the boil, then simmer for 4–7 minutes, until just tender.

6 Carefully transfer the spears to a large colander to drain, then lay them on a tea towel and pat dry. Arrange on a large serving platter or individual plates and spoon over a little sauce. Scatter the orange rind over the sauce and serve at once.

Cook's tip

This sauce is a kind of hollandaise and needs gentle treatment. If the egg yolk mixture thickens too quickly, remove from the heat and plunge the base of the pan into cold water to prevent the sauce from curdling. The sauce should keep over hot water for 1 hour, but don't let it get too hot.

GLAZED CARROTS AND TURNIPS *Navets à la Nivernaise*

In France when a dish is described on a menu as "à la nivernaise", it indicates the presence of carrots and onions. Here the addition of turnips adds a bitter-sweet contrast.

SERVES 6

40g/1½oz/3 tbsp butter
450g/1lb baby carrots, well-scrubbed, or medium carrots, cut into 2.5cm/1in sticks
450g/1lb young turnips, peeled and cut into quarters or eighths
225g/½lb baby onions, peeled
125ml/4fl oz/½ cup beef or chicken stock or water
15–30ml/1–2 tbsp sugar
1.5ml/¼ tsp dried thyme
15–30ml/1–2 tbsp chopped fresh parsley

1 In a large heavy frying pan, melt 30g/1oz/2 tbsp of the butter over a medium heat. Add the carrots, turnips and onions and toss to coat, then add the stock or water and stir in the sugar and thyme.

2 ▲ Bring the vegetables to the boil over a medium-high heat, then cover and simmer over a medium heat for 8–10 minutes until the vegetables begin to soften, shaking the pan occasionally to prevent the vegetables sticking. Check the pan once or twice during cooking and add a little more liquid if needed.

3 ▼ Uncover the pan and increase the heat to evaporate any remaining liquid, stirring frequently, until vegetables are lightly coated with the glaze. Add the remaining butter and the chopped parsley to the pan and stir until the butter melts.

CREAMY SPINACH PURÉE *Purée d'Epinards*

Crème fraîche, the thick French soured cream, or béchamel sauce usually give this spinach recipe its creamy richness, but try this quick, light alternative.

SERVES 4

675g/1½lb leaf spinach, stems removed
120g/4oz full- or medium-fat soft cheese
milk (if needed)
freshly grated nutmeg
salt and freshly ground black pepper

1 Rinse the spinach, spin or shake lightly and place in a deep frying pan or wok with just the water clinging to the leaves. Cook, uncovered, over a medium heat for 3–4 minutes until wilted. Drain the spinach in a colander or large sieve, pressing with the back of a spoon; the spinach doesn't need to be completely dry.

2 ▼ In a food processor fitted with the metal blade, purée the spinach and soft cheese until well blended, then transfer to a bowl. If the purée is too thick to fall easily from a spoon, add a little milk, spoonful by spoonful.

3 ▲ Season the spinach with salt, pepper and nutmeg. Transfer the spinach to a heavy pan and reheat gently over a low heat.

Cabbage Charlotte *Charlotte de Chou et de Pommes de Terre*

This delicious dish takes its name from the steep-sided container with heart-shaped handles in which it is cooked, but any straight-sided dish, such as a soufflé dish, will do.

Serves 6

450g/1lb green or savoy cabbage
30g/1oz/2 tbsp butter
1 medium onion, chopped
550g/1¼lb potatoes, peeled and quartered
1 large egg, beaten
15–30ml/1–2 tbsp milk, if needed
salt and freshly ground black pepper

1 Preheat the oven to 190°C/375°F/Gas 5. Lightly butter a 1.2 litre/2 pint/5 cup charlotte mould. Line the base with greaseproof paper and butter again.

2 Bring a large saucepan of salted water to the boil. Remove 5–6 large leaves from the cabbage and add to the pan. Cook the leaves for about 2 minutes until softened and bright green, then plunge them into cold water. Chop the remaining cabbage.

3 Melt the butter in a heavy frying pan and cook the onion for 2–3 minutes until just softened. Stir in the chopped cabbage and cook, covered, over a medium heat for 10–15 minutes until tender and pale golden, stirring frequently.

4 ▲ Put the potatoes in a large saucepan and add enough cold water to cover. Salt the water generously and bring to the boil over a medium-high heat. Cook until the potatoes are tender, then drain. Mash them with the beaten egg and a little milk, if needed, until smooth and creamy, then stir in the cabbage mixture. Season with salt and pepper.

5 ▲ Dry the cabbage leaves and cut out the thickest part of the centre vein. Use the leaves to line the mould, saving one leaf for the top. Spoon the potato mixture into the dish, smoothing it evenly, then cover with the remaining cabbage leaf. Cover tightly with foil. Put the mould in a shallow roasting tin or a baking dish and pour in boiling water to come halfway up the side of the mould. Bake for 40 minutes.

6 To serve, remove the foil and place a serving plate over the mould. Holding the plate tightly against the mould, turn over together. Lift off the mould and peel off the paper.

Braised Red Cabbage

Chou Rouge Braisé

The combination of red wine vinegar and sugar gives this dish a sweet, yet tart flavour. In France it is often served with game, but it is also delicious with pork, duck or cold sliced meats.

Serves 6–8

30ml/2 tbsp vegetable oil
2 medium onions, thinly sliced
2 eating apples, peeled, cored and thinly sliced
1 head red cabbage (about 900g–1.2kg/2–2½lb), trimmed, cored, halved and thinly sliced
60ml/4 tbsp red wine vinegar
15–30ml/1–2 tbsp sugar
1.5ml/¼ tsp ground cloves
5–10ml/1–2 tsp mustard seeds
55g/2oz/⅓ cup raisins or currants
about 125ml/4fl oz/½ cup red wine or water
15–30ml/1–2 tbsp redcurrant jelly (optional)
salt and freshly ground black pepper

1 ▲ In a large stainless steel saucepan or flameproof casserole, heat the oil over a medium heat. Add the onions and cook for 7–10 minutes until golden.

2 ▲ Stir in the apples and cook, stirring, for 2–3 minutes until they are just softened.

3 ▲ Add the cabbage, red wine vinegar, sugar, cloves, mustard seeds, raisins or currants, red wine or water and salt and pepper, stirring until well mixed. Bring to the boil over a medium-high heat, stirring occasionally.

4 ▼ Cover and cook over a medium-low heat for 35–40 minutes until the cabbage is tender and the liquid is just absorbed, stirring occasionally. Add a little more red wine or water if the pan boils dry before the cabbage is tender. Just before serving, stir in the redcurrant jelly, if using, to sweeten and glaze the cabbage.

FESTIVE BRUSSELS SPROUTS *Choux de Bruxelles Braisées*

In this recipe Brussels sprouts are braised with chestnuts, which are very popular in France.

SERVES 4–6

225g/½lb chestnuts
125ml/4fl oz/½ cup milk
550g/1¼lb/4 cups small tender Brussels sprouts
30g/1oz/2 tbsp butter
1 shallot, finely chopped
30–45ml/2–3 tbsp dry white wine or water

COOK'S TIP

Fresh chestnuts have a wonderful texture and flavour, but bottled or canned unsweetened whole chestnuts make an adequate substitute. They are available in delicatessens and some large supermarkets.

1 Using a small knife, score a cross in the base of each chestnut. Over a medium-high heat, bring a saucepan of water to the boil, drop in the chestnuts and boil for 6–8 minutes. Remove the pan from heat.

2 ▲ Using a slotted spoon, remove a few chestnuts, leaving the others immersed in water until ready to peel. Holding them in a tea towel, remove the outer shell with a knife and then peel off the inner skin.

3 Rinse the pan, return the peeled chestnuts to it and add the milk. Top up with enough water to completely cover the chestnuts. Simmer over a medium heat for 12–15 minutes until the chestnuts are just tender. Drain and set aside.

4 Remove any wilted or yellow leaves from the Brussels sprouts. Trim the root end but leave intact or the leaves will separate. Using a small knife, score a cross in the base of each sprout so they cook evenly.

5 ▲ In a large heavy frying pan, melt the butter over a medium heat. Stir in the chopped shallot and cook for 1–2 minutes until just softened, then add the Brussels sprouts and wine or water. Cook, covered, over a medium heat for 6–8 minutes, shaking the pan and stirring occasionally, adding a little more water if necessary.

6 ▲ Add the poached chestnuts and toss gently to combine, then cover and cook for 3–5 minutes more until the chestnuts and Brussels sprouts are tender.

French Beans with Tomatoes *Haricots Verts à la Provençale*

This colourful combination of Provençal flavours makes a pleasant change from plain green beans. Served cool or at room temperature, it is good as a starter or hors d'oeuvre.

Serves 4

450g/1lb ripe tomatoes
15ml/1 tbsp olive oil
1 shallot, finely chopped
1 or 2 garlic cloves, very finely chopped
225g/½lb French beans, trimmed and cut into 2 or 3 pieces
30ml/2 tbsp chopped fresh basil
salt and freshly ground black pepper

1 ▲ Bring a large saucepan of water to the boil. Score a shallow cross in the base of each tomato and plunge them into the boiling water for about 45 seconds, then plunge into cold water. Peel off the skins, halve the tomatoes and scoop out and discard the seeds. Chop coarsely.

2 ▲ Heat the oil in a heavy saucepan over a medium heat, add the shallot and garlic and cook for 2–3 minutes until just softened.

3 ▼ Add the chopped tomatoes and continue cooking for about 10 minutes until the liquid has evaporated and the tomatoes are soft, stirring frequently. Season with salt and pepper.

4 ▲ Bring a large saucepan of salted water to the boil, then add the beans and cook for 4–6 minutes until just tender. Drain the beans and stir into the tomato mixture, then cook for 1–2 minutes until heated through. Serve immediately or, if preferred, allow to cool for an hour or two and serve at room temperature.

PEAS WITH LETTUCE AND ONION *Petits Pois à la Française*

Fresh peas vary enormously in the time they take to cook – the tastiest and sweetest will be young and just picked. Frozen peas normally need less cooking time than fresh.

SERVES 4–6

15g/½oz/1 tbsp butter
1 small onion, finely chopped
1 small round lettuce
450g/1lb/3½ cups shelled fresh peas (from about 1.5kg/3½lb peas), or thawed frozen peas
45ml/3 tbsp water
salt and freshly ground black pepper

1 Melt the butter in a heavy saucepan. Add the onion and cook over a medium-low heat for about 3 minutes until just softened.

2 ▼ Cut the lettuce in half through the core, then place cut side down on a board and slice into thin strips. Place the lettuce strips on top of the onion and add the peas and water. Season lightly with salt and pepper.

3 ▲ Cover the pan tightly and cook the lettuce and peas over a low heat until the peas are tender – fresh peas will take 10–20 minutes, frozen peas about 10 minutes.

BROAD BEANS WITH CREAM *Fèves à la Crème*

In France, tiny new broad beans are eaten raw with a little salt, just like radishes. More mature beans are usually cooked and skinned, revealing the bright green kernel inside.

SERVES 4–6

450g/1lb shelled broad beans (from about 2kg/4½lb broad beans)
90ml/6 tbsp crème fraîche or whipping cream
salt and freshly ground black pepper
finely snipped chives, to garnish

1 ▼ Bring a large pan of salted water to the boil over a medium-high heat and add the beans.

2 Bring back to the boil, then reduce the heat slightly and boil the beans gently for about 8 minutes until just tender. Drain and refresh in cold water, then drain again.

3 ▲ To remove the skins, make an opening along one side of each bean with the tip of a knife and gently squeeze out the kernel.

4 ▲ Put the skinned beans in a saucepan with the cream and seasoning, cover and heat through gently. Sprinkle with the snipped chives and serve at once.

VARIATION

If you can find them, fresh flageolet or lima beans may be served in the same way.

LENTILS WITH BACON

Lentilles Braisées aux Lardons

The best lentils grown in France come from Le Puy, in the Auvergne. They are very small and the colour of dark slate – look for them in delicatessens and large supermarkets.

SERVES 6–8

450g/1lb/2½ cups brown or green lentils, well rinsed and picked over
15ml/1 tbsp olive oil
225g/½lb bacon, diced
1 onion, finely chopped
2 garlic cloves, finely chopped
2 tomatoes, peeled, seeded and chopped
2.5ml/½ tsp dried thyme
1 bay leaf
about 350ml/12fl oz/1½ cups beef or chicken stock
30–45ml/2–3 tbsp double cream (optional)
salt and freshly ground black pepper
15–30ml/1–2 tbsp chopped fresh parsley, to garnish

1 ▼ Put the lentils in a large saucepan and cover with cold water. Bring to the boil over a high heat and boil gently for 15 minutes. Drain and set aside.

2 In a heavy frying pan, heat the oil over a medium heat. Add the bacon and cook for 5–7 minutes until crisp, then transfer the bacon to a plate.

3 ▲ Stir the onion into the fat in the pan and cook for 2–3 minutes until just softened. Add the garlic and cook for 1 minute, then stir in the tomatoes, thyme, salt and pepper, bay leaf and lentils.

4 ▲ Add the stock and cover the pan. Cook over a medium-low heat for 25–45 minutes, until the lentils are just tender, stirring occasionally. Add a little more stock or water to the pan, if needed.

5 ▲ Uncover the pan and allow any excess liquid to evaporate. Add the reserved bacon, and cream, if using, and heat through for 1–2 minutes. Serve hot, with a scattering of chopped parsley on top.

FRENCH SCALLOPED POTATOES *Pommes de Terre Dauphinoise*

These potatoes taste far richer than you would expect even with only a little cream – they are delicious with just about everything, but in France, they are nearly always served with roast lamb.

SERVES 6

1kg/2¼lb potatoes
900ml/1½ pints/3⅔ cups milk
pinch of freshly grated nutmeg
1 bay leaf
15–30ml/1–2 tbsp butter, softened
2 or 3 garlic cloves, very finely chopped
45–60ml/3–4 tbsp crème fraîche or whipping cream (optional)
salt and freshly ground black pepper

1 ▲ Preheat the oven to 180°C/350°F/Gas 4. Cut the potatoes into fairly thin slices.

2 ▲ Put the potatoes in a large saucepan and pour over the milk, adding more to cover if needed. Add the salt and pepper, nutmeg and the bay leaf. Bring slowly to the boil over a medium heat and simmer for about 15 minutes until the potatoes just start to soften, but are not completely cooked, and the milk has thickened.

3 ▼ Generously butter a 36cm/14in oval gratin dish or a 2 litre/3¼ pint/8 cup shallow baking dish and sprinkle the garlic over the base.

COOK'S TIP

If cooked ahead, this dish will keep hot in a low oven for an hour or so, if necessary, without suffering; moisten the top with a little extra cream, if you like.

4 ▲ Using a slotted spoon, transfer the potatoes to the gratin or baking dish. Taste the milk and adjust the seasoning, then pour over enough of the milk to come just to the surface of the potatoes, but not cover them. Spoon a thin layer of cream over the top, or, if you prefer, add more of the thickened milk to cover.

5 Bake the potatoes for about 1 hour until the milk is absorbed and the top is a deep golden brown.

Sautéed Potatoes

Pommes de Terre Sautées au Romarin

These rosemary-scented, crisp golden potatoes are a favourite in French households.

Serves 6

1.3kg/3lb baking potatoes
60–90ml/4–6 tbsp oil, bacon dripping or clarified butter
2 or 3 fresh rosemary sprigs, leaves removed and chopped
salt and freshly ground black pepper

1 Peel the potatoes and cut into 2.5cm/1in pieces. Place them in a bowl, cover with cold water and leave to soak for 10–15 minutes. Drain, rinse and drain again, then dry thoroughly in a tea towel.

2 In a preferably non-stick large heavy frying pan or wok, heat about 60ml/4 tbsp of the oil, dripping or butter over a medium-high heat, until very hot, but not smoking.

3 ▲ Add the potatoes and cook for 2 minutes without stirring so that they seal completely and brown on one side.

4 Shake the pan and toss the potatoes to brown on another side and continue to stir and shake the pan until potatoes are evenly browned on all sides. Season with salt and pepper.

5 ▼ Add a little more oil, dripping or butter and continue cooking the potatoes over a medium-low to low heat for 20–25 minutes until tender when pierced with a knife, stirring and shaking the pan frequently. About 5 minutes before the end of cooking, sprinkle the potatoes with the chopped rosemary.

Straw Potato Cake

Pommes Paillasson

These potatoes are so named in France because of their resemblance to a woven straw doormat. You could make several small cakes instead of a large one – just adjust the cooking time accordingly.

Serves 4

450g/1lb baking potatoes
25ml/1½ tbsp melted butter
15ml/1 tbsp vegetable oil, plus more if needed
salt and freshly ground black pepper

1 Peel the potatoes and grate them coarsely, then immediately toss them with the melted butter and season with salt and pepper.

2 ▲ Heat the oil in a large frying pan. Add the potato mixture and press down to form an even layer that covers the pan. Cook over a medium heat for 7–10 minutes until the base is well browned.

3 Loosen the potato cake by shaking the pan or running a thin palette knife under it.

4 ▼ To turn it over, invert a large baking tray over the frying pan and holding it tightly against the pan, turn them both over together. Lift off the frying pan, return it to the heat and add a little oil if it looks dry. Slide the potato cake into the frying pan and continue cooking until crisp and browned on both sides. Serve hot.

Salines
DE
Guérande
LE SEL DE LA VIE

Garlic Mashed Potatoes *Purée de Pommes de Terre à l'Ail*

These creamy mashed potatoes are perfect with all kinds of roast or sautéed meats – and although it seems a lot of garlic, the flavour is sweet and subtle when cooked in this way.

Serves 6–8

2 garlic bulbs, separated into cloves, unpeeled
120g/4oz/½ cup unsalted butter
1.3kg/3lb baking potatoes
125–175ml/4–6fl oz/½–¾ cup milk
salt and white pepper

Cook's tip

This recipe makes a very light, creamy purée. Use less milk to achieve a firmer purée, more for a softer purée. Be sure the milk is almost boiling or it will cool the potato mixture. Keep the potato purée warm in a bowl over simmering water.

1 Bring a small saucepan of water to the boil over a high heat. Add the garlic cloves and boil for 2 minutes, then drain and peel.

2 ▲ In a heavy frying pan, melt half the butter over a low heat. Add the blanched garlic cloves, then cover and cook gently for 20–25 minutes until very tender and just golden, shaking the pan and stirring occasionally. Do not allow the garlic to scorch or brown.

3 ▲ Remove the pan from the heat to cool slightly. Spoon the garlic and any butter into a blender or a food processor fitted with the metal blade and process until smooth. Tip into a small bowl, press clear film on to the surface to prevent a skin forming and set aside.

4 Peel and quarter the potatoes, place in a large saucepan and add enough cold water to just cover them. Salt the water generously and bring to the boil over a high heat. Cook the potatoes until tender, then drain and work through a food mill or press through a sieve back into the saucepan. Return the pan to a medium heat and, using a wooden spoon, stir the potatoes for 1–2 minutes to dry out completely. Remove the pan from the heat.

5 ▲ Warm the milk over a medium-high heat until bubbles form around the edge. Gradually beat the milk, remaining butter and reserved garlic purée into the potatoes, then season with salt, if needed, and white pepper.

PROVENÇAL VEGETABLE STEW *Ratatouille*

This classic combination of the vegetables that grow abundantly in the south of France is infinitely flexible. Use the recipe as a guide for making the most of what you have on hand.

SERVES 6

2 medium aubergines (about 450g/1lb total)
60–75ml/4–5 tbsp olive oil
1 large onion, halved and sliced
2 or 3 garlic cloves, very finely chopped
1 large red or yellow pepper, seeded and cut into thin strips
2 large courgettes, cut into 1cm/½in slices
675g/1½lb ripe tomatoes, peeled, seeded and chopped, or 400g/14oz/2 cups canned chopped tomatoes
5ml/1 tsp dried herbes de Provence
salt and freshly ground black pepper

1 ▲ Preheat the grill. Cut the aubergine into 2cm/¾in slices, then brush the slices with olive oil on both sides and grill until lightly browned, turning once. Cut the slices into cubes.

2 ▲ Heat 15ml/1 tbsp of the olive oil in a large heavy saucepan or flameproof casserole and cook the onion over a medium-low heat for about 10 minutes until lightly golden, stirring frequently. Add the garlic, pepper and courgettes and cook for a further 10 minutes, stirring occasionally.

3 ▼ Add the tomatoes and aubergine cubes, dried herbs and salt and pepper and simmer gently, covered, over a low heat for about 20 minutes, stirring occasionally. Uncover and continue cooking for a further 20–25 minutes, stirring occasionally, until all the vegetables are tender and the cooking liquid has thickened slightly. Serve hot or at room temperature.

VARIATION

To remove the pepper skin and add flavour to the ratatouille, quarter the pepper and grill, skin-side up, until blackened. Enclose in a sturdy polythene bag and set aside until cool. Peel off the skin, then remove the core and seeds and cut into strips. Add to the mixture with the cooked aubergine.

COURGETTE AND TOMATO BAKE *Tian Provençal*

This dish has been made for centuries in Provence and it gets its name from the shallow casserole, tian, *in which it is traditionally cooked. In the days before home kitchens had ovens, the assembled dish was carried to the baker's to make use of the heat remaining after the bread was baked.*

SERVES 4

15ml/1 tbsp olive oil, plus more for drizzling
1 large onion (about 225g/8oz), sliced
1 garlic clove, finely chopped
450g/1lb tomatoes
450g/1lb courgettes
5ml/1 tsp dried herbes de Provence
30ml/2 tbsp grated Parmesan cheese
salt and freshly ground black pepper

1 Preheat the oven to 180°C/350°F/Gas 4. Heat the oil in a heavy saucepan over a low heat and cook the onion and garlic for about 20 minutes until soft and golden. Spread over the base of a 30cm/12in shallow baking dish.

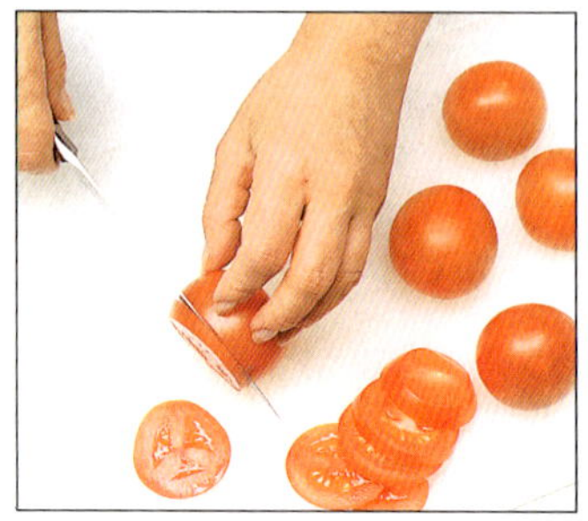

2 ▲ Cut the tomatoes crossways into 6mm/¼in thick slices. (If the tomatoes are very large, cut the slices in half.)

3 Cut the courgettes diagonally into slices about 1cm/½in thick.

4 ▼ Arrange alternating rows of courgettes and tomatoes over the onion mixture and sprinkle with herbs, cheese and salt and pepper. Drizzle with olive oil, then bake for 25 minutes until the vegetables are tender. Serve hot or warm.

BAKED TOMATOES WITH GARLIC *Tomatoes à la Provençale*

These tomatoes, epitomizing the flavour of Provence, are perfect with roast meat or poultry. You can prepare them a few hours ahead, then cook them while carving the roast.

SERVES 4

2 large tomatoes
45ml/3 tbsp dry breadcrumbs
2 garlic cloves, very finely chopped
30ml/2 tbsp chopped fresh parsley
30–45ml/2–3 tbsp olive oil
salt and freshly ground black pepper
flat leaf parsley sprigs, to garnish

1 Preheat the oven to 220°C/425°F/Gas 7. Cut the tomatoes in half crossways and arrange them cut side up on a foil-lined baking sheet.

2 ▲ Mix together the breadcrumbs, garlic, parsley and salt and pepper and spoon over the tomato halves.

3 ▼ Drizzle generously with olive oil and bake the tomatoes at the top of the oven for about 8–10 minutes until lightly browned. Serve at once, garnished with parsley sprigs.

BROCCOLI TIMBALES

Timbales de Brocoli

This elegant but easy to make dish can be made with almost any puréed vegetable, such as carrot or celeriac. To avoid last-minute fuss, make the timbales a few hours ahead and cook while the first course is being eaten. Or, serve them on their own as a starter with a little white wine butter sauce.

SERVES 4

350g/¾lb broccoli florets
45ml/3 tbsp crème fraîche or whipping cream
1 egg, plus 1 egg yolk
15ml/1 tbsp chopped spring onion
pinch of freshly grated nutmeg
salt and freshly ground black pepper
white wine butter sauce, to serve (optional)
fresh chives, to garnish

1 ▼ Preheat the oven to 190°C/375°F/Gas 5. Lightly butter four 175ml/6fl oz ramekins. Line the bases with greaseproof paper and butter the paper.

2 Steam the broccoli in the top of a covered steamer over boiling water for 8–10 minutes until very tender.

3 ▲ Put the broccoli in a food processor fitted with the metal blade and process with the cream, egg and egg yolk until smooth.

4 ▲ Add the spring onion and season with salt, pepper and nutmeg. Pulse to mix.

5 ▲ Spoon the purée into the ramekins and place them in a baking dish. Add boiling water to come halfway up the sides, then bake for 25 minutes, until just set. Invert on to warmed plates and peel off the paper. If serving as a starter, pour a little sauce around each timbale and garnish with chives.

Cauliflower Cheese

Choufleur au Gratin

A vegetable gratin is a classic supper dish in French homes. It also makes a great accompaniment to plain roast meat or chicken. If you wish, prepare it in individual gratin dishes.

Serves 4–6

450g/1lb cauliflower, broken into florets
45g/1½oz/3 tbsp butter
45g/1½oz/4 tbsp plain flour
350ml/12fl oz/1½ cups milk
1 bay leaf
pinch of freshly grated nutmeg
15ml/1 tbsp Dijon mustard
175g/6oz/1½ cups grated Gruyère or Emmenthal cheese
salt and freshly ground black pepper

1 ▲ Preheat the oven to 180°C/350°F/Gas 4. Lightly butter a large gratin dish or shallow baking dish.

2 ▲ Bring a large saucepan of salted water to the boil, add the cauliflower florets and cook for 6–8 minutes until just tender. Alternatively, bring water to the boil in the base of a covered steamer and steam the cauliflower over boiling water for 12–15 minutes until just tender.

3 ▲ Melt the butter in a heavy saucepan over a medium heat, add the flour and cook until just golden, stirring occasionally. Pour in half the milk, stirring vigorously until smooth, then stir in the remaining milk and add the bay leaf. Season with salt, pepper and nutmeg. Reduce the heat to medium-low, cover and simmer gently for about 5 minutes, stirring occasionally, then remove the pan from the heat. Discard the bay leaf, add half the cheese and stir until melted.

4 ▼ Arrange the cauliflower in the dish. Pour over the cheese sauce and sprinkle with the remaining cheese. Bake for about 20 minutes until bubbly and well browned.

Variations

If you wish, add diced ham or cooked bacon to the cauliflower before covering with the cheese sauce, or use broccoli florets in place of cauliflower.

Oven-Braised Chicory

Endives Braisées au Four

Chicory is often used raw in salads, yet it is delicious cooked, too. Slow-braising accentuates its unique flavour, giving it a rich, slightly bitter-sweet taste – perfect with pork and veal.

Serves 6

55g/2oz/4 tbsp butter, softened
6 large or 12 small chicory
15ml/1 tbsp sugar
15–30ml/1–2 tbsp fresh lemon juice
60ml/4 tbsp chicken stock or water

Variation

To make Chicory au Gratin, prepare as above. Preheat the grill. Stir 40g/1½oz grated Gruyère or Emmenthal cheese into 60ml/4 tbsp crème fraîche or double cream. Spoon over the top and grill until golden and bubbly.

1 Preheat the oven to 170°C/325°F/Gas 3. Spread half the butter over the base of a shallow baking dish just large enough to hold the chicory in a single layer.

2 ▲ Discard any wilted or bruised outer leaves from the chicory and, using a stainless steel knife, trim the root end. For particularly large chicory, core out the bitter centre stem of the root. Wipe with kitchen paper (do not wash them).

3 ▲ Place the chicory in the dish. Spread over the remaining butter, sprinkle with sugar and a little lemon juice and pour over the stock or water. Cover with foil and bake for 30–45 minutes until tender.

4 Serve immediately or, if you like, arrange the chicory in a warmed serving dish and reduce the juices over a high heat, pour the juices over the chicory and serve.

Celeriac Purée

Purée de Céleri-rave

Many chefs add potato to celeriac purée, but this recipe highlights the pure flavour of the vegetable. If you have any leftovers, thin with stock or milk to make a lovely soup!

Serves 4

1 large celeriac (about 750g/1¾lb), peeled
15g/½oz/1 tbsp butter
pinch of freshly grated nutmeg
salt and freshly ground black pepper

1 Cut the celeriac into large cubes, put in a saucepan with enough cold water to cover and add a little salt. Bring to the boil over a medium-high heat and cook gently for 10–15 minutes until tender.

2 ▲ Drain the celeriac, reserving a little of the cooking liquid, and place in a food processor fitted with the metal blade. Process until smooth, adding a little of the cooking liquid if it needs thinning.

3 ▼ Stir in the butter and season to taste with salt, pepper and nutmeg. Reheat, if necessary, before serving.

RICE PILAF *Riz Pilaf*

In France the word pilaf refers to the cooking method of sautéing a food in fat before adding liquid. This method produces perfect rice every time.

SERVES 6–8

40g/1½oz/3 tbsp butter or 45–60ml/ 3–4 tbsp oil
1 medium onion, finely chopped
450g/1lb/2 cups long grain rice
750ml/1¼ pints/3 cups chicken stock or water
2.5ml/½ tsp dried thyme
1 small bay leaf
salt and freshly ground black pepper
15–30ml/1–2 tbsp chopped fresh parsley, dill or chives, to garnish

COOK'S TIP

Once cooked, the rice will remain hot for a half an hour, tightly covered. Or, spoon into a microwave-safe bowl, cover and microwave on High (full power) for about 5 minutes until hot.

1 ▼ In a large heavy saucepan, melt the butter or heat the oil over a medium heat. Add the onion and cook for 2–3 minutes until just softened, stirring all the time. Add the rice and cook for 1–2 minutes until the rice becomes translucent but does not begin to brown, stirring frequently.

2 ▲ Add the stock or water, dried thyme and bay leaf and season with salt and pepper. Bring to the boil over a high heat, stirring frequently. Just as the rice begins to boil, cover the surface with a round of foil or greaseproof paper and cover the saucepan. Reduce the heat to very low and cook for 20 minutes (do not lift the cover or stir). Serve hot, garnished with fresh herbs.

SAUTÉED WILD MUSHROOMS *Champignons Sauvages à la Bordelaise*

This is a quick dish to prepare and makes an ideal accompaniment to all kinds of roast and grilled meats. Use any combination of wild or cultivated "wild" mushrooms you can find.

SERVES 6

900g/2lb mixed fresh wild and cultivated mushrooms, such as morels, porcini, chanterelles, oyster or shiitake
30ml/2 tbsp olive oil
30g/1oz/2 tbsp unsalted butter
2 garlic cloves, finely chopped
3 or 4 shallots, finely chopped
45–60ml/3–4 tbsp chopped fresh parsley, or a mixture of fresh herbs
salt and freshly ground black pepper

1 Wash and carefully dry any very dirty mushrooms. Trim the stems and cut the mushrooms into quarters or slice if very large.

2 ▲ In a large heavy frying pan, heat the oil over a medium-high heat. Add the butter and swirl to melt, then stir in the mushrooms and cook for 4–5 minutes until beginning to brown.

3 ▼ Add the garlic and shallots and cook for a further 4–5 minutes until the mushrooms are tender and any liquid given off has evaporated. Season with salt and pepper and stir in the parsley or mixed herbs.

EGGS AND CHEESE

In French households eggs and cheese form a basic part of everyday meals. They are absolutely essential in French cooking – not only as cooking ingredients, but also as separate courses in their own right. Eggs are popular as a starter at lunchtime or as a supper dish, often served baked or made into creamy omelettes, or combined with cheese to make a soufflé or quiche. While cheese, as a separate course, is always served after the main course, and before any dessert. The choice is huge – France produces more kinds of cheeses than any other country, and every region has its own varieties.

OMELETTE WITH HERBS *Omelette aux Fines Herbes*

Omelettes are often served as a starter or supper dish in France and fines herbes *combined with tangy, delicately soured cream make a simple but delicious filling.*

SERVES 1

2 eggs
15g/½oz/1 tbsp butter
15ml/1 tbsp crème fraîche or soured cream
5ml/1 tsp chopped fresh mixed herbs (such as tarragon, chives, parsley or marjoram)
salt and freshly ground black pepper

1 Beat together the eggs and salt and pepper until well mixed.

VARIATIONS

Other omelette fillings could include sautéed sliced mushrooms, diced ham or crumbled crisp bacon, creamed spinach or thick tomato sauce and grated cheese.

2 ▲ Melt the butter in an omelette pan or small non-stick frying pan over a medium-high heat until foamy and light nutty brown, then pour in the eggs.

3 As the egg mixture starts to set on the base of the pan, lift up the sides using a fork or palette knife and tilt the pan to allow the uncooked egg to run underneath.

4 ▲ When the egg is too set to run but still soft, spoon the crème fraîche or soured cream down the centre and sprinkle with the herbs.

5 To serve the omelette, hold the pan over a warmed plate. With a fork or palette knife lift one edge of the omelette and fold it over the middle. Tilt the pan to help the omelette fold over on itself in thirds and slide it out on to the plate.

EGG-STUFFED TOMATOES *Tomates Farcies d'Oeuf*

This simple dish is just the kind of thing you might find in charcuteries *all over France. It is easy to make at home and makes a delicious starter or a light lunch.*

SERVES 4

175ml/6fl oz/¾ cup mayonnaise
30ml/2 tbsp chopped fresh chives
30ml/2 tbsp chopped fresh basil
30ml/2 tbsp chopped fresh parsley
4 hard-boiled eggs
4 ripe medium tomatoes
salt
lettuce, to serve

1 In a small bowl, blend together the mayonnaise and herbs and set aside.

2 Using an egg slicer or sharp knife, cut the eggs into thin slices.

3 ▼ Place the tomatoes core-end down and make deep cuts to within 1.2cm/½in of the base. (There should be the same number of cuts in each tomato as there are slices of egg; the white ends of the eggs can be discarded.)

4 ▲ Fan open the tomatoes and sprinkle with salt, then insert an egg slice into each slit.

5 Place each stuffed tomato on a plate with lettuce and serve with the herb mayonnaise.

Provençal Chard Omelette *Trouchia*

This traditional flat omelette can also be made with fresh spinach, but chard leaves are typical in Provence. It is delicious served with small black Niçoise olives.

Serves 6

675g/1½lb chard leaves without stalks
60ml/4 tbsp olive oil
1 large onion, sliced
5 eggs
salt and freshly ground black pepper
sprig of fresh parsley, to garnish

1 Wash the chard well in several changes of water and pat dry. Stack four or five leaves at a time and slice across into thin ribbons. Steam the chard until wilted, then drain in a sieve and press out any liquid with the back of a spoon.

2 ▼ Heat 30ml/2 tbsp of the olive oil in a large frying pan. Add the onion and cook over a medium-low heat for about 10 minutes until soft, stirring occasionally. Add the chard and cook for a further 2–4 minutes until the leaves are tender.

3 ▲ In a large bowl, beat the eggs and season with salt and pepper, then stir in the cooked vegetables.

4 Heat the remaining 30ml/2 tbsp of oil in a large non-stick frying pan over a medium-high heat. Pour in the egg mixture and reduce the heat to medium-low. Cook the omelette, covered, for 5–7 minutes until the egg mixture is set around the edges and almost set on top.

5 ▲ To turn the omelette over, loosen the edges and slide it on to a large plate. Place the frying pan over the omelette and, holding them tightly, carefully invert the pan and plate together. Lift off the plate and continue cooking for a further 2–3 minutes. Slide the omelette on to a serving plate and serve hot or at room temperature, cut into wedges.

BAKED EGGS WITH CREAMY LEEKS *Oeufs en Cocotte aux Poireaux*

The French have traditionally enjoyed eggs prepared in many different ways. Vary this simple yet elegant dish by using other vegetables, such as puréed spinach, or ratatouille, as a base.

SERVES 4

15g/½oz/1 tbsp butter, plus extra for greasing
225g/½lb small leeks, thinly sliced (about 2 cups)
75–90ml/5–6 tbsp whipping cream
freshly grated nutmeg
4 eggs
salt and freshly ground black pepper

1 ▲ Preheat the oven to 190°C/375°F/Gas 5. Generously butter the base and sides of four ramekins or individual soufflé dishes.

2 ▲ Melt the butter in a small frying pan and cook the leeks over a medium heat, stirring frequently, until softened but not browned.

3 ▼ Add 45ml/3 tbsp of the cream and cook gently for about 5 minutes until the leeks are very soft and the cream has thickened a little. Season with salt, pepper and nutmeg.

VARIATION

For an even quicker dish, put 15ml/1 tbsp of cream in each dish with some chopped herbs. Break in the eggs, add 15ml/1 tbsp cream and a little grated cheese, then bake.

4 ▲ Arrange the ramekins in a small roasting tin and divide the leeks among them. Break an egg into each, spoon 5–10ml/1–2 tsp of the remaining cream over each egg and season lightly.

5 Pour boiling water into the baking dish to come halfway up the sides of the ramekins or soufflé dishes. Bake for about 10 minutes, until the whites are set and the yolks are still soft, or a little longer if you prefer them more well done.

SCRAMBLED EGGS WITH PEPPERS *Pipérade à la Basquaise*

This dish comes from the Basque country in the Pyrenees, piper *being Basquaise for pepper.*

SERVES 4

60ml/4 tbsp bacon fat, duck fat or olive oil
2 onions, coarsely chopped
3 or 4 green or red peppers (or mixed), cored and chopped
2 garlic cloves, finely chopped
small pinch of chilli powder or cayenne pepper, to taste
900g/2lb ripe tomatoes, peeled, seeded and chopped
2.5ml/½ tsp dried oregano or thyme
8 eggs, lightly beaten
salt and freshly ground black pepper
chopped fresh parsley, to garnish

1 Heat the fat or oil in a large heavy frying pan over a medium-low heat. Add the onions and cook, stirring occasionally, for 5–7 minutes until they are softened but not browned.

2 ▲ Stir in the peppers, garlic and chilli powder or cayenne. Cook for a further 5 minutes until the peppers soften, stirring frequently.

COOK'S TIP

Make sure that you cook the peppers until the pan is almost completely dry before adding the eggs, otherwise the finished dish will be too wet.

3 Stir in the tomatoes and season with salt and pepper and the oregano or thyme. Cook over a medium heat for 15–20 minutes until the peppers are soft, the liquid has evaporated and the mixture is thick. Stir occasionally to prevent the mixture burning and sticking to the pan.

4 ▲ Add the beaten eggs to the vegetables and stir over a low heat for 5–8 minutes until the mixture is thickened and softly set. Scatter over the parsley and serve.

SCRAMBLED EGGS WITH CAVIAR *Oeufs Brouillés au Caviar*

In France, scrambled eggs are cooked slowly so they are rich, smooth and creamy – never dry.

SERVES 4

40g/1½oz/3 tbsp butter, cut into small pieces
8 eggs, plus 1 egg yolk
15ml/1 tbsp crème fraîche, soured cream or double cream
15–30ml/1–2 tbsp snipped fresh chives
4 slices lightly toasted brioche, buttered, plus more to serve
55g/2oz caviar
salt and white pepper
fresh chives, to garnish

1 In a large heavy frying pan or saucepan, melt half the butter over a medium-low heat.

2 ▲ Beat the eggs and egg yolk well and season with salt and pepper. Pour into the pan and cook gently, stirring constantly until the mixture begins to thicken and set; this may take 10–12 minutes or longer. Gradually stir in the remaining butter, lifting the pan from the heat occasionally to slow the cooking.

3 ▼ When the eggs are just set, take the pan off the heat and stir in the cream and chives. Arrange the buttered brioche slices on plates and divide the scrambled egg among them. Top each serving with a spoonful of caviar. Garnish with chives and serve with extra toasted brioche.

POACHED EGGS WITH SPINACH *Oeufs Pochés à la Florentine*

This classic recipe may be served as a starter, but is also excellent for a light lunch or brunch.

SERVES 4

30g/1oz/2 tbsp butter
450g/1lb young spinach leaves
2.5ml/½ tsp vinegar
4 eggs
salt and freshly ground black pepper
FOR THE HOLLANDAISE SAUCE
175g/6oz/¾ cup butter, cut into pieces
2 egg yolks
15ml/1 tbsp lemon juice
15ml/1 tbsp water
salt and white pepper

COOK'S TIP

Hollandaise sauce is quick and easy to make in a blender or food processor. If you wish, you can make it an hour or two in advance and keep it warm in a wide-mouthed vacuum flask.

1 To make the hollandaise sauce, melt the butter in a small saucepan over a medium heat until it bubbles, then remove from the heat.

2 ▲ Put the egg yolks, lemon juice and water into a blender or food processor and whizz to blend. With the machine running, slowly pour in the hot butter in a thin stream. Stop pouring when you reach the milky solids at the bottom. Season with salt and pepper and more lemon juice if needed. Transfer the sauce to a serving bowl, cover and keep warm.

3 ▲ Melt the butter in a heavy frying pan over a medium heat. Add the spinach and cook until wilted, stirring occasionally. Season and keep warm.

4 ▲ To poach the eggs, bring a medium pan of lightly salted water to the boil and add the vinegar. Break an egg into a saucer and slide the egg into the water. Reduce the heat and simmer for a few minutes until the white is set and the yolk is still soft. Remove with a slotted spoon and drain. Trim any untidy edges with scissors and keep warm. Cook the remaining eggs in the same way.

5 To serve, spoon the spinach on to warmed plates and make an indentation in each mound. Place the eggs on top and pour over a little hollandaise sauce.

GOAT'S CHEESE SOUFFLÉ

Soufflé au Fromage de Chèvre

Make sure everyone is seated before the soufflé comes out of the oven because it will begin to deflate almost immediately. This recipe works equally well with strong blue cheeses such as Roquefort.

SERVES 4–6

30g/1oz/2 tbsp butter
30g/1oz/3 tbsp plain flour
175ml/6fl oz/¾ cup milk
1 bay leaf
freshly grated nutmeg
grated Parmesan cheese, for sprinkling
40g/1½oz herb and garlic soft cheese
150g/5oz firm goat's cheese, diced
6 egg whites, at room temperature
1.5ml/¼ tsp cream of tartar
salt and freshly ground black pepper

1 Melt the butter in a heavy saucepan over a medium heat. Add the flour and cook until slightly golden, stirring occasionally. Pour in half the milk, stirring vigorously until smooth, then stir in the remaining milk and add the bay leaf. Season with a pinch of salt and plenty of pepper and nutmeg. Reduce the heat to medium-low, cover and simmer gently for about 5 minutes, stirring occasionally.

2 ▲ Preheat the oven to 190°C/ 375°F/ Gas 5. Generously butter a 1.5 litre/2½ pint soufflé dish and sprinkle with Parmesan cheese.

3 ▼ Remove the sauce from the heat and discard the bay leaf. Stir in both cheeses.

4 In a clean greasefree bowl, using an electric mixer or balloon whisk, beat the egg whites slowly until they become frothy. Add the cream of tartar, increase the speed and continue beating until they form soft peaks, then stiffer peaks that just flop over a little at the top.

5 ▲ Stir a spoonful of beaten egg whites into the cheese sauce to lighten it, then pour the cheese sauce over the remaining whites. Using a rubber spatula or large metal spoon, gently fold the sauce into the whites until the mixtures are just combined, cutting down through the centre to the bottom, then along the side of the bowl and up to the top.

6 Gently pour the soufflé mixture into the prepared dish and bake for 25–30 minutes until puffed and golden brown. Serve at once.

Twice-Baked Soufflés

Soufflés Renversés

These little soufflés are served upside-down! They are remarkably easy to make and can be prepared up to a day in advance, then reheated in the sauce – perfect for easy entertaining.

Serves 6

20g/¾oz/1½ tbsp butter
30ml/2 tbsp plain flour
150ml/¼ pint/⅔ cup milk
1 small bay leaf
freshly grated nutmeg
2 eggs, separated, plus 1 egg white, at room temperature
85g/3oz/⅔ cup grated Gruyère cheese
1.5ml/¼ tsp cream of tartar
salt and freshly ground black pepper
For the tomato cream sauce
300ml/½ pint/1¼ cups whipping cream
10ml/2 tsp tomato purée
1 ripe tomato, peeled, seeded and finely diced
salt and cayenne pepper

1 Preheat the oven to 190°C/375°F/Gas 5. Generously butter six 175ml/6fl oz/¾ cup ramekins or dariole moulds, then line the bases with buttered greaseproof or non-stick baking paper.

2 ▲ In a heavy saucepan over a medium heat, melt the butter, stir in the flour and cook until just golden, stirring occasionally. Pour in about half the milk, whisking vigorously until smooth, then whisk in the remaining milk and add the bay leaf. Season with a little salt and plenty of pepper and nutmeg. Bring to the boil and cook, stirring constantly, for about 1 minute.

3 ▲ Remove the sauce from the heat and discard the bay leaf. Beat the egg yolks, one at a time, into the hot sauce, then stir in the cheese until it is melted. Set aside.

4 In a large, clean greasefree bowl, whisk the egg whites slowly until they become frothy. Add the cream of tartar, then increase the speed and whisk until they form peaks that just flop over at the top.

5 ▲ Whisk a spoonful of beaten egg whites into the cheese sauce to lighten it. Pour the cheese sauce over the remaining whites. Using a rubber spatula or large metal spoon, gently fold the sauce into the whites.

Cook's tip

If making ahead, cool the cooked soufflés, then cover and chill. Bring the soufflés back to room temperature before baking.

6 ▲ Spoon the soufflé mixture into the prepared dishes, filling them about three-quarters full. Put the dishes in a shallow baking dish and pour in boiling water to come halfway up the sides of the dishes. Bake for about 18 minutes until puffed and golden brown. Let the soufflés cool in the dishes long enough to deflate.

7 ▲ To make the sauce, bring the cream just to the boil in a small saucepan. Reduce the heat, stir in the tomato purée and diced tomato and cook for 2–3 minutes. Season with salt and cayenne pepper. Spoon a thin layer of sauce into a gratin dish just large enough to hold the soufflés. Run a knife around the edge of the soufflés and invert to unmould. Remove the lining paper if necessary. Pour the remaining sauce over the soufflés and bake for 12–15 minutes until well browned.

Farine

ALSATIAN LEEK AND ONION TARTLETS *Tartlettes Alsaciennes*

The savoury filling in these tartlets is traditional to north-east France where many types of quiche are popular. Baking in individual tins makes for easier serving and looks attractive too.

SERVES 6

30g/1oz/2 tbsp butter, cut into 8 pieces
1 onion, thinly sliced
2.5ml/½ tsp dried thyme
450g/1lb leeks, thinly sliced
55g/2 oz/5 tbsp grated Gruyère or Emmenthal cheese
3 eggs
300ml/½ pint/1¼ cups single cream
pinch of freshly grated nutmeg
salt and freshly ground black pepper
lettuce and parsley leaves and cherry tomatoes, to serve

FOR THE PASTRY
175g/6oz/1⅓ cup plain flour
85g/3oz/6 tbsp cold butter
1 egg yolk
30–45ml/2–3 tbsp cold water
2.5ml/½ tsp salt

1 To make the pastry, sift the flour into a bowl and add the butter. Using your fingertips or a pastry blender, rub or cut the butter into the flour until the mixture resembles fine breadcrumbs.

2 ▲ Make a well in the flour mixture. In a small bowl, beat together the egg yolk, water and salt. Pour into the well and, using a fork, lightly combine the flour and liquid until the dough begins to stick together. Form into a flattened ball. Wrap and chill for 30 minutes.

3 ▲ Lightly butter six 10cm/4in tartlet tins. On a lightly floured surface, roll out the dough until about 3mm/⅛in thick, then using a 12.5cm/5in cutter, cut as many rounds as possible. Gently ease the pastry rounds into the tins, pressing the pastry firmly into the base and sides. Reroll the trimmings and line the remaining tins. Prick the bases and chill for 30 minutes.

4 ▲ Preheat the oven to 190°C/375°F/Gas 5. Line the pastry cases with foil and fill with baking beans. Place them on a baking sheet and bake for 6–8 minutes until the pastry edges are golden. Lift out the foil and beans and bake the pastry cases for a further 2 minutes until the bases appear dry. Transfer to a wire rack to cool. Reduce the oven to 180°C/350°F/Gas 4.

5 ▲ In a large frying pan, melt the butter over a medium heat, then add the onion and thyme and cook for 3–5 minutes until the onion is just softened, stirring frequently. Add the leeks and cook for 10–12 minutes until they are soft and tender. Divide the mixture among the pastry cases and sprinkle each with cheese, dividing it evenly.

6 ▲ In a medium bowl, beat together the eggs, cream, nutmeg and salt and pepper. Place the pastry cases on a baking sheet and pour in the egg mixture. Bake for 15–20 minutes until set and golden. Transfer the tartlets to a wire rack to cool slightly, then remove them from the tins and serve warm or at room temperature with lettuce and parsley leaves and cherry tomatoes.

CHEESE AND ONION FLAN *Flamiche au Fromage*

A strong flavoured washed rind cheese such as Epoisses, Maroilles, *or* Livarot, *is traditional in this tart but* Munster *or* Port Salut *will also produce a pleasant, if milder, result.*

SERVES 4

15g/½oz/1 tbsp butter
1 onion, halved and sliced
2 eggs
250ml/8fl oz/1 cup single cream
225g/8oz strong-flavoured semi-soft cheese, rind removed (about 175g/6oz without rind), sliced
salt and freshly ground black pepper
lettuce and parsley leaves, to serve

FOR THE YEAST DOUGH

10ml/2 tsp active dry yeast
125ml/4fl oz/½ cup milk
5ml/1 tsp sugar
1 egg yolk
225g/8oz/1¾ cups plain flour, plus more for kneading
2.5ml/½ tsp salt
55g/2oz//4 tbsp butter, softened

1 First make the yeast dough. Place the yeast in a small bowl. Warm the milk in a saucepan until it is at body temperature and stir into the yeast with the sugar, stirring until the yeast has dissolved. Leave the yeast mixture to stand for 3 minutes, then beat in the egg yolk.

2 Put the flour and salt in a food processor fitted with the metal blade and pulse twice to combine. With the machine running, slowly pour in the yeast mixture. Scrape down the sides and continue processing for 2–3 minutes. Add the butter and process for another 30 seconds.

3 Transfer the dough to a lightly oiled bowl. Cover with a cloth and allow to rise in a warm place for about 1 hour until doubled in bulk, then punch down.

4 On a lightly floured surface, roll the dough into a 30cm/12in round. Use to line a 23cm/9in flan tin or dish. Trim any overhanging dough so that it is about 3mm/⅛in outside the rim of the tin or dish. Set aside and leave the dough to rise again for about ½ hour, or until puffy.

5 ▲ Meanwhile, melt the butter in a heavy saucepan and fry the onion, covered, over a medium-low heat for about 15 minutes, until softened, stirring occasionally. Uncover the pan and continue cooking, stirring frequently, until the onion is very soft and caramelized.

6 Preheat the oven to 180°C/350°F/Gas 4. Beat together the eggs and cream. Season with salt and pepper and stir in the cooked onion.

7 ▲ Arrange the cheese on the base of the dough. Pour over the egg mixture and bake for 30–35 minutes until the bread base is golden and the centre just set. Cool on a wire rack before serving hot or warm with lettuce and parsley leaves.

Cheese and Bacon Quiche *Quiche Savoyarde*

Gruyère is probably the most important French cheese for cooking. Made in the rugged Alpine dairy country of the Savoie, *it is firm and has a rich nutty flavour.*

Serves 6–8

340g/12oz shortcrust pastry
15ml/1 tbsp Dijon mustard
175g/6oz/6 rindless streaky bacon rashers, chopped
1 onion, chopped
3 eggs
350ml/12fl oz/1½ cups single cream
150g/5oz Gruyère cheese, diced
salt and freshly ground black pepper
fresh parsley, to garnish

1 ▲ Preheat the oven to 200°C/400°F/Gas 6. Roll out the pastry thinly and use to line a 23cm/9in flan tin. Prick the base of the pastry case and line with foil. Fill with baking beans and bake for 15 minutes. Remove the foil and beans, brush the case with mustard and bake for a further 5 minutes, then transfer to a wire rack. Reduce the oven to 180°C/350°F/Gas 4.

2 ▲ In a frying pan, cook the bacon over a medium heat, until crisp and browned, stirring occasionally.

3 ▲ Remove the bacon with a slotted spoon and drain on kitchen paper. Pour off most of the fat from the pan, add the onion and cook over a medium-low heat for about 15 minutes until very soft and golden, stirring occasionally.

4 Beat together the eggs and cream and season with salt and pepper.

5 ▼ Sprinkle half the cheese over the pastry, spread the onion over the cheese and add the bacon, then top with the remaining cheese.

6 Pour on the egg mixture and bake for 35–45 minutes until set. Transfer to a wire rack to cool slightly. Serve warm, garnished with parsley.

Cheese and Ham Croissants *Croissants au Fromage et Jambon*

These hot croissant "sandwiches" are an upmarket version of classic café fare. They make a simple tasty lunch – try using different combinations of ham and cheese – or serve them for breakfast.

Serves 2

2 large croissants
30g/1oz/2 tbsp butter, softened
Dijon mustard
2 slices Bayonne or Parma ham
55–85g/2–3oz Camembert or Brie (rind removed), sliced 6mm/¼ in thick
lettuce, tomatoes and chives, to serve

1 Preheat the oven to 200°C/400°F/Gas 6. Split the croissants lengthways and spread each side with butter and a little mustard.

2 ▼ Place a piece of ham on the bottom half of each croissant, trimming to fit. Place slices of cheese on the ham and cover with the croissant tops.

3 ▲ Place the croissants on a baking sheet and cover them loosely with foil, then bake for 3–5 minutes until the cheese begins to melt. Serve with lettuce, tomatoes and chives.

Cheese Puff Ring *Gougère*

This light savoury pastry comes from Burgundy, where it is traditionally served with red wine.

Serves 6–8

100g/3½oz/¾ cup plain flour
1.5ml/¼ tsp salt
pinch of cayenne pepper
pinch of freshly grated nutmeg
175ml/6fl oz/¾ cup water
85g/3oz/6 tbsp butter, cut into pieces
3 eggs
85g/3oz Gruyère cheese, cut into 6mm/¼in cubes

1 Preheat the oven to 200°C/400°F/Gas 6. Lightly grease a baking sheet. Sift together the flour, salt, cayenne pepper and nutmeg.

Variation

Stir in 15–30ml/1–2 tbsp chopped fresh parsley or chives, or chopped spring onions before baking.

2 ▲ In a medium saucepan, bring the water and butter to the boil. Remove from the heat and add the dry ingredients all at once. Beat with a wooden spoon for about 1 minute until the mixture is well blended and starts to pull away from the sides of the pan.

3 Place the pan over a low heat and cook for 2 minutes, beating constantly, then remove the pan from the heat.

4 Beat the eggs together in a small bowl and then very gradually (one tablespoon at a time), beat into the mixture, beating thoroughly after each addition until the dough is smooth and shiny. It should pull away and fall slowly when dropped from a spoon – you may not need all the beaten egg. Add the cubed cheese and stir to mix well.

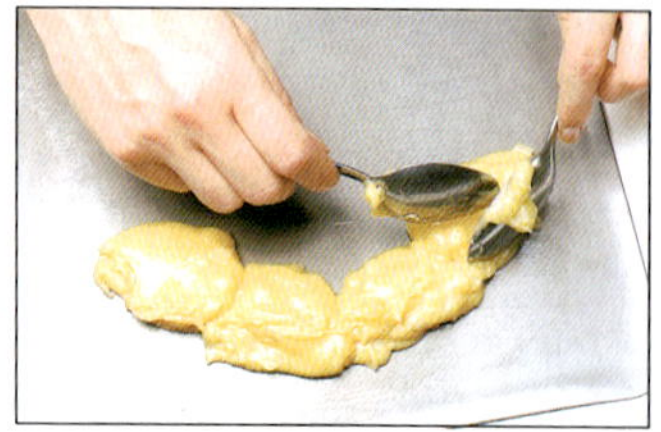

5 ▲ Using two large tablespoons, drop adjoining mounds of dough on to the baking sheet to form a 25cm/10in circle. Bake for 25–30 minutes until well browned. Cool slightly on a wire rack and serve warm.

premier
à Brême

Grilled Goat's Cheese Salad *Salade de Chèvre*

Here is the salad and cheese course on one plate – or serve it as a quick and satisfying starter or light lunch. The fresh tangy flavour of goat's cheese contrasts with the mild salad leaves.

Serves 4

2 firm round whole goat's cheeses, such as Crottin de Chavignol *(about 70–120g/2½–4oz each)*
4 slices French bread
extra virgin olive oil, for drizzling
175g/6oz/5–6 cups mixed salad leaves, including soft and bitter varieties
snipped fresh chives, to garnish
For the vinaigrette dressing
½ garlic clove
5ml/1 tsp Dijon mustard
5ml/1 tsp white wine vinegar
5ml/1 tsp dry white wine
45ml/3 tbsp extra virgin olive oil
salt and freshly ground black pepper

1 ▼ To make the dressing, rub a large salad bowl with the cut side of the garlic clove. Combine the mustard, vinegar and wine, salt and pepper in the bowl. Whisk in the oil, 15ml/1 tbsp at a time, to form a thick vinaigrette.

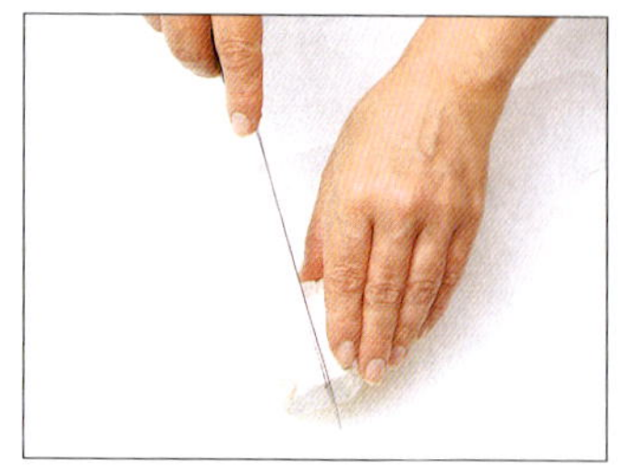

2 ▲ Cut the goat's cheeses in half crossways using a sharp knife.

3 ▲ Preheat the grill to hot. Arrange the bread slices on a baking sheet and toast the bread on one side. Turn over and place a piece of cheese, cut side up, on each slice. Drizzle with olive oil and grill until the cheese is lightly browned.

4 ▲ Add the leaves to the salad bowl and toss to coat them with the dressing. Divide the salad among four plates, top each with a goat's cheese croûton and serve, garnished with chives.

ROQUEFORT AND CUCUMBER MOUSSE *Mousse au Roquefort*

This cool and refreshing mousse makes a perfect summer starter. Other blue-veined cheeses, such as bleu d'Auvergne *or* fourme d'Ambert, *may be used instead of* Roquefort.

SERVES 6

18cm/7in piece cucumber
10ml/2 tsp powdered gelatine
75ml/5 tbsp cold water
100g/3½oz Roquefort cheese
200g/7oz full-, medium- or low-fat soft cheese
45ml/3 tbsp crème fraîche or soured cream
cayenne or white pepper
seedless red and green grapes and mint leaves, to garnish

1 ▲ Peel the cucumber and cut lengthways into quarters. Remove the seeds and cut the cucumber strips into 2.5cm/1in pieces.

2 Sprinkle the gelatine over the cold water in a small heatproof bowl. Let the gelatine stand to soften for about 2 minutes, then place the bowl in a shallow pan of simmering water. Heat until the gelatine is dissolved, stirring occasionally.

3 In a food processor fitted with the metal blade, process the cheeses and cream until smooth. Add the dissolved gelatine and process to blend. Add the cucumber and pulse to chop finely without completely reducing it to a purée. Season with cayenne or white pepper.

4 ▼ Rinse a 1.5 litre/2½ pint dish or mould with cold water. Carefully spoon the mixture into the dish or mould and tap gently to remove air bubbles. Chill for 4–6 hours or overnight until well set.

5 ▲ To turn out, run a knife around the edge of the dish or mould, dip in hot water for 10–15 seconds and wipe the wet base. Place a large plate over the top of the dish and invert both together, shaking firmly to release the mousse. Garnish with grapes and mint leaves.

The Cheeseboard

Le plateau de fromages

Although all cheese is made from milk, the end products vary enormously. The different methods of cheesemaking, and types of milk, produce different textures, flavours and characteristics.

Charles De Gaulle once said "How can I govern a country which produces more than 300 cheeses?". The French perhaps more than any other country are a nation of cheese lovers, each region produces a variety of cheeses reflecting the local tastes and, appropriately enough, they seem to marry well with the local wines, as well as the fruit and nuts of the area.

Cheeses are made from cow's, goat's and ewe's milk and vary from fine fresh creamy cheeses such as those from Normandy like *Brillat Savarin* or *Explorateur*, to blues like *Roquefort* from the mountains of the Causses and *Bleu d'Auvergne*, to hard cheeses of the Alps, *Gruyère* and *Emmenthal*, which are much used in quiches and ideal for cooking.

In most homes, the daily meal ends with cheese and perhaps some fruit, but unless it is a special occasion or a restaurant meal, dessert is less common – cheese is the dessert. A cheeseboard need not contain a bewildering selection; far better to search out one or two really good cheeses in perfect condition and present them with good fruit and bread, as the French do.

Some government regulations prohibit the entry of cheese made from unpasteurized milk and aged less than 60 days, but nonetheless, a few importers have managed to offer "raw milk" or "farmhouse" *Brie*, *Camembert* and other regional cheeses. It is unfortunate that while pasteurization makes cheese safer, it also neutralizes the flavour slightly, producing less tasty imitations of what may be available in France.

Ideally cheese should be stored in a cool cellar, offering conditions much like those in which they are aged. However, most of us have to make do with the fridge. Store cheese, well wrapped in clear film, in the part of the fridge where it is least cold, or in the specified area. Before serving, remove from the fridge and unwrap. Allow about 1 hour for the cheese to come to room temperature.

CHEESE AND FRUIT COMBINATIONS

Semi-firm cheeses such as *Gruyère*, *Emmenthal*, *Cantal*, *Comté* and *Mimolette* are delicious with almost all varieties of crisp apples and with walnuts.

Serve semi-soft cheeses such as *Morbier*, *Munster*, *Port-Salut*, *Gaperon*, *Doux de Montagne*, *Tomme de Savoie*, *Raclette* and *Reblochon*, with apricots, ripe red, yellow or purple plums, slices of ripe cantaloupe melon or, better still, slices of mango and papaya.

Blue cheeses such as *Roquefort*, *Bleu de Bresse* or *Bleu d'Auvergne* classically go with fresh fruit, but also go well with fresh figs or with dried fruit such as apricots, dates and figs.

Soft ripening cheeses such as *Brie*, *Camembert*, *Chaource*, *Coulommiers* and *Vacherin Mont d'Or* pair well with black or white grapes, mangoes and cherries.

Double- and triple-cream cheeses such as *Brillat-Savarin*, *Explorateur*, *St. André*, *Belle Etoile* and *Gratte-Paille* are good with melon, kiwi, ripe papaya, apricots, wild strawberries and toasted nuts and are especially good served with walnut bread.

Cheeses made from goat's or sheep's milk can be mild and creamy or strong and tangy. They go well with pears, grapes, peaches and figs as well as strawberries and blackberries.

Offer a balanced selection when serving several cheeses, varying the colours, flavours and textures; perhaps a soft creamy white cheese such as a *Neufchâtel*, a more distinctive cheese with a nutty flavour like the orange-rinded *Chaumes* from Bordeaux, an ash covered goat's cheese such as *Montrachet* or *St Maure* from Burgundy and a strong blue like *Roquefort* or *Fourme d'Ambert*.

For a special occasion during the winter holidays, serve the famous *Vacherin* from near the Swiss border. This is a rich cheese, so soft when ripe that the cheese is served with the top crust removed and a spoon used to scoop out the centre! Otherwise when cutting portions of cheese, remember to keep the shape of the cheese. For example, cutting thin wedges from a wedge shaped piece, rectangular pieces from a square cheese and cut wedges from a round or pyramid. Try not to cut off the "nose" of the cheese leaving only the rind edge for others!

Marinated Goat's Cheese
Chèvre mariné

This makes a delicious and unusual cheese course – serve while the marinade is still warm. If you can find them, small individual goat's cheeses are ideal.

SERVES 6–8

- *2 or 3 garlic cloves, thinly sliced*
- *2 small bay leaves*
- *1 or 2 rosemary sprigs, leaves removed*
- *2.5ml/½ tsp dried thyme*
- *15ml/1 tbsp black, white, green and pink peppercorns, lightly crushed*
- *2.5ml/½ tsp mustard seeds, lightly crushed*
- *2.5ml/½ tsp fennel seeds, lightly crushed*
- *125ml/4fl oz/½ cup extra virgin olive oil*
- *6–8 individual goat's cheeses or 2* Montrachet *logs or other soft mild goat's cheese (450g/1lb total weight), cut into 6 or 8 pieces each*
- *French bread, sliced and toasted, to serve*

Mix together the garlic, herbs, peppercorns, mustard and fennel seeds and oil in a small bowl. Place over a medium-low heat for about 5 minutes and then set aside for 5–10 minutes, for the flavours to infuse. Arrange the goat's cheese rounds on a platter and pour over the marinade. Serve warm with toasted French bread.

FISH AND SHELLFISH

With a coastline bordering two seas and a vast network of rivers, fish and shellfish play a leading role in French cuisine. Coastal areas are rightly renowned for their fish and shellfish, but fish is enjoyed all over France, and a great deal of effort is spent in making sure that fresh fish is available in markets throughout the country. Despite their reputation for rich, complicated cooking, the French tend to treat fish and shellfish fairly simply, usually poaching, baking, sautéing or grilling it. And, of course, nothing is wasted from the catch – even small bony fish are used to make *bouillon* for soups, sauces and stews.

TROUT WITH ALMONDS *Truites aux Amandes*

This simple and quick recipe doubles easily – you can cook the trout in two frying pans or in batches. In Normandy, hazelnuts might be used in place of almonds.

SERVES 2

2 trout (about 350g/12oz each), cleaned
40g/1½oz/⅓ cup plain flour
55g/2oz/4 tbsp butter
30g/1oz/¼ cup flaked or sliced almonds
30ml/2 tbsp dry white wine
salt and freshly ground black pepper

1 Rinse the trout and pat dry. Put the flour in a large polythene bag and season with salt and pepper. Place the trout, one at a time, in the bag and shake to coat with flour. Shake off the excess flour from the fish and discard the remaining flour.

2 ▲ Melt half the butter in a large frying pan over a medium heat. When it is foamy, add the trout and cook for 6–7 minutes on each side, until golden brown and the flesh next to the bone is opaque. Transfer the fish to warmed plates and cover to keep warm.

3 ▼ Add the remaining butter to the pan and cook the almonds until just lightly browned. Add the wine to the pan and boil for 1 minute, stirring constantly, until slightly syrupy. Pour or spoon over the fish and serve at once.

TUNA WITH GARLIC, TOMATOES AND HERBS *Thon St Remy*

St Rémy is a beautiful village in Provence in the South of France. Herbs, such as thyme, rosemary and oregano, grow wild on the nearby hillsides and feature in many of the recipes from this area.

SERVES 4

4 tuna steaks, about 2.5cm/1in thick (175–200g/6–7oz each)
30–45ml/2–3 tbsp olive oil
3 or 4 garlic cloves, finely chopped
60ml/4 tbsp dry white wine
3 ripe plum tomatoes, peeled, seeded and chopped
5ml/1 tsp dried herbes de Provence
salt and freshly ground black pepper
fresh basil leaves, to garnish

COOK'S TIP

Tuna is often served pink in the middle like beef. If you prefer it cooked through, reduce the heat and cook for an extra few minutes.

1 ▼ Season the tuna steaks with salt and pepper. Set a heavy frying pan over a high heat until very hot, add the oil and swirl to coat. Add the tuna steaks and press down gently, then reduce the heat to medium and cook for 6–8 minutes, turning once, until just slightly pink in the centre.

2 ▲ Transfer the steaks to a serving plate and cover to keep warm. Add the garlic to the pan and fry for 15–20 seconds, stirring all the time, then pour in the wine and boil until it is reduced by half. Add the tomatoes and dried herbs and cook for 2–3 minutes until the sauce is bubbly. Season with pepper and pour over the fish steaks. Serve, garnished with fresh basil leaves.

Halibut with Tomato Vinaigrette *Flétan Sauce Vièrge*

Sauce vièrge, *an uncooked mixture of tomatoes, aromatic fresh herbs and olive oil, can either be served at room temperature or, as in this dish,* tiède *(slightly warm).*

Serves 2

3 large ripe beefsteak tomatoes, peeled, seeded and chopped
2 shallots or 1 small red onion, finely chopped
1 garlic clove, crushed
90ml/6 tbsp chopped mixed fresh herbs, such as parsley, coriander, basil, tarragon, chervil or chives
125ml/4fl oz/½ cup extra virgin olive oil
4 halibut fillets or steaks (175–200g/6–7oz each)
salt and freshly ground black pepper
green salad, to serve

1 ▼ In a medium bowl, mix together the tomatoes, shallots or onion, garlic and herbs. Stir in the oil and season with salt and freshly ground pepper. Cover the bowl and leave the sauce at room temperature for about 1 hour to allow the flavours to blend.

2 ▲ Preheat the grill. Line a grill pan with foil and brush the foil lightly with oil.

3 ▲ Season the fish with salt and pepper. Place the fish on the foil and brush with a little extra oil. Grill for 5–6 minutes until the flesh is opaque and the top lightly browned.

4 ▲ Pour the sauce into a saucepan and heat gently for a few minutes. Serve the fish with the sauce and a green salad.

SALMON WITH GREEN PEPPERCORNS *Saumon au Poivre Vert*

A fashionable discovery of nouvelle cuisine*, green peppercorns add piquancy to all kinds of sauces and stews. Available pickled in jars or cans, they are great to keep on hand in your store cupboard.*

SERVES 4

15g/½oz/1 tbsp butter
2 or 3 shallots, finely chopped
15ml/1 tbsp brandy (optional)
60ml/4 tbsp dry white wine
90ml/6 tbsp fish or chicken stock
125ml/4fl oz/½ cup whipping cream
30–45ml/2–3 tbsp green peppercorns in brine, rinsed
15–30ml/1–2 tbsp vegetable oil
4 pieces salmon fillet (175–200g/6–7oz each)
salt and freshly ground black pepper
fresh parsley, to garnish

1 ▲ Melt the butter in a heavy saucepan over a medium heat. Add the shallots and cook for about 1–2 minutes until just softened.

2 ▲ Add the brandy, if using, and the white wine, then add the stock and boil to reduce by three-quarters, stirring occasionally.

3 ▲ Reduce the heat, then add the cream and half the peppercorns, crushing them slightly with the back of a spoon. Cook very gently for 4–5 minutes until the sauce is slightly thickened, then strain and stir in the remaining peppercorns. Keep the sauce warm over a very low heat, stirring occasionally, while you cook the salmon.

4 ▼ In a large heavy frying pan, heat the oil over a medium-high heat until very hot. Lightly season the salmon and cook for 3–4 minutes, until the flesh is opaque throughout. To check, pierce the fish with the tip of a sharp knife; the juices should run clear. Arrange the fish on warmed plates and pour over the sauce. Garnish with parsley.

Grilled Red Mullet with Herbs *Rouget Grillé aux Herbes*

In Provence this fish is often charcoal-grilled with herbs from the region or dried fennel branches.

Serves 4

olive oil, for brushing
4 red mullet (225–275g/8–10oz each), cleaned and scaled
fresh herb sprigs, such as parsley, dill, basil or thyme
30–45ml/2–3 tbsp pastis (anise liqueur)

1 About one hour before cooking, light a charcoal fire: when ready the coals should be grey with no flames. Generously brush a hinged grilling rack with olive oil.

2 ▲ Brush each fish with a little olive oil and stuff the cavity with a few herb sprigs, breaking them to fit if necessary. Secure the fish in the grilling rack. Lay the dried fennel sticks over the coals and grill the fish for about 15–20 minutes, turning once during cooking.

3 ▼ Remove the fish to a warmed, flameproof serving dish. Pour the pastis into a small saucepan and heat for a moment or two, then tilt the pan and carefully ignite with a long match. Pour evenly over the fish and serve at once.

Salmon Steaks with Sorrel Sauce *Saumon à l'Oseille*

Salmon and sorrel are traditionally paired in France – the sharp flavour of the sorrel balances the richness of the fish. If sorrel is not available, use finely chopped watercress instead.

Serves 2

2 salmon steaks (about 250g/8oz each)
5ml/1 tsp olive oil
15g/½oz/1 tbsp butter
2 shallots, finely chopped
45ml/3 tbsp whipping cream
100g/3½oz fresh sorrel leaves, washed and patted dry
salt and freshly ground black pepper
fresh sage, to garnish

Cook's tip

If preferred, cook the salmon steaks in a microwave oven for about 4–5 minutes, tightly covered, or according to the manufacturer's guidelines.

1 Season the salmon steaks with salt and pepper. Brush a non-stick frying pan with the oil.

2 ▲ In a small saucepan, melt the butter over a medium heat and fry the shallots, stirring frequently, until just softened. Add the cream and the sorrel to the shallots and cook until the sorrel is completely wilted, stirring constantly.

3 ▲ Meanwhile, place the frying pan over a medium heat until hot. Add the salmon steaks and cook for about 5 minutes, turning once, until the flesh is opaque next to the bone. If you're not sure, pierce with the tip of a sharp knife; the juices should run clear. Arrange the salmon steaks on two warmed plates, garnish with sage and serve with the sorrel sauce.

51

SEA BASS WITH CITRUS FRUIT

Bar Rôti aux Agrumes

Along the Mediterranean coast, sea bass is called loup de mer*; elsewhere in France it is known as* bar. *Its delicate flavour is complemented by citrus fruits and fruity French olive oil.*

SERVES 6

1 small grapefruit
1 orange
1 lemon
1 sea bass (about 1.35kg/3lb), cleaned and scaled
6 fresh basil sprigs
6 fresh dill sprigs
plain flour, for dusting
45ml/3 tbsp olive oil
4–6 shallots, peeled and halved
60ml/4 tbsp dry white wine
15g/½oz/1 tbsp butter
salt and freshly ground black pepper
fresh dill, to garnish

1 ▲ With a vegetable peeler, remove the rind from the grapefruit, orange and lemon. Cut into thin julienne strips, cover and set aside. Peel off the white pith from the fruits and, working over a bowl to catch the juices, cut out the segments from the grapefruit and orange and set aside for the garnish. Slice the lemon thickly.

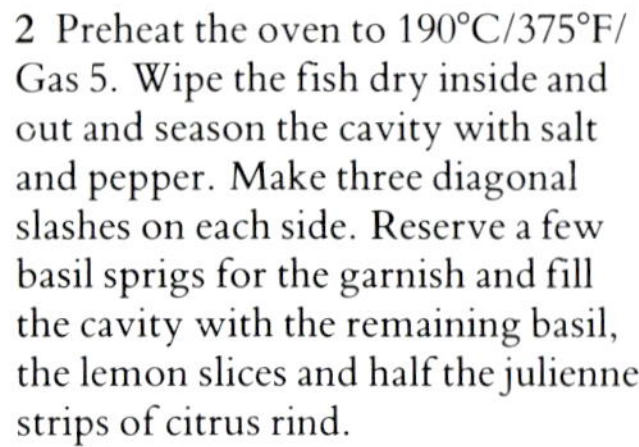

2 Preheat the oven to 190°C/375°F/Gas 5. Wipe the fish dry inside and out and season the cavity with salt and pepper. Make three diagonal slashes on each side. Reserve a few basil sprigs for the garnish and fill the cavity with the remaining basil, the lemon slices and half the julienne strips of citrus rind.

3 ▲ Dust the fish lightly with flour. In a roasting tin or flameproof casserole large enough to hold the fish, heat 30ml/2 tbsp of the olive oil over a medium-high heat and cook the fish for about 1 minute until the skin just crisps and browns on one side. Add the shallots.

4 Place the fish in the oven and bake for about 15 minutes, then carefully turn the fish over and stir the shallots. Drizzle the fish with the remaining oil and bake for a further 10–15 minutes until the flesh is opaque throughout.

5 Carefully transfer the fish to a heated serving dish and remove and discard the cavity stuffing. Pour off any excess oil and add the wine and 30–45ml/2–3 tbsp of the fruit juices to the pan. Bring to the boil over a high heat, stirring. Stir in the remaining julienne strips of citrus rind and boil for 2–3 minutes, then whisk in the butter. Spoon the shallots and sauce around the fish and garnish with dill and the reserved basil and grapefruit and orange segments.

MONKFISH WITH TOMATOES *Lotte à la Provençale*

Monkfish, also known as angler fish, was once scorned by fisherman because of its huge ugly head, yet now it is prized for its rich meaty texture – and is sometimes called "poor man's lobster".

SERVES 4

750g/1¾lb monkfish tail, skinned and filleted
plain flour, for dusting
45–60ml/3–4 tbsp olive oil
125ml/4fl oz/½ cup dry white wine or fish stock
3 ripe tomatoes, peeled, seeded and chopped
2.5ml/½ tsp dried thyme
16 black olives (preferably Niçoise), stoned
15–30ml/1–2 tbsp capers, rinsed
15ml/1 tbsp chopped fresh basil
salt and freshly ground black pepper
pine nuts, to garnish

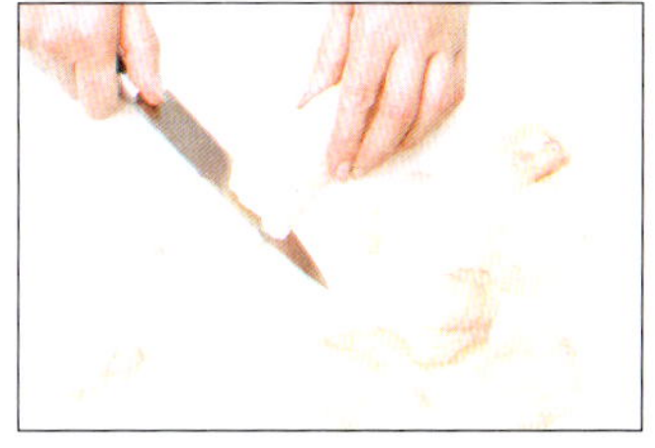

1 ▲ Using a thin, sharp knife, remove any pinkish membrane from the monkfish tail. Holding the knife at a 45° angle, cut the fillets diagonally into 12 slices.

2 ▲ Season the slices with salt and pepper and dust lightly with flour, shaking off any excess.

3 ▲ Heat a large heavy frying pan over a high heat until very hot. Add 45ml/3 tbsp of the oil and swirl to coat. Add the monkfish slices and reduce the heat to medium-high. Cook the monkfish for 1–2 minutes on each side, adding a little more oil if necessary, until lightly browned and the flesh is opaque. Transfer the fish to a warmed plate and keep warm while you make the sauce.

4 ▼ Add the wine or fish stock to the pan and boil for 1–2 minutes, stirring constantly. Add the tomatoes and thyme and cook for 2 minutes, then stir in the olives, capers and basil and cook for a further minute to heat through. Arrange three pieces of fish on each of four warmed plates. Spoon over the sauce and garnish with pine nuts.

PAN-FRIED SOLE

Sole Meunière

This simple recipe is perfect for fresh Dover sole and makes the most of its delicate flavour – lemon sole fillets are a less expensive, but equally tasty alternative.

SERVES 2

340g/¾lb skinless Dover sole or lemon sole fillets
125ml/4fl oz/½ cup milk
55g/2oz/⅓ cup plain flour
15ml/1 tbsp vegetable oil, plus more if needed
15g/½oz/1 tbsp butter
15ml/1 tbsp chopped fresh parsley
salt and freshly ground black pepper
lemon wedges, to serve

1 ▼ Rinse the fish fillets and pat dry using kitchen paper.

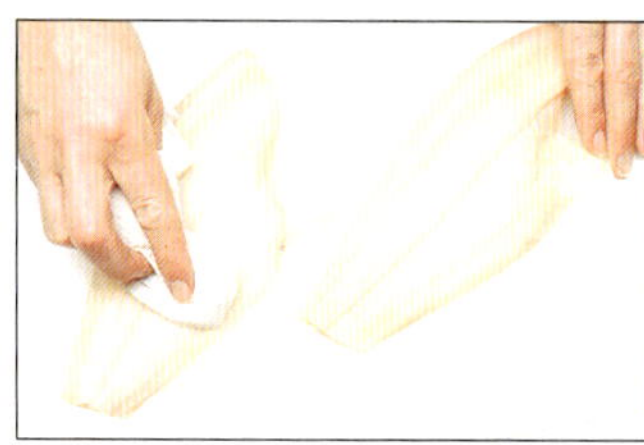

2 ▲ Put the milk into a shallow dish about the same size as a fish fillet. Put the flour in another shallow dish and season with salt and freshly ground black pepper.

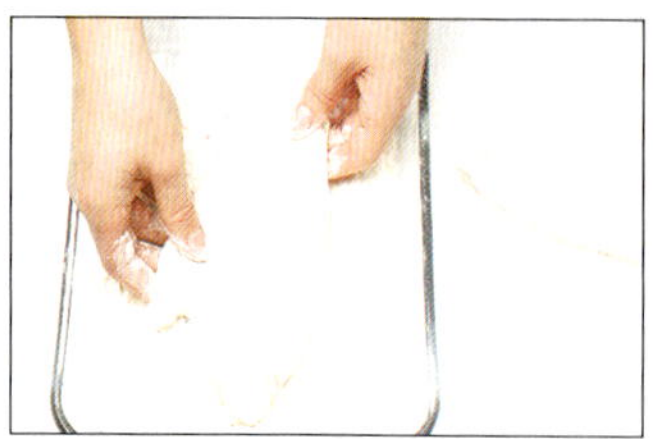

3 ▲ Heat the oil in a large frying pan over a medium-high heat and add the butter. Dip a fish fillet into the milk, then into the flour, turning to coat well, then shake off excess.

4 ▲ Put the coated fillets into the pan in a single layer. (Do not crowd the pan; cook in batches, if necessary.) Fry the fish gently for 3–4 minutes until lightly browned, turning once. Sprinkle the fish with chopped parsley and serve with wedges of lemon.

BREADED SOLE BATONS

Goujonettes de Sole

Goujons *are tiny fish which are fried and eaten whole. In this dish, sole fillets are cut into strips that, when cooked, resemble* goujons. *The French even bring a sense of style to fish fingers!*

SERVES 4

275g/10oz lemon sole fillets, skinned
2 eggs
120g/4oz/1½ cups fine fresh breadcrumbs
85g/3oz/6 tbsp plain flour
salt and freshly ground black pepper
vegetable oil, for frying
tartar sauce and lemon, to serve

1 ▲ Cut the fish fillets into long diagonal strips about 2cm/¾in wide.

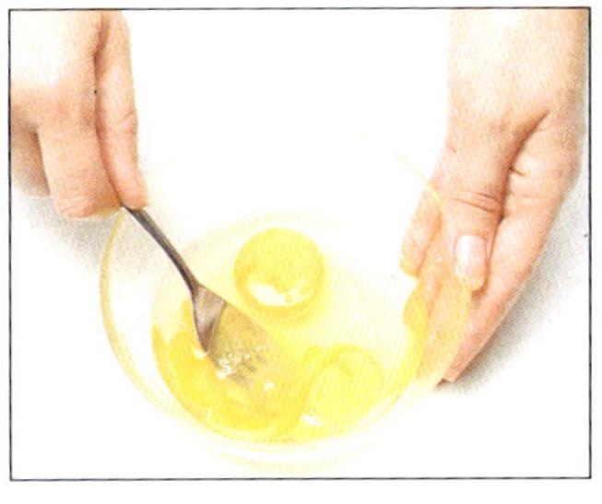

2 ▲ Break the eggs into a shallow dish and beat well with a fork. Place the breadcrumbs in another shallow dish. Put the flour in a large polythene bag and season with salt and freshly ground black pepper.

3 ▼ Dip the fish strips in the egg, turning to coat well. Place on a plate and then taking a few at a time, shake them in the bag of flour. Dip the fish strips in the egg again and then in the breadcrumbs, turning to coat well. Place on a tray in a single layer, not touching. Let the coating set for at least 10 minutes.

4 ▲ Heat 1cm/⅜in oil in a large frying pan over a medium-high heat. When the oil is hot (a cube of bread will sizzle) fry the fish strips for about 2–2½ minutes in batches, turning once, taking care not to overcrowd the pan. Drain on kitchen paper and keep warm. Serve the fish with tartar sauce and lemon.

SOLE WITH PRAWNS AND MUSSELS *Filets de Sole à la Dieppoise*

This classic regional speciality takes its name from the Normandy port of Dieppe, renowned for fish and seafood. The recipe incorporates another great product of the region – cream.

SERVES 6

85g/3oz/6 tbsp butter
8 shallots, finely chopped
300ml/½ pint/1¼ cups dry white
1kg/2¼lb mussels, scrubbed and debearded
225g/8oz button mushrooms, quartered
250ml/8fl oz/1 cup fish stock
12 skinless lemon or Dover sole fillets (about 85–150g/3–5oz each)
30ml/2 tbsp plain flour
60ml/4 tbsp crème fraîche or double cream
250g/8oz cooked, peeled prawns
salt and white pepper
fresh parsley sprigs, to garnish

1 ▲ In a large heavy flameproof casserole, melt 15g/½oz/1 tbsp of the butter over a medium-high heat. Add half the shallots and cook for about 2 minutes until just softened, stirring frequently. Add the white wine and bring to the boil, then add the mussels and cover tightly. Cook the mussels over a high heat, shaking and tossing the pan occasionally, for 4–5 minutes until the shells open. Discard any mussels that do not open.

2 ▲ Transfer the mussels to a large bowl. Strain the mussel cooking liquid through a muslin-lined sieve and set aside. When cool enough to handle, reserve a few mussels in their shells for the garnish. Then remove the rest from their shells and set aside, covered.

3 ▲ Melt half the remaining butter in a large heavy frying pan over a medium heat. Add the remaining shallots and cook for 2 minutes until just softened, stirring frequently. Add the mushrooms and fish stock and bring just to the simmer. Season the fish fillets with salt and pepper. Fold or roll them and slide gently into the stock. Cover and poach for 5–7 minutes until the flesh is opaque. Transfer the fillets to a warmed serving dish and cover to keep warm. Increase the heat and boil the liquid until reduced by one-third.

4 ▲ Melt the remaining butter in a small saucepan over a medium heat. Add the flour and cook for 1–2 minutes, stirring constantly; do not allow the flour mixture to brown. Gradually whisk in the reduced fish cooking liquid, the reserved mussel liquid and pour in any liquid from the fish, then bring to the boil, stirring constantly.

5 ▲ Reduce the heat to medium-low and cook the sauce for 5–7 minutes, stirring frequently. Whisk in the crème fraîche or double cream and keep stirring over a low heat until well blended. Adjust the seasoning then add the reserved mussels and the prawns to the sauce. Cook gently for 2–3 minutes to heat through then spoon the sauce over the fish and serve garnished with fresh parsley sprigs.

TURBOT IN PARCHMENT

Turbot en Papillote

Cooking in parcels is not new, but it is an ideal way to cook fish. Serve this dish plain or with a little hollandaise sauce and let each person open their own parcel to savour the aroma.

SERVES 4

2 carrots, cut into thin julienne strips
2 courgettes, cut into thin julienne strips
2 leeks, cut into thin julienne strips
1 fennel bulb, cut into thin julienne strips
2 tomatoes, peeled, seeded and diced
30ml/2 tbsp chopped fresh dill, tarragon, or chervil
4 turbot fillets (about 200g/7oz each), cut in half
20ml/4 tsp olive oil
60ml/4 tbsp white wine or fish stock
salt and freshly ground black pepper

1 ▼ Preheat the oven to 190°C/375°F /Gas 5. Cut four pieces of non-stick baking paper, about 45cm/18in long. Fold each piece in half and cut into a heart shape.

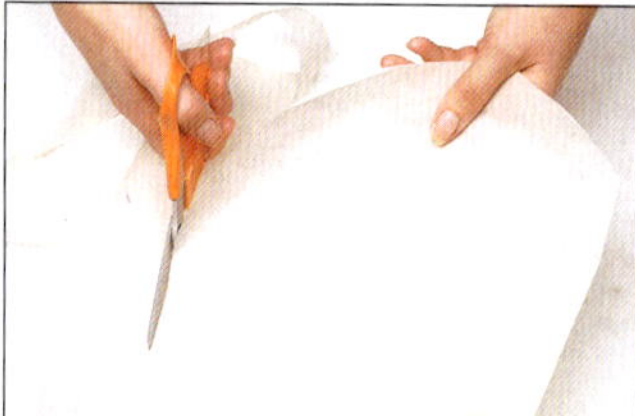

2 ▲ Open the paper hearts. Arrange one quarter of each of the vegetables next to the fold of each heart. Sprinkle with salt and pepper and half the chopped herbs. Arrange two pieces of turbot fillet over each bed of vegetables, overlapping the thin end of one piece and the thicker end of the other. Sprinkle the remaining herbs, the olive oil and wine or stock evenly over the fish.

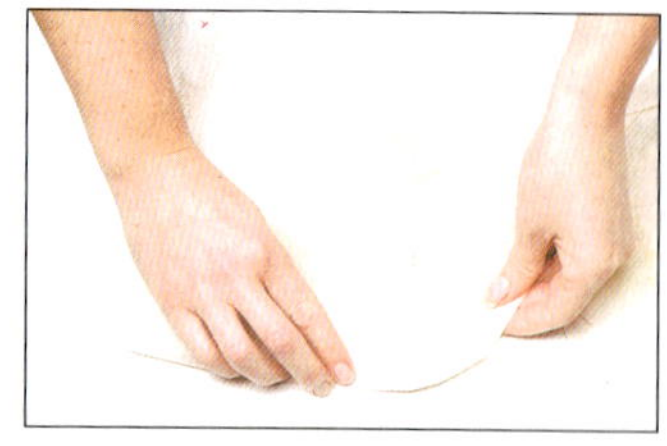

3 ▲ Fold the top half of one of the paper hearts over the fish and vegetables and, beginning at the rounded end, fold the edges of the paper over, twisting and folding to form an airtight packet. Repeat with the remaining three. (The parcels may be assembled up to 4 hours ahead and chilled.)

4 Slide the parcels on to one or two baking sheets and bake for about 10 minutes, or until the paper is lightly browned and well puffed. Slide each parcel on to a warmed plate and serve immediately.

Cod with Lentils and Leeks *Morue aux Lentilles et Poireaux*

This unusual dish, discovered in a Parisian charcuterie, is great for entertaining. You can cook the vegetables ahead of time and let it bake while the first course is served.

Serves 4

150g/5oz/1 cup green lentils
1 bay leaf
1 garlic clove, finely chopped
grated rind of 1 orange
grated rind of 1 lemon
pinch of ground cumin
15g/½oz/1 tbsp butter
450g/1lb leeks, thinly sliced or cut into julienne strips
300ml/½ pint/1¼ cups whipping cream
15ml/1 tbsp lemon juice, or to taste
750g/1¾lb thick skinless cod or haddock fillets
salt and freshly ground black pepper

1 Rinse the lentils and put them in a large saucepan with the bay leaf and garlic. Add enough water to cover by 5cm/2in. Bring to the boil, and boil gently for 10 minutes, then reduce the heat and simmer for a further 15–30 minutes until the lentils are just tender.

2 ▲ Drain the lentils and discard the bay leaf, then stir in half the orange rind and all the lemon rind and season with ground cumin and salt and pepper. Transfer to a shallow baking dish or gratin dish. Preheat the oven to 190°C/375°F/Gas 5.

3 ▼ Melt the butter in a medium saucepan over a medium heat, then add the leeks and cook, stirring frequently, until just softened. Add 225ml/8fl oz/1 cup of the cream and the remaining orange rind and cook gently for 15–20 minutes until the leeks are completely soft and the cream has thickened slightly. Stir in the lemon juice and season with salt and plenty of pepper.

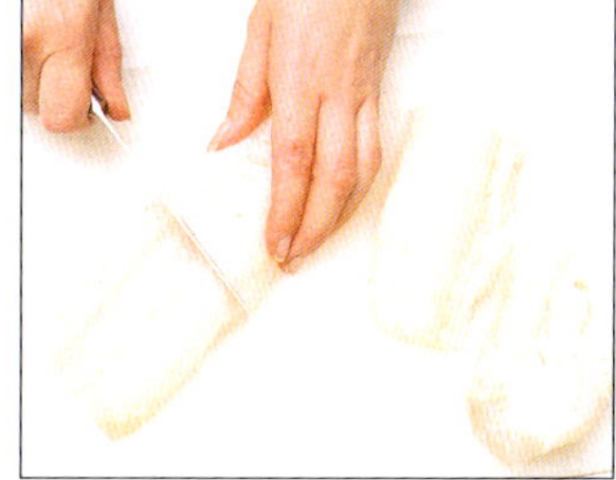

4 ▲ Cut the fish into four pieces, then, with your fingertips, locate and pull out any small bones. Season the fish with salt and pepper, place on top of the lentil mixture and press down slightly into the lentils. Cover each piece of fish with quarter of the leek mixture and pour 15ml/1 tbsp of the remaining cream over each. Bake for about 30 minutes until the fish is cooked through and the topping is lightly golden.

MEDITERRANEAN BAKED FISH

Poisson au Suquet

This informal fish bake is said to have originated with the fishermen on the Côte d'Azur who would cook the remains of their catch for lunch in the still-warm baker's oven.

SERVES 4

3 medium potatoes
2 onions, halved and sliced
30ml/2 tbsp olive oil, plus more for drizzling
2 garlic cloves, very finely chopped
675g/1½lb thick skinless fish fillets, such as turbot or sea bass
1 bay leaf
1 thyme sprig
3 tomatoes, peeled and thinly sliced
30ml/2 tbsp orange juice
60ml/4 tbsp dry white wine
2.5ml/½ tsp saffron threads, steeped in 60ml/4 tbsp boiling water
salt and freshly ground black pepper

1 ▼ Cook the potatoes in boiling salted water for 15 minutes, then drain. When the potatoes are cool enough to handle, peel off the skins and slice them thinly.

2 ▲ Meanwhile, in a heavy frying pan, fry the onions in the oil over a medium-low heat for about 10 minutes, stirring frequently. Add the garlic and continue cooking for a few minutes until the onions are soft and golden.

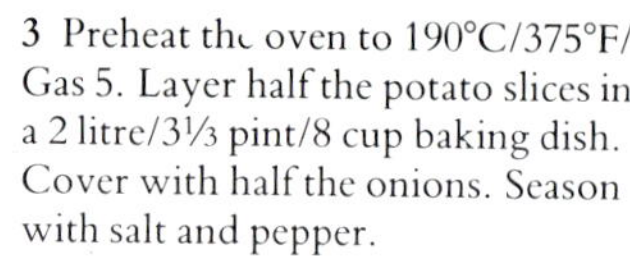

3 Preheat the oven to 190°C/375°F/Gas 5. Layer half the potato slices in a 2 litre/3⅓ pint/8 cup baking dish. Cover with half the onions. Season with salt and pepper.

4 ▲ Place the fish fillets on top of the vegetables and tuck in the herbs between them. Top with the tomato slices and then the remaining onions and potatoes.

5 Pour over the orange juice, wine and saffron liquid, season with salt and pepper and drizzle a little extra olive oil on top. Bake uncovered for about 30 minutes until the potatoes are tender and the fish is cooked.

Fish with Butter Sauce *Filets de Poisson Beurre Blanc*

This classic French butter sauce livens up steamed or poached fish. For a dinner party, make it shortly before the guests arrive and keep warm in a vacuum flask until ready to serve.

Serves 4

750g/1¾lb skinless white fish fillets, such as sole, plaice, sea bass or perch
salt and white pepper
For the butter sauce
2 shallots, finely chopped
90ml/6 tbsp white wine vinegar
15ml/1 tbsp whipping cream
175g/6oz /¾ cup unsalted butter, cut into 12 pieces
15ml/1 tbsp chopped fresh tarragon or chives
fresh tarragon sprigs, to garnish

1 ▲ To make the sauce, put the shallots and vinegar in a small heavy saucepan and boil over a high heat until the liquid has almost evaporated, leaving only about 15ml/1 tbsp, then stir in the cream.

2 ▲ Reduce the heat to medium and add the butter, one piece at a time, whisking constantly until it melts before adding the next (lift the pan off the heat if the butter melts faster than it can be incorporated).

3 ▲ Season the sauce with salt and pepper to taste and whisk in the tarragon or chives. (If you prefer a smooth sauce, strain before adding the herbs.) Cover the pan and set aside in a warm place.

4 ▼ Bring some water to the boil in the bottom of a covered steamer. Season the fish fillets with salt and pepper, then steam for 3–5 minutes until the flesh is opaque. The time will depend on the thickness of the fish. Serve the fish with the sauce, garnished with fresh tarragon.

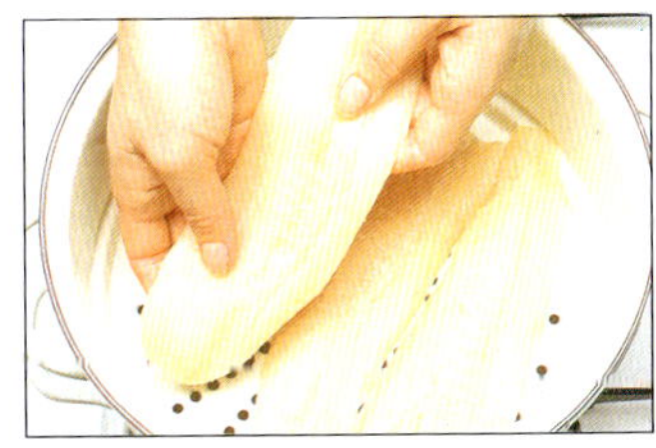

FISH TERRINE

Terrine de Poisson

This colourful layered terrine makes a spectacular presentation for a special occasion. It is typical of those found in the best charcuteries *in France and great for entertaining since it is prepared ahead.*

SERVES 6

450g/1lb skinless white fish fillets
225–275g/8–10oz thinly sliced smoked salmon
2 cold egg whites
1.5ml/¼ tsp each salt and white pepper
pinch of freshly grated nutmeg
250ml/8fl oz/1 cup whipping cream
55g/2 oz/2 cups (packed) small tender spinach leaves
lemon mayonnaise, to serve

1 Cut the white fish fillets into 2.5cm/1in pieces, removing any bones as you work. Spread out the fish pieces on a plate, cover with clear film. Place in the freezer for about 15 minutes until very cold.

2 ▲ Lightly grease a 1.2 litre/2 pint/5 cup terrine or loaf tin and line the base with non-stick baking paper, then line the base and sides of the tin with smoked salmon slices, letting them overhang the edge. Preheat the oven to 180°C/350°F/Gas 4.

3 Remove the fish from the freezer, then process in a food processor until it is a very smooth purée, stopping the machine and scraping down the sides two or three times.

4 Add the egg whites, one at a time, then add the salt, pepper and nutmeg. With the machine running, pour in the cream and stop as soon as it is blended. (If overprocessed, the cream will thicken too much.)

5 Transfer the fish mixture to a large glass bowl. Put the spinach leaves into the food processor and purée. Add one-third of the fish mixture to the spinach and process until just combined, scraping down the sides once or twice.

6 ▲ Spread half the plain fish mixture in the base of the tin and smooth it level. Spoon the green fish mixture over the top and smooth the surface, then cover with the remaining plain mixture and smooth the top. Fold the overhanging pieces of salmon over the top to enclose the mixture. Tap the tin to settle the mixture and remove any air pockets, then cover the terrine with a double layer of foil.

7 Put the terrine in a roasting tin and pour in enough boiling water to come halfway up the sides of the terrine. Bake for about 1 hour, until a skewer inserted in the centre comes out clean. Allow to cool, wrap well and chill until firm or overnight.

8 To serve the terrine, turn out on to a board and slice. Arrange slices on individual plates and serve with lemon mayonnaise.

Mussels Steamed in White Wine *Moules Marinières*

This is the best and easiest way to serve the small tender mussels, bouchots*, which are farmed along much of the French coast line. In Normandy the local sparkling dry cider is often used instead of white wine. Serve with plenty of crusty French bread to dip in the juices.*

Serves 4

2kg/4½lb mussels
300ml/½ pint/1¼ cups dry white wine
4–6 large shallots, finely chopped
bouquet garni
freshly ground black pepper

1 ▲ Discard any broken mussels and those with open shells that refuse to close when tapped. Under cold running water, scrape the mussel shells with a knife to remove any barnacles and pull out the stringy "beards". Soak the mussels in several changes of cold water for at least 1 hour.

2 ▲ In a large heavy flameproof casserole combine the wine, shallots, bouquet garni and plenty of pepper. Bring to the boil over a medium-high heat and cook for 2 minutes.

3 ▲ Add the mussels and cook, tightly covered, for 5 minutes, or until the mussels open, shaking and tossing the pan occasionally. Discard any mussels that do not open.

4 Using a slotted spoon, divide the mussels among warmed soup plates. Tilt the casserole a little and hold for a few seconds to allow any sand to settle to the bottom.

5 Spoon or pour the cooking liquid over the mussels, dividing it evenly, then serve at once.

Variation

For Mussels with Cream Sauce (*Moules à la Crème*), cook as above, but transfer the mussels to a warmed bowl and cover to keep warm. Strain the cooking liquid through a muslin-lined sieve into a large saucepan and boil for about 7–10 minutes to reduce by half. Stir in 90ml/6 tbsp whipping cream and 30ml/2 tbsp chopped parsley, then add the mussels. Cook for about 1 minute more to reheat the mussels.

MEDITERRANEAN FISH STEW *Bouillabaisse*

Different variations of bouillabaisse *abound along the Mediterranean coast – every village seems to have its own version – and almost any combination of fish and shellfish can be used.*

SERVES 8

2.5kg/6lb white fish, such as sea bass, snapper or monkfish, filleted and skinned (choose thick fish)
45ml/3 tbsp extra virgin olive oil
grated rind of 1 orange
1 garlic clove, very finely chopped
pinch of saffron threads
30ml/2 tbsp pastis (anise liqueur)
1 small fennel bulb, finely chopped
1 large onion, finely chopped
225g/½lb small new potatoes, sliced
900g/2lb large raw Mediterranean prawns, peeled
croûtons, to serve

FOR THE STOCK
1–1.3kg/2–3lb fish heads, bones and trimmings
30ml/2 tbsp olive oil
2 leeks, sliced
1 onion, halved and sliced
1 red pepper, cored and sliced
675g/1½lb ripe tomatoes, cored and quartered
4 garlic cloves, sliced
bouquet garni
rind of ½ orange, removed with a vegetable peeler
2 or 3 pinches saffron threads

FOR THE ROUILLE
30g/1oz/⅔ cup soft white breadcrumbs
1 or 2 garlic cloves, very finely chopped
½ red pepper, roasted
5ml/1 tsp tomato purée
125ml/4fl oz/½ cup extra virgin olive oil

COOK'S TIP

Be sure to ask the fishmonger for the heads, tails and trimmings from your fish fillets and avoid strong-flavoured oily fish, such as mackerel. To reduce last-minute work, you can make the *rouille*, croûtons and stock early in the day while the fish marinates.

1 ▲ Cut the fish fillets into serving pieces, then trim off any thin parts and reserve for the stock. Put the fish in a bowl with 30ml/2 tbsp of the olive oil, the orange rind, garlic, saffron and pastis. Turn to coat well, cover and chill.

2 ▲ To make the stock, rinse the fish heads and bones under cold running water. Heat the olive oil in a large, preferably stainless steel, saucepan or flameproof casserole. Add the leeks, onion and pepper and cook over a medium heat for about 5 minutes until the onion starts to soften, stirring occasionally. Add the fish heads, bones and trimmings, with any heads or shells from the prawns. Then add the tomatoes, garlic, bouquet garni, orange rind, saffron and enough cold water to cover the ingredients by 2.5cm/1in.

3 Bring to the boil, skimming any foam that rises to the surface, then reduce the heat and simmer, covered, for ½ hour, skimming once or twice more. Strain the stock.

4 ▲ To make the *rouille*, soak the breadcrumbs in water then squeeze dry. Put the breadcrumbs in a food processor with the garlic, roasted red pepper and tomato puree and process until smooth. With the machine running, slowly pour the oil through the feed tube, scraping down the sides once or twice.

5 ▲ To finish the bouillabaise, heat the remaining 15ml/1 tbsp of olive oil in a wide flameproof casserole over a medium heat. Cook the fennel and onion for about 5 minutes until the onion just softens, then add the stock. Bring to the boil, add the potatoes and cook for 5–7 minutes. Reduce the heat to medium and add the fish, starting with the thickest pieces and adding the thinner ones after 2 or 3 minutes. Add the prawns and continue simmering gently until all the fish and shellfish is cooked.

6 Transfer the fish, shellfish and potatoes to a heated tureen or soup plates. Adjust the seasoning and ladle the soup over. Serve with croûtons spread with *rouille*.

Sautéed Scallops *Coquilles Saint Jacques Meunières*

Scallops go well with all sorts of sauces, but simple cooking is the best way to enjoy their flavour.

Serves 2

450g/1lb shelled scallops
30g/1oz/2 tbsp butter
30ml/2 tbsp dry white vermouth
15ml/1 tbsp finely chopped fresh parsley
salt and freshly ground black pepper

1 Rinse the scallops under cold running water to remove any sand or grit and pat dry using kitchen paper. Season them lightly with salt and pepper.

2 ▼ In a frying pan large enough to hold the scallops in one layer, heat half the butter until it begins to colour. Sauté the scallops for 3–5 minutes, turning, until golden brown on both sides and just firm to the touch. Remove to a serving platter and cover to keep warm.

3 ▲ Add the vermouth to the hot frying pan, swirl in the remaining butter, add the parsley and pour the sauce over the scallops. Serve immediately.

Garlicky Scallops and Prawns *Fruits de Mer à la Provençale*

Scallops and prawns are found all along the Atlantic and Mediterranean coasts of France and are enjoyed in every region. This method of cooking is typical in Provence.

Serves 2–4

6 large shelled scallops
6–8 large raw prawns, peeled
plain flour, for dusting
30–45ml/2–3 tbsp olive oil
1 garlic clove, finely chopped
15ml/1 tbsp chopped fresh basil
30–45ml/2–3 tbsp lemon juice
salt and freshly ground black pepper

Variation

To make a richer sauce, transfer the cooked scallops and prawns to a warmed plate. Pour in 60ml/4 tbsp dry white wine and boil to reduce by half. Add 15g/½oz/1 tbsp unsalted butter, whisking until it melts and the sauce thickens slightly. Pour over the scallops and prawns.

1 ▼ Rinse the scallops under cold running water to remove any sand or grit. Pat them dry using kitchen paper and cut in half crossways. Season the scallops and prawns with salt and pepper and dust lightly with flour, shaking off excess.

2 Heat the oil in a large frying pan over a high heat and add the scallops and prawns.

3 ▲ Reduce heat to medium-high and cook for 2 minutes, then turn the scallops and prawns and add the garlic and basil, shaking pan to distribute them evenly. Cook for a further 2 minutes until golden and just firm to the touch. Sprinkle over the lemon juice and toss to blend.

Scallops with Mushrooms *Coquilles Saint Jacques au Gratin*

This dish has been a classic on bistro menus since Hemingway's days in Paris – it makes an appealing starter, or serve it as a rich and elegant main course.

Serves 2–4

250ml/8fl oz/1 cup dry white wine
125ml/4fl oz/½ cup water
2 shallots, finely chopped
1 bay leaf
450g/1lb shelled scallops, rinsed
40g/1½oz /3 tbsp butter
40g/1½oz/3 tbsp plain flour
90ml/6 tbsp whipping cream
freshly grated nutmeg
175g/6oz mushrooms, thinly sliced
45–60ml/3–4 tbsp dry breadcrumbs
salt and freshly ground black pepper

1 ▼ Combine the wine, water, shallots and bay leaf in a medium saucepan. Bring to the boil, then reduce the heat to medium-low and simmer for 10 minutes. Add the scallops, cover and simmer for 3–4 minutes until they are opaque.

2 Remove the scallops from the cooking liquid with a slotted spoon and boil the liquid until reduced to 175ml/6fl oz. Strain the liquid.

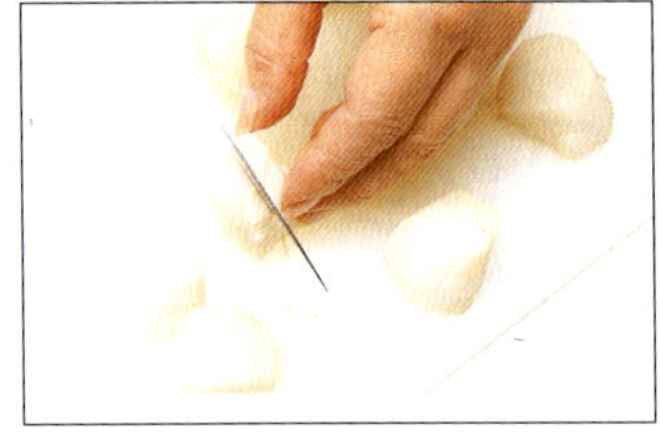

3 ▲ Carefully pull off the tough muscle from the side of the scallops and discard. Slice the scallops in half crossways.

4 ▲ Melt 30g/1oz/2 tbsp of the butter in a heavy saucepan over a medium-high heat. Stir in the flour and cook for 2 minutes. Add the reserved cooking liquid, whisking vigorously until smooth, then whisk in the cream and season with salt, pepper and nutmeg. Reduce the heat to low and simmer for 10 minutes, stirring frequently.

5 Melt the remaining butter in a frying pan over a medium-high heat. Add the mushrooms and cook for about 5 minutes until lightly browned, stirring frequently. Stir the mushrooms into the sauce.

6 Preheat the grill. Add the scallops to the sauce and adjust the seasoning. Spoon the mixture into four individual gratin dishes, large scallop shells or a flameproof baking dish and sprinkle with breadcrumbs. Grill until golden brown and bubbly.

PRAWNS WITH CURRY SAUCE *Crevettes en Brochette à l'Indienne*

In France any dish called à l'Indienne *contains Indian spices. This sauce is great with grilled prawns, but you can make it with chicken stock for serving with chicken, game, veal or pork.*

SERVES 4

16 large raw prawns, peeled
grated rind and juice of 1 orange
juice of 1 lemon or lime
30ml/2 tbsp olive oil
1 garlic clove, crushed
5ml/1 tsp hot chilli sauce or curry powder, or to taste
2.5ml/½ tsp ground coriander
2.5ml/½ tsp ground cumin

FOR THE CURRY SAUCE

15ml/1 tbsp olive oil
2 shallots, finely chopped
1 or 2 garlic cloves, crushed
5ml/1 tsp curry powder or paste
1.5ml/¼ tsp ground coriander
1.5ml/¼ tsp ground cumin
60ml/4 tbsp fish stock
225ml/8fl oz/1 cup whipping cream
15ml/1 tbsp chopped fresh coriander or mint

1 ▲ Put the prawns in a bowl with the orange rind and juice, lemon or lime juice, oil, garlic, chilli sauce or curry powder, ground coriander and cumin. Stir well, then cover and leave to marinate for 30 minutes.

2 To make the curry sauce, heat the oil in a medium saucepan over a medium heat. Add the shallots and cook for 1–2 minutes, stirring, until just softened. Stir in the garlic and curry powder or paste, ground coriander and cumin and cook for 1–2 minutes, stirring constantly.

3 ▲ Add the fish stock and bring to the boil. Reduce by half, then add the cream and simmer for 8–10 minutes until slightly thickened. Stir in the fresh coriander or mint. Reduce the heat to low and keep warm, stirring occasionally.

4 ▼ Preheat the grill and line a grill pan with foil. Thread the prawns on to four metal or damp wooden skewers. Place the skewers on the grill pan and grill for 3–4 minutes, turning once. Spoon a little sauce on to four dinner plates. Place a skewer on each plate, and serve at once.

Seafood in Puff Pastry

Feuilletés aux Fruits de Mer

This classic combination of seafood in a creamy sauce served in a puff pastry case is found as a starter on the menus of many elegant restaurants in France.

Serves 6

350g/12oz rough puff or puff pastry
1 egg beaten with 15ml/1 tbsp water, to glaze
60ml/4 tbsp dry white wine
2 shallots, finely chopped
450g/1lb mussels, scrubbed and debearded
15g/½oz/1 tbsp butter
450g/1lb shelled scallops, cut in half crossways
450g/1lb raw prawns, peeled
175g/6oz cooked lobster meat, sliced

For the sauce

225g/8oz/1 cup unsalted butter, diced
2 shallots, finely chopped
250ml/8fl oz/1 cup fish stock
90ml/6 tbsp dry white wine
15–30ml/1–2 tbsp cream
lemon juice
salt and white pepper
fresh dill sprigs, to garnish

1 ▼ Lightly grease a large baking sheet and sprinkle with a little water. On a lightly floured surface, roll out the pastry into a rectangle slightly less than 6mm/¼in thick. Using a sharp knife, cut into six diamond shapes about 12.5cm/5in long. Transfer to the baking sheet. Brush pastry with egg glaze. Using the tip of a knife, score a line 1.2cm/½in from the edge, then lightly mark the centre in a criss-cross pattern.

2 Chill the pastry cases for 30 minutes. Preheat the oven to 220°C/425°F/Gas 7. Bake for about 20 minutes until puffed and brown. Transfer to a wire rack and, while still hot, remove each lid, cutting along the scored line to free it. Scoop out any uncooked dough from the bases and discard, then leave the cases to cool completely.

3 In a large saucepan, bring the wine and shallots to the boil over a high heat. Add the mussels to the pan and cook, tightly covered, for 4–6 minutes until the shells open, shaking the pan occasionally. Remove any mussels that do not open. Reserve six mussels for the garnish, then remove the rest from their shells and set aside in a bowl, covered. Strain the cooking liquid through a muslin-lined sieve and reserve for the sauce.

4 ▲ In a heavy frying pan, melt the butter over a medium heat. Add the scallops and prawns, cover tightly and cook for 3–4 minutes, shaking and stirring occasionally, until they feel just firm to the touch; do not overcook.

5 Using a slotted spoon, transfer the scallops and prawns to the bowl with the mussels and add any cooking juices to the mussel liquid.

6 ▲ To make the sauce, melt 30g/1oz /2 tbsp of the butter in a heavy saucepan. Add the shallots and cook for 2 minutes. Pour in the fish stock and boil for about 15 minutes over a high heat until reduced by three-quarters. Add the white wine and reserved mussel liquid and boil for 5–7 minutes until reduced by half. Lower the heat to medium and whisk in the remaining butter, a little at a time, to make a smooth thick sauce (lift the pan from the heat if the sauce begins to boil). Whisk in the cream and season with salt, if needed, pepper and lemon juice. Keep warm over a very low heat, stirring frequently.

7 Warm the pastry cases in a low oven for about 10 minutes. Put the mussels, scallops and prawns in a large saucepan. Stir in quarter of the sauce and reheat gently over a low heat. Gently stir in the lobster meat and cook for a further minute.

8 Arrange the pastry case bases on individual plates. Divide the seafood mixture equally among them and top with the lids. Garnish each with a mussel and a dill sprig and spoon the remaining sauce around the edges or serve separately.

Shellfish with Seasoned Broth *Fruits de Mer à la Nage*

Leave one or two mussels and prawns in their shells to add a flamboyant touch to this elegant dish.

Serves 4

675g/1½lb mussels, scrubbed and debearded
1 small fennel bulb, thinly sliced
1 onion, finely sliced
1 leek, thinly sliced
1 small carrot, cut in julienne strips
1 garlic clove
1 litre/1⅔ pints/4 cups water
pinch of curry powder
pinch of saffron
1 bay leaf
450g/1lb raw large prawns, peeled
450g/1lb small shelled scallops
175g/6oz cooked lobster meat, sliced (optional)
15–30ml/1–2 tbsp chopped fresh chervil or parsley
salt and freshly ground black pepper

1 ▼ Put the mussels in a large heavy saucepan or flameproof casserole and cook, tightly covered, over a high heat for 4–6 minutes until the shells open, shaking the pan or casserole occasionally. When cool enough to handle, discard any mussels that did not open and remove the rest from their shells. Strain the cooking liquid through a muslin-lined sieve and reserve.

2 ▲ Put the fennel, onion, leek, carrot and garlic in a saucepan and add the water, reserved mussel liquid, spices and bay leaf. Bring to the boil, skimming any foam that rises to the surface, then reduce the heat and simmer gently, covered, for 20 minutes until the vegetables are tender. Remove the garlic clove.

3 ▲ Add the prawns, scallops and lobster meat, if using, then after 1 minute, add the mussels. Simmer gently for about 3 minutes until the scallops are opaque and all the shellfish is heated through. Adjust the seasoning, then ladle into a heated tureen or shallow soup plates and sprinkle with herbs.

Cook's tip

If you like, you can cook and shell the mussels and simmer the vegetables in the broth ahead of time, then finish the dish just before serving.

Lobster Thermidor *Homard Thermidor*

Lobster Thermidor takes its name from the 11th month of the French Revolutionary calendar, which falls in mid-summer, although this rich dish it is equally delicious in cooler weather, too. Serve one lobster per person as a main course or one filled shell each for a starter.

Serves 2–4

2 live lobsters (about 675g/1½lb each)
20g/¾oz/1½ tbsp butter
30ml/2 tbsp plain flour
30ml/2 tbsp brandy
125ml/4fl oz/½ cup milk
90ml/6 tbsp whipping cream
15ml/1 tbsp Dijon mustard
lemon juice
salt and white pepper
grated Parmesan cheese, for sprinkling
fresh parsley and dill, to garnish

1 ▲ Bring a large saucepan of salted water to the boil. Put the lobsters into the pan head first and cook for 8–10 minutes.

2 ▲ Cut the lobsters in half lengthways and discard the dark sac behind the eyes, then pull out the string-like intestine from the tail. Remove the meat from the shells, reserving the coral and liver, then rinse the shells and wipe dry. Cut the meat into bite-size pieces.

3 ▲ Melt the butter in a heavy saucepan over a medium-high heat. Stir in the flour and cook, stirring, until slightly golden. Pour in the brandy and milk, whisking vigorously until smooth, then whisk in the cream and mustard.

4 Push the lobster coral and liver through a sieve into the sauce and whisk to blend. Reduce the heat to low and simmer gently for about 10 minutes, stirring frequently, until thickened. Season with salt, if needed, pepper and lemon juice.

5 Preheat the grill. Arrange the lobster shells in a gratin dish or shallow flameproof baking dish.

6 Stir the lobster meat into the sauce and divide the mixture evenly among the shells. Sprinkle lightly with Parmesan and grill until golden. Serve garnished with herbs.

POULTRY AND GAME

Poultry is immensely popular in France and fresh, free-range birds, like the excellent chickens from Bresse, are widely prized. These birds are expensive, but with their usual regard for quality, the French are prepared to pay a little more for something special. The very best are often cooked simply by roasting or sautéeing so that their quality can be appreciated. There is a huge variety of other poultry, too – capons, cocks, different sizes of poussins, several kinds of ducks, geese, guinea fowl, as well as feathered game such as quail, partridge and mallard, which can often be seen hanging outside the poulterer's shop.

ROAST CHICKEN WITH LEMON AND HERBS *Poulet Rôti*

In France, the evocative sight and smell of chickens roasting on their spits can often be found in charcuteries. *A well-flavoured chicken is essential – use a free-range or corn-fed bird, if possible.*

SERVES 4

1.3kg/3lb chicken
1 unwaxed lemon, halved
small bunch thyme sprigs
1 bay leaf
15g/½oz/1 tbsp butter, softened
60–90ml/4–6 tbsp chicken stock or water
salt and freshly ground black pepper

COOK'S TIP

Be sure to save the carcasses of roast poultry for stock. Freeze them until you have several, then simmer with aromatic vegetables, herbs and water.

1 Preheat the oven to 200°C/400°F/Gas 6. Season the chicken inside and out with salt and pepper.

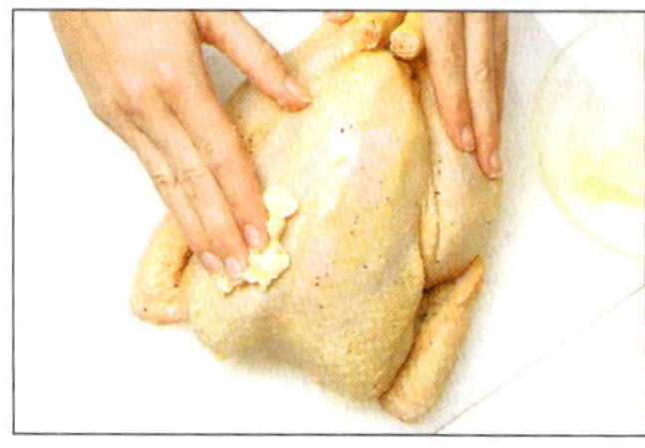

2 ▲ Squeeze the juice of one lemon half and then place the juice, the squeezed lemon half, the thyme and bay leaf in the chicken cavity. Tie the legs with string and rub the breast with butter.

3 ▲ Place the chicken on a rack in a roasting tin. Squeeze over the juice of the other lemon half. Roast the chicken for 1 hour, basting two or three times, until the juices run clear when the thickest part of the thigh is pierced with a knife.

4 ▲ Pour the juices from the cavity into the roasting tin and transfer the chicken to a carving board. Cover loosely with foil and leave to stand for 10–15 minutes before carving.

5 ▲ Skim off the fat from the cooking juices. Add the stock or water and boil over a medium heat, stirring and scraping the base of the pan, until slightly reduced. Strain and serve with the chicken.

GRILLED POUSSINS WITH CITRUS GLAZE *Poussins Grillés*

This recipe is suitable for many kinds of small birds, including pigeons, snipe and partridges. It would also work with quail, but decrease the cooking time and spread the citrus mixture over, rather than under, the fragile skin.

SERVES 4

2 poussins (about 750g/1½lb each)
55g/2oz/4 tbsp butter, softened
30ml/2 tbsp olive oil
2 garlic cloves, crushed
2.5ml/½ tsp dried thyme
1.5ml/¼ tsp cayenne pepper, or to taste
grated rind and juice of 1 unwaxed lemon
grated rind and juice of 1 unwaxed lime
30ml/2 tbsp honey
salt and freshly ground black pepper
tomato salad, to serve
fresh dill, to garnish

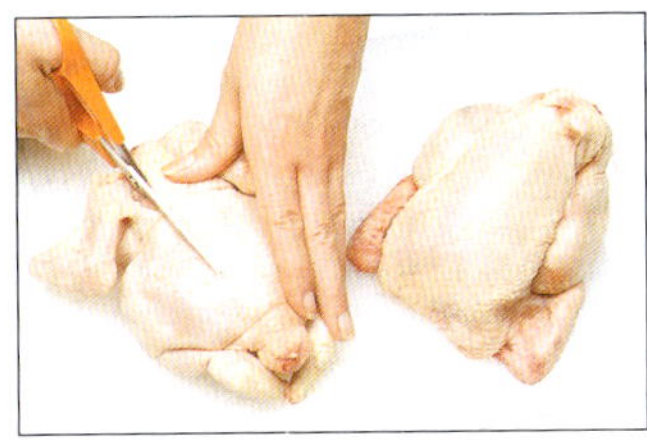

1 ▲ Using kitchen scissors, cut along both sides of the backbone of each bird; remove and discard. Cut the birds in half along the the breast bone, then using a rolling pin, press down to flatten.

2 ▲ Beat the butter in a small bowl, then beat in 15ml/1 tbsp of the olive oil, the garlic, thyme, cayenne, salt and pepper, half the lemon and lime rind and 15ml/1 tbsp each of the lemon and lime juice.

3 ▼ Using your fingertips, carefully loosen the skin of each poussin breast. With a round-bladed knife or small palette knife, spread the butter mixture evenly between the skin and breast meat.

COOK'S TIP

If smaller poussins, about 450g/1lb each, are available, serve one per person. Increase the butter to 85g/3oz/6 tbsp, if necessary.

4 ▲ Preheat the grill and line a grill pan with foil. In a small bowl, mix together the remaining olive oil, lemon and lime juices and the honey. Place the bird halves, skin side up, on the grill pan and brush with the juice mixture.

5 Grill for 10–12 minutes, basting once or twice with the juices. Turn over and grill for 7–10 minutes, basting once, or until juices run clear when the thigh is pierced with a knife. Serve with the tomato salad, garnished with dill.

OLD-FASHIONED CHICKEN FRICASSÉE *Fricassée de Poulet*

A fricassée is a classic dish in which poultry or meat is first seared in fat, then braised with liquid until cooked. This recipe is finished with a little cream – leave it out if you wish.

SERVES 4–6

1.2–1.3kg/2½–3lb chicken, cut into pieces
55g/2oz/4 tbsp butter
30ml/2 tbsp vegetable oil
30g/1oz/3 tbsp plain flour
250ml/8fl oz/1 cup dry white wine
750ml/1¼ pints/3 cups chicken stock
bouquet garni
1.5ml/¼ tsp white pepper
225g/8oz button mushrooms, trimmed
5ml/1 tsp lemon juice
16–24 small white onions, peeled
125ml/4fl oz/½ cup water
5ml/1 tsp sugar
90ml/6 tbsp whipping cream
salt
30ml/2 tbsp chopped fresh parsley, to garnish

1 ▲ Wash the chicken pieces, then pat dry with kitchen paper. Melt half the butter with the oil in a large, heavy flameproof casserole over a medium heat. Add half the chicken pieces and cook for 10 minutes, turning occasionally, or until just golden in colour. Transfer to a plate, then cook the remaining pieces in the same way.

COOK'S TIP

This dish can be made ahead and kept hot in a warm oven for up to an hour before serving.

2 ▲ Return the seared chicken pieces to the casserole. Sprinkle with the flour, turning the pieces to coat. Cook over a low heat for about 4 minutes, turning occasionally.

3 ▲ Pour in the wine, bring to the boil and add the stock. Push the chicken pieces to one side and scrape the base of the casserole, stirring until well blended.

4 ▲ Bring the liquid to the boil, add the bouquet garni and season with a pinch of salt and white pepper. Cover and simmer over a medium heat for 25–30 minutes until the chicken is tender and the juices run clear when the thickest part of the meat is pierced with a knife.

5 ▲ Meanwhile, in a frying pan, heat the remaining butter over a medium-high heat. Add the mushrooms and lemon juice and cook for 3–4 minutes until the mushrooms are golden, stirring. Transfer the mushrooms to a bowl, add the onions, water and sugar to the pan, swirling to dissolve the sugar. Simmer for about 10 minutes, until just tender. Tip the onions and any juices into the bowl with the mushrooms and set aside.

6 When the chicken is cooked, transfer the pieces to a deep serving dish and cover with foil to keep warm. Discard the bouquet garni. Add any cooking juices from the vegetables to the casserole. Bring to the boil and boil, stirring frequently, until the sauce is reduced by half.

7 ▲ Whisk the cream into the sauce and cook for 2 minutes. Add the mushrooms and onions and cook for a further 2 minutes. Adjust the seasoning, then pour the sauce over the chicken, sprinkle with parsley and serve.

Chicken with garlic *Poulet à l'Ail*

Use fresh new season's garlic if you can find it – there's no need to peel the cloves if the skin is not papery. In France, sometimes the cooked garlic cloves are spread on toasted country bread.

Serves 8

2kg/4½lb chicken pieces
1 large onion, halved and sliced
3 large garlic bulbs (about 200g/7oz), separated into cloves and peeled
150ml/¼ pint/⅔ cup dry white wine
175ml/6fl oz/¾ cup chicken stock
4–5 thyme sprigs, or 2.5ml/½ tsp dried thyme
1 small rosemary sprig, or a pinch of ground rosemary
1 bay leaf
salt and freshly ground black pepper

1 Preheat the oven to 190°C/375°F/Gas 5. Pat the chicken pieces dry and season with salt and pepper.

2 ▼ Put the chicken, skin side down in a large flameproof casserole and set over a medium-high heat. Turn frequently and transfer the chicken to a plate when browned. Cook in batches if necessary and pour off the fat after browning.

3 ▲ Add the onion and garlic to the casserole and cook over a medium-low heat, covered, until lightly browned, stirring frequently.

4 Add the wine to the casserole, bring to the boil and return the chicken to the casserole. Add the stock and herbs and bring back to the boil. Cover and transfer to the oven. Cook for 25 minutes, or until the chicken is tender and the juices run clear when the thickest part of the thigh is pierced with a knife.

5 ▲ Remove the chicken pieces from the pan and strain the cooking liquid. Discard the herbs, transfer the solids to a food processor and purée until smooth. Remove any fat from the cooking liquid and return to the casserole. Stir in the garlic and onion purée, return the chicken to the casserole and reheat gently for 3–4 minutes before serving.

CHICKEN CHASSEUR

Poulet Sauté Chasseur

A chicken sauté is one of the classics of French cooking. Quick to prepare, it lends itself to endless variation. Since this dish reheats successfully, it is also convenient for entertaining.

SERVES 4

40g/1½oz/¼ cup plain flour
1.2kg/2½lb chicken pieces
15ml/1 tbsp olive oil
3 small onions or large shallots, sliced
175g/6oz mushrooms, quartered
1 garlic clove, crushed
60ml/4 tbsp dry white wine
125ml/4fl oz/½ cup chicken stock
340g/¾lb tomatoes, peeled, seeded and chopped, or 250ml/8fl oz/1 cup canned chopped tomatoes
salt and freshly ground black pepper
fresh parsley, to garnish

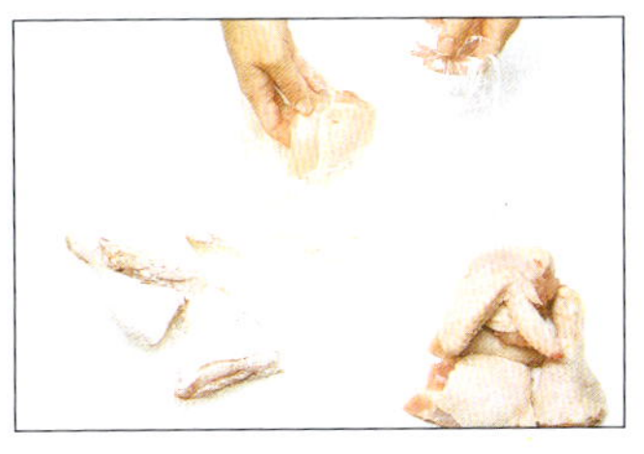

1 ▲ Put the flour into a polythene bag and season with salt and pepper. One at a time, drop the chicken pieces into the bag and shake to coat with flour. Tap off the excess and transfer to a plate.

2 ▲ Heat the oil in a heavy flameproof casserole. Fry the chicken over a medium-high heat until golden brown, turning once. Transfer to a plate and keep warm.

3 ▲ Pour off all but 15ml/1 tbsp of fat from the pan. Add the onions or shallots, mushrooms and garlic. Cook until golden, stirring frequently.

COOK'S TIP

To prepare ahead, reduce the cooking time by 5 minutes. Leave to cool and chill. Reheat gently for 15–20 minutes.

4 ▼ Return the chicken to the casserole with any juices. Add the wine and bring to the boil, then stir in the stock and tomatoes. Bring back to the boil, reduce the heat, cover and simmer over a low heat for about 20 minutes until the chicken is tender and the juices run clear when the thickest part of the meat is pierced with a knife. Tilt the pan and skim off any fat that has risen to the surface, then adjust the seasoning before serving.

Chicken with Prawns

Poulet aux Crevettes

This unusual combination of ingredients has its origins in Burgundy, where it is traditionally made with crayfish. Prawns give a similar result and are often easier to obtain.

Serves 4

1.3kg/3lb chicken, cut into 8 pieces
10ml/2 tsp vegetable oil
12 large raw prawns or live crayfish, with heads if possible
1 small onion, halved and sliced
30ml/2 tbsp plain flour
175ml/6fl oz/¾ cup dry white wine
30ml/2 tbsp brandy
300ml/½ pint/1¼ cups chicken stock
3 medium tomatoes, cored and quartered
1 or 2 garlic cloves, finely chopped
bouquet garni
90ml/6 tbsp whipping cream
salt and freshly ground black pepper
fresh parsley, to garnish

1 Wash the chicken pieces, then pat dry with kitchen paper and season with salt and pepper.

2 Heat the oil in a large flameproof casserole and cook the prawns or crayfish over a high heat until they turn a bright colour. Remove the prawns or crayfish, cool slightly and then peel away the heads and shells and reserve. Chill the peeled tails.

3 Add the chicken to the casserole, skin side down and cook over a medium-high heat for 10–12 minutes until golden brown, turning to colour evenly and cooking in batches if necessary. Transfer the chicken to a plate and pour off all but 15ml/1 tbsp of the fat.

4 In the same casserole, cook the onion over a medium-high heat until golden, stirring frequently. Sprinkle with flour and continue cooking for 2 minutes, stirring frequently, then add the wine and brandy and bring to the boil, stirring constantly.

Cook's tip

To prepare ahead, cook as directed up to step 6. Cool and chill the chicken and sauce. To serve, reheat the chicken and sauce over a medium-low heat for about 30 minutes. Add the prawn or crayfish tails and heat through.

5 Add the stock, prawn or crayfish heads and shells, tomatoes, garlic and bouquet garni with the chicken pieces and any juices. Bring to the boil, then reduce the heat to very low. Cover the casserole and simmer for 20–25 minutes until the chicken is tender and the juices run clear when the thickest part of the meat is pierced with a knife.

6 Remove the chicken pieces from the casserole and strain the cooking liquid, pressing down on the shells and vegetables to extract as much liquid as possible. Skim off the fat from the cooking liquid and return the liquid to the pan. Add the cream and boil until it is reduced by one-third and slightly thickened.

7 Return the chicken pieces to the pan and simmer for 5 minutes. Just before serving, add the prawns or crayfish tails and heat through. Arrange on warmed plates, pour over some of the sauce and garnish with fresh parsley.

CHICKEN BRAISED IN RED WINE *Coq au Vin*

This classic dish was originally made with an old rooster, marinated then slowly braised until very tender. White wine may be used instead of red – as in Alsace, where the local riesling is used.

SERVES 4

1.6–1.8kg/3½–4lb chicken, cut in pieces
25ml/1½ tbsp olive oil
225g/½lb baby onions
15g/½oz/1 tbsp butter
225g/½lb mushrooms, quartered if large
30ml/2 tbsp plain flour
750ml/1¼ pints/3 cups dry red wine
250ml/8fl oz/1 cup chicken stock, or more to cover
bouquet garni
salt and freshly ground black pepper

COOK'S TIP

Avoid large flat mushrooms – although they have a lovely flavour, they will make the sauce murky.

1 ▲ Pat the chicken pieces dry and season with salt and pepper. Put the chicken in a large heavy frying pan, skin side down, and cook over a medium-high heat for 10–12 minutes, or until golden brown. Transfer to a plate.

2 Meanwhile, heat the oil in a large flameproof casserole over a medium-low heat, add the onions and cook, covered, until evenly browned, stirring frequently.

3 ▲ In a heavy frying pan, melt the butter over a medium heat and sauté the mushrooms, stirring, until golden brown.

4 Sprinkle the onions with flour and cook for 2 minutes, stirring frequently, then add the wine and boil for 1 minute, stirring. Add the chicken, mushrooms, stock and bouquet garni. Bring to the boil, reduce the heat to very low and simmer, covered, for 45–50 minutes until the chicken is tender and the juices run clear when the thickest part of the meat is pierced with a knife. (Alternatively, bake in a preheated oven 170°C/325°F/Gas 3 for the same amount of time.)

5 ▲ Transfer the chicken pieces and vegetables to a plate. Strain the cooking liquid, skim off the fat and return the liquid to the pan. Boil to reduce by one-third, then return the chicken and vegetables to the casserole and simmer for 3–4 minutes to heat through.

CHICKEN AND PISTACHIO PÂTÉ *Ballotine de Volaille aux Pistaches*

This simplified version of a classic of French charcuterie *can be made using a whole boned bird, or chicken pieces. Serve it for an elegant picnic or a cold buffet accompanied by a herb mayonnaise.*

SERVES 10–12

900g/2lb boneless chicken meat
1 skinless boneless chicken breast (about 175g/6oz)
30g/1oz/⅔ cup fresh white breadcrumbs
125ml/4fl oz/½ cup whipping cream
1 egg white
4 spring onions, finely chopped
1 garlic clove, finely chopped
85g/3oz cooked ham, cut into 1cm/⅜in cubes
55g/2oz/½ cup shelled pistachio nuts
45ml/3 tbsp chopped fresh tarragon
pinch of grated nutmeg
3.5ml/¾ tsp salt
7.5ml/1½ tsp pepper
green salad, to serve

1 ▲ Trim all the fat, tendons and connective tissue from the 900g/2lb chicken meat and cut into 5cm/2in cubes. Put in a food processor fitted with the metal blade and pulse to chop the meat to a smooth purée, in two or three batches (depending on capacity). Or alternatively pass the meat through the medium or fine blade of a mincer. Remove any white stringy bits.

2 Preheat the oven to 180°C/350°F/Gas 4. Cut the chicken breast fillet into 1cm/⅜in cubes.

3 ▼ In a large mixing bowl, soak the breadcrumbs in the cream. Add the puréed chicken, egg white, spring onions, garlic, ham, pistachio nuts, tarragon, nutmeg and salt and pepper. Using a wooden spoon or your fingers, mix until very well combined.

COOK'S TIP

You could use turkey meat in place of some or all of the chicken. A 2kg/4½lb chicken or whole turkey breast yields about 900g/2lb of boneless meat.

4 ▲ Lay out a piece of extra-wide strong foil about 45cm/18in long on a work surface and lightly brush oil on a 30cm/12in square in the centre. Spoon the chicken mixture on to the foil to form a log shape about 30cm/12in long and about 9cm/3½in thick across the width of the foil. Bring together the long sides of the foil and fold over securely to enclose. Twist the ends of the foil and tie with string.

5 Transfer to a baking dish and bake for 1½ hours. Leave to cool in the dish and chill until cold, preferably overnight. Serve the pâté sliced with green salad.

Tarragon Chicken Breasts *Suprêmes de Poulet à l'Estragon*

The classic French version of this dish uses a whole chicken, but boneless breasts are quick to cook and elegant. The combination of dried and fresh tarragon makes a wonderfully aromatic sauce.

Serves 4

4 skinless boneless chicken breasts (about 150–175g/5–6oz each)
125ml/4fl oz/½ cup dry white wine
about 300ml/½ pint/1¼ cups chicken stock
15ml/1 tbsp dried tarragon
1 garlic clove, finely chopped
175ml/6fl oz/¾ cup whipping cream
15ml/1 tbsp chopped fresh tarragon
salt and freshly ground black pepper
fresh tarragon sprigs, to garnish

Cook's tip

Tarragon is traditionally paired with chicken, but you could of course use chopped fresh basil or parsley instead.

1 ▼ Season the chicken breasts lightly with salt and pepper and put them in a saucepan just large enough to hold them in one layer. Pour over the wine and stock, adding more stock to cover, if necessary, then add the dried tarragon and the garlic. Bring the stock just to a simmer over a medium heat and cook gently for 8–10 minutes until the juices run clear when the chicken is pierced with a knife.

2 ▲ With a slotted spoon, transfer the chicken to a plate and cover to keep warm. Strain the cooking liquid into a small saucepan, skim off any fat and boil to reduce by two-thirds.

3 Add the cream and boil to reduce by half. Stir in the fresh tarragon and adjust the seasoning. Slice the chicken breasts, spoon over a little sauce and garnish with tarragon.

Chicken Breasts with Grapes *Suprêmes de Volaille Veronique*

When grapes are used in a dish, it is often called "Veronique" *or sometimes* "à la vigneronne" *after the wife of the grape grower. Here they are cooked with chicken in a creamy sauce.*

Serves 4

4 boneless chicken breasts (about 200g/7oz each), well trimmed
30g/1oz/2 tbsp butter
1 large or 2 small shallots, chopped
125ml/4fl oz/½ cup dry white wine
250ml/8fl oz/1 cup chicken stock
125ml/4fl oz/½ cup whipping cream
150g/5oz/1 cup (about 30) seedless green grapes
salt and freshly ground black pepper
fresh parsley, to garnish

1 Season the chicken breasts. Melt half the butter in a frying pan over a medium-high heat and cook the chicken breasts for 4–5 minutes on each side until golden.

2 ▲ Transfer the chicken breasts to a plate and cover to keep warm. Add the remaining butter and sauté the shallots until just softened, stirring frequently. Add the wine, bring to the boil and boil to reduce by half, then add the stock and continue boiling to reduce by half again.

3 ▼ Add the cream to the sauce, bring back to the boil, and add any juices from the chicken. Add the grapes and cook gently for 5 minutes. Slice the chicken breasts and serve with the sauce, garnished with parsley.

CHICKEN WITH OLIVES

Poulet à la Provençale

Chicken breasts or turkey, veal or pork escalopes may be flattened for quick and even cooking. You can buy them ready-prepared in France, but they are easy to do at home.

SERVES 4

6 ripe plum tomatoes
4 skinless boneless chicken breasts (about 150–175g/5–6oz each)
1.5ml/¼ tsp cayenne pepper
75–105ml/5–7 tbsp extra virgin olive oil
1 garlic clove, finely chopped
16–24 stoned black olives
small handful fresh basil leaves
salt

1 ▼ Carefully remove the fillets (the long finger-shaped muscle on the back of each breast) and reserve for another use.

2 Place each chicken breast between two sheets of greaseproof paper or clear film and pound with the flat side of a meat hammer or roll out with a rolling pin to flatten to about 1.2cm/½in thick. Season with salt and the cayenne pepper.

3 Heat 45–60ml/3–4 tbsp of olive oil in a large heavy frying pan over a medium-high heat. Add the chicken and cook for 4–5 minutes until golden brown and just cooked, turning them once. Transfer the chicken to warmed serving plates and keep warm while you cook the tomatoes and olives.

4 ▲ Wipe out the frying pan and return to the heat. Add another 30–45ml/2–3 tbsp of olive oil and fry the garlic for 1 minute until golden and fragrant. Stir in the olives, cook for a further 1 minute, then stir in the tomatoes. Shred the basil leaves and stir into the olive and tomato mixture, then spoon it over the chicken and serve at once.

COOK'S TIP

If the tomato skins are at all tough, remove them by scoring the base of each tomato with a knife, then plunging them into boiling water for 45 seconds. The skin should simply peel off.

CHICKEN WITH RED WINE VINEGAR *Poulet au Vinaigre*

This dish is an easy version of the modern classic invented by one of the masters of French cooking, the late Fernand Point of the Michelin-starred restaurant near Lyons, La Pyramide.

SERVES 4

4 skinless boneless chicken breasts (200g/7oz each)
55g/2oz/4 tbsp unsalted butter
freshly ground black pepper
8–12 shallots, trimmed and halved
60ml/4 tbsp red wine vinegar
2 garlic cloves, finely chopped
60ml/4 tbsp dry white wine
125ml/4fl oz/½ cup chicken stock
15ml/1 tbsp chopped fresh parsley
green salad, to serve

1 ▲ Cut each chicken breast in half crossways to make eight pieces.

2 Melt half the butter in a large heavy-based frying pan over a medium heat. Add the chicken and cook for 3–5 minutes until golden brown, turning once, then season with pepper.

3 ▲ Add the shallot halves to the pan, cover and cook over a low heat for 5–7 minutes, shaking the pan and stirring the pieces occasionally.

4 ▲ Transfer the chicken pieces to a plate. Add the vinegar and cook, stirring frequently, for about 1 minute until the liquid is almost evaporated. Add the garlic, wine and stock and stir to blend.

5 Return the chicken to the pan with any accumulated liquid. Cover and simmer for 2–3 minutes until the chicken is tender and the juices run clear when the meat is pierced with a knife.

6 Transfer the chicken and shallots to a serving dish and cover to keep warm. Increase the heat and boil the cooking liquid until it has reduced by half.

7 Remove the pan from the heat. Gradually add the remaining butter, whisking until the sauce is slightly thickened and glossy. Stir in the parsley and pour the sauce over the chicken pieces and shallots. Serve at once with a green salad.

VARIATIONS

You could use different flavoured vinegars. Try tarragon vinegar and substitute fresh tarragon for the parsley, or use raspberry vinegar and garnish with a few fresh raspberries.

Chicken with Morels *Suprêmes de Volaille Farcies aux Morilles*

Morels are among the most tasty dried mushrooms and, although expensive, a little goes a long way. Of course, you can use fresh morels (about 275g/10oz) in place of the dried ones, or substitute chanterelles, shiitake or oyster mushrooms.

Serves 4

45g/1½oz dried morel mushrooms
250ml/8fl oz/1 cup chicken stock
55g/2oz/4 tbsp butter
5 or 6 shallots, thinly sliced
100g/3½oz button mushrooms, thinly sliced
1.5ml/¼ tsp dried thyme
175ml/6fl oz/¾ cup double or whipping cream
30–45ml/2–3 tbsp brandy
4 skinless boneless chicken breasts (about 200g/7oz each)
15ml/1 tbsp vegetable oil
175ml/6fl oz/¾ cup Champagne or dry sparkling wine
salt and freshly ground black pepper

1 ▲ Put the morels in a strainer and rinse well under cold running water, shaking to remove as much sand as possible. Put them in a saucepan with the stock and bring to the boil over a medium-high heat. Remove the pan from the heat and leave to stand for 1 hour.

2 Remove the morels from the cooking liquid and strain the liquid through a very fine sieve or muslin-lined strainer and reserve for the sauce. Reserve a few whole morels and slice the rest.

3 ▲ Melt half the butter in a frying pan over a medium heat. Add the shallots and cook for 2 minutes until softened, then add the morels and mushrooms and cook, stirring frequently, for 2–3 minutes. Season and add the thyme, brandy and 100ml/3½fl oz/⅓ cup of the cream. Reduce the heat and simmer gently for 10–12 minutes until any liquid has evaporated, stirring occasionally. Remove the morel mixture from the pan and set aside.

4 ▲ Pull off the fillets from the chicken breasts (the finger-shaped piece on the underside) and reserve for another use. Make a pocket in each chicken breast by cutting a slit along the thicker edge, taking care not to cut all the way through.

5 Using a small spoon, fill each pocket with one-quarter of the mushroom mixture, then if necessary, close with a cocktail stick.

6 ▲ Melt the remaining butter with the oil in a heavy frying pan over a medium-high heat and cook the chicken breasts on one side for 6–8 minutes until golden. Transfer the chicken breasts to a plate. Add the Champagne or sparkling wine to the pan and boil to reduce by half. Add the strained morel cooking liquid and boil to reduce by half again.

7 ▲ Add the remaining cream and cook over a medium heat for 2–3 minutes until the sauce thickens slightly and coats the back of a spoon. Adjust the seasoning. Return the chicken to the pan with any accumulated juices and the reserved whole morels and simmer for 3–5 minutes over a medium-low heat until the chicken breasts are hot and the juices run clear when the meat is pierced with a knife.

Turkey Escalopes with Capers *Escalopes en Capilotade*

A staple of bistro cooking, these thin slices of poultry or meat, called escalopes *or sometimes* paillards*, cook very quickly and can be served with all kinds of interesting sauces.*

Serves 2

4 thin turkey breast escalopes (about 85g/3oz each)
1 large unwaxed lemon
2.5ml/½ tsp chopped fresh sage
60–75ml/4–5 tbsp extra virgin olive oil
55g/2oz/½ cup fine dry breadcrumbs
15ml/1 tbsp capers, rinsed and drained
salt and freshly ground black pepper
sage leaves and lemon wedges, to garnish

1 ▼ Place the turkey escalopes between two sheets of greaseproof paper or clear film and pound with the flat side of a meat hammer or roll with a rolling pin to flatten to about a 6mm/¼in thickness.

2 ▲ With a vegetable peeler, remove four pieces of lemon rind. Cut them into thin julienne strips, cover with clear film and set aside. Grate the remainder of the lemon rind and squeeze the lemon. Put the grated rind in a large shallow dish and add the sage, salt and pepper. Stir in 15ml/1 tbsp of the lemon juice, reserving the rest, and about 15ml/1 tbsp of the olive oil, then add the turkey, turn to coat and marinate for 30 minutes.

3 ▲ Place the breadcrumbs in another shallow dish and dip the escalopes in the crumbs, coating both sides. In a heavy frying pan heat 30ml/2 tbsp of the olive oil over a high heat, add the escalopes and cook for 2–3 minutes, turning once, until golden. Transfer to two warmed plates and keep warm.

4 Wipe out the pan, add the remaining oil, the lemon julienne and the capers, stirring, and heat through. Spoon a little sauce over the turkey and garnish with sage leaves and lemon.

GUINEA FOWL WITH CABBAGE *Pintade au Chou*

Guinea fowl is a domesticated relative of pheasant, so you can substitute pheasant or even chicken in this recipe. In some parts of France, such as Burgundy, garlic sausage may be added.

SERVES 4

1.2–1.3kg/2½–3lb guinea fowl
15ml/1 tbsp vegetable oil
15g/½oz/1 tbsp butter
1 large onion, halved and sliced
1 large carrot, halved and sliced
1 large leek, sliced
450g/1lb green cabbage, such as savoy, sliced or chopped
125ml/4fl oz/½ cup dry white wine
125ml/4fl oz/½ cup chicken stock
1 or 2 garlic cloves, finely chopped
salt and freshly ground black pepper

1 Preheat the oven to 180°C/350°F/Gas 4. Tie the legs of the guinea fowl with string.

2 ▲ Heat half the oil in a large flameproof casserole over a medium-high heat and cook the guinea fowl until golden brown on all sides. Transfer to a plate.

3 Pour out the fat from the casserole and add the remaining oil with the butter. Add the onion, carrot and leek and cook over a low heat, stirring occasionally, for 5 minutes. Add the cabbage and cook for about 3–4 minutes until slightly wilted, stirring occasionally. Season the vegetables with salt and pepper.

4 ▼ Place the guinea fowl on its side on the vegetables. Add the wine and bring to the boil, then add the stock and garlic. Cover and transfer to the oven. Cook for 25 minutes, then turn the bird on to the other side and cook for 20–25 minutes until it is tender and the juices run clear when the thickest part of the thigh is pierced with a knife.

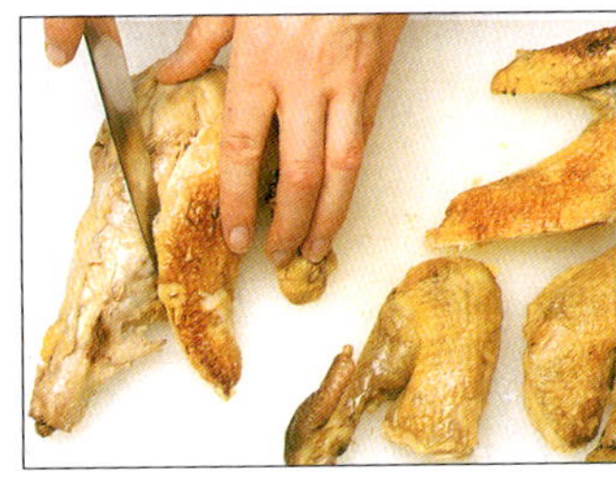

5 ▲ Transfer the bird to a board and leave to stand for 5–10 minutes, then cut into four or eight pieces. With a slotted spoon, transfer the cabbage to a warmed serving dish and place the guinea fowl on top. Skim any fat from the cooking juices and serve separately.

Roast Pheasant with Port

Faisan Rôti au Porto

Roasting the pheasant in foil keeps the flesh particularly moist. This recipe is best for very young birds and, if you have a choice, request the more tender female birds.

Serves 4

2 oven-ready hen pheasants (about 675g/1½lb each)
55g/2oz/4 tbsp unsalted butter, softened
8 fresh thyme sprigs
2 bay leaves
6 streaky bacon rashers
15ml/1 tbsp plain flour
175ml/6fl oz/¾ cup game or chicken stock, plus more if needed
15ml/1 tbsp redcurrant jelly
45–60ml/3–4 tbsp port
freshly ground black pepper

1 Preheat the oven to 230°C/450°F/Gas 8. Line a large roasting tin with a sheet of strong foil large enough to enclose the pheasants. Lightly brush the foil with oil.

2 ▼ Wipe the pheasants with damp kitchen paper and remove any extra fat or skin. Using your fingertips, carefully loosen the skin of the breasts. With a round-bladed knife or small palette knife, spread the butter between the skin and breast meat of each bird. Tie the legs securely with string then lay the thyme sprigs and a bay leaf over the breast of each bird.

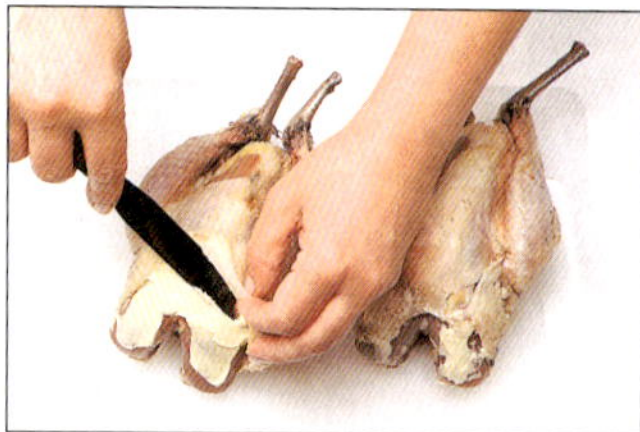

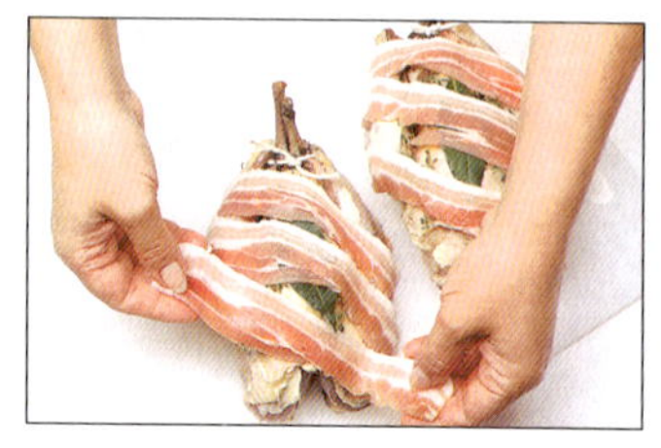

3 ▲ Lay bacon rashers over the breasts, place the birds in the foil-lined tin and season with pepper. Bring together the long ends of the foil, fold over securely to enclose, then seal the ends.

4 Roast the birds for 20 minutes, then reduce the oven temperature to 190°C/375°F/Gas 5 and cook for a further 40 minutes. Uncover the birds and roast 10–15 minutes more or until they are browned and the juices run clear when the thigh of a bird is pierced with a knife. Transfer the birds to a board and leave to stand, covered with clean foil, for 10 minutes before carving.

5 ▲ Pour the juices from the foil into the roasting tin and skim off any fat. Sprinkle in the flour and cook over a medium heat, stirring until smooth. Whisk in the stock and redcurrant jelly and bring to the boil. Simmer until the sauce thickens slightly, adding more stock if needed, then stir in the port and adjust the seasoning. Strain and serve with the pheasant.

Pheasant Breast with Apples *Faisan à la Normande*

The Normandy countryside is full of picturesque apple orchards and herds of grazing cows. Many regional dishes contain apples or Calvados and rich Normandy cream.

Serves 2

2 boneless pheasant breasts
30g/1oz/2 tbsp butter
1 onion, thinly sliced
1 eating apple, peeled and quartered
10ml/2 tsp sugar
60ml/4 tbsp Calvados
60ml/4 tbsp chicken stock
1.5ml/¼ tsp dried thyme
1.5ml/¼ tsp white pepper
125ml/4fl oz/½ cup whipping cream
salt
sautéed potatoes, to serve

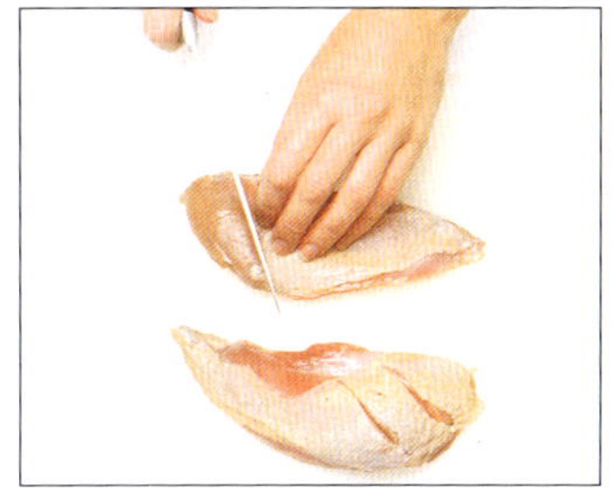

1 ▲ With a sharp knife, score the thick end of each pheasant breast.

2 In a medium heavy frying pan melt half of the butter over a medium heat. Add the onion and cook for 8–10 minutes until golden, stirring occasionally. Using a slotted spoon, transfer the onion to a plate.

3 Cut each apple quarter crossways into thin slices. Melt half of the remaining butter in the pan and add the apple slices. Sprinkle with the sugar and cook the apple slices slowly for 5–7 minutes until golden and caramelized, turning occasionally. Transfer the apples to the plate with the onion, then wipe out the pan.

4 ▲ Add the remaining butter to the pan and increase the heat to medium-high. Add the pheasant breasts, skin side down, and cook for 3–4 minutes until golden. Turn and cook for a further 1–2 minutes until the juices run slightly pink when the thickest part of the meat is pierced with a knife. Transfer to a board and cover to keep warm.

5 Add the Calvados to the pan and boil over a high heat until reduced by half. Add the stock, thyme, a little salt and the white pepper and reduce by half again. Stir in the cream, bring to the boil and cook for 1 minute. Add the reserved onion and apple slices to the pan and cook for 1 minute.

6 Slice each pheasant breast diagonally and arrange on warmed plates. Spoon over a little sauce with the onion and apples.

Cook's tip

If you can't find Calvados, substitute Cognac, cider or apple juice instead.

Quail with Fresh Figs

Cailles aux Figues Fraîches

The fig trees in the South of France are laden with ripe purple fruit in early autumn, coinciding with the quail shooting season. However, you can buy farmed quail all year.

Serves 4

8 oven-ready quail (150g/5oz each)
6 firm ripe figs, quartered
15g/½oz/1 tbsp butter
90ml/6 tbsp white Pineau de Charantes or dry sherry
300ml/½ pint/1¼ cups chicken stock
1 garlic clove, finely chopped
2–3 thyme sprigs
1 bay leaf
7.5ml/1½ tsp cornflour blended with 15ml/1 tbsp water
salt and freshly ground black pepper
green salad, to serve

1 ▼ Season the quail inside and out with salt and pepper. Put a fig quarter in the cavity of each quail and tie the legs with string.

2 ▲ Melt the butter in a deep frying pan or heavy flameproof casserole over a medium-high heat. Add the quail and cook for 5–6 minutes, turning to brown all sides evenly; cook in batches if necessary.

3 ▲ Add the Pineau de Charantes or sherry and boil for 1 minute, then add the stock, garlic, thyme and bay leaf. Bring to the boil, reduce the heat and simmer gently, covered, for 20 minutes.

4 Add the remaining fig quarters and continue cooking for a further 5 minutes until the juices run clear when the thigh of a quail is pierced with a knife. Transfer the quail and figs to a warmed serving dish, cut off the trussing string and cover to keep warm.

5 Bring the sauce to the boil, then stir in the blended cornflour. Cook gently for 3 minutes, stirring frequently, until the sauce is thickened, then strain into a sauce boat. Serve the quail and figs with the sauce and a green salad.

DUCK WITH ORANGE SAUCE *Canard à la Bigarade*

Commercially raised ducks tend to be much fattier than wild ducks. In this recipe, the initial slow cooking and pricking the skin of the duck helps to draw out the excess fat.

SERVES 2–3

2kg/4½lb duck
2 oranges
100g/3½oz/½ cup caster sugar
90ml/6 tbsp white wine vinegar or cider vinegar
125ml/4fl oz/½ cup Grand Marnier or orange liqueur
salt and freshly ground black pepper
watercress and orange slices, to garnish

1 ▲ Preheat the oven to 150°C/300°F/Gas 2. Trim off all the excess fat and skin from the duck and prick the skin all over with a fork. Season the duck inside and out with salt and pepper and tie the legs with string.

2 ▲ Place the duck on a rack in a large roasting tin. Cover tightly with foil and cook in the oven for 1½ hours. With a vegetable peeler, remove the rind in wide strips from the oranges, then stack two or three strips at a time and slice into very thin julienne strips. Squeeze the juice from the oranges.

3 ▼ Place the sugar and vinegar in a small heavy saucepan and stir to dissolve the sugar. Boil over a high heat, without stirring, until the mixture is a rich caramel colour, remove the pan from the heat and, standing well back, carefully add the orange juice, pouring it down the side of the pan. Swirl the pan to blend, then bring back to the boil and add the orange rind and liqueur. Simmer for 2–3 minutes.

4 Remove the duck from the oven and pour off all the fat from the tin. Raise the oven temperature to 200°C/400°F/Gas 6.

5 ▲ Roast the duck, uncovered, for 25–30 minutes, basting three or four times with the caramel mixture, until the duck is golden brown and the juices run clear when the thigh is pierced with a knife.

6 Pour the juices from the cavity into the casserole and transfer the duck to a carving board. Cover loosely with foil and leave to stand for 10–15 minutes. Pour the roasting juices into the pan with the rest of the caramel mixture, skim off the fat and simmer gently. Serve the duck, with the sauce, garnished with watercress and orange slices.

ROAST WILD DUCK WITH JUNIPER *Canard aux Genièvres*

Wild duck should be served slightly underdone or the meat will be very tough. There is little meat on the leg, so one duck will serve only two people – keep the legs for making a tasty stock.

SERVES 2

15ml/1 tbsp juniper berries, fresh if possible
1 oven-ready wild duck (preferably a mallard)
30g/1oz/2 tbsp butter, softened
45ml/3 tbsp gin
125ml/4fl oz/½ cup duck or chicken stock
125ml/4fl oz/½ cup whipping cream
salt and freshly ground black pepper
watercress, to garnish

1 Preheat the oven to 230°C/450°F/Gas 8. Reserve a few juniper berries for garnishing and put the remainder in a heavy polythene bag. Crush coarsely with a rolling pin.

2 ▲ Wipe the duck with damp kitchen paper and remove any excess fat or skin. Tie the legs with string, then spread the butter over the duck. Sprinkle with salt and pepper and press the crushed juniper berries on to the skin.

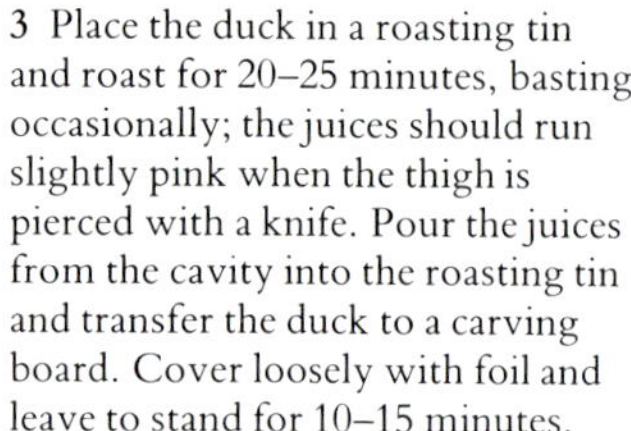

3 Place the duck in a roasting tin and roast for 20–25 minutes, basting occasionally; the juices should run slightly pink when the thigh is pierced with a knife. Pour the juices from the cavity into the roasting tin and transfer the duck to a carving board. Cover loosely with foil and leave to stand for 10–15 minutes.

4 ▲ Skim off as much fat as possible from the roasting tin, leaving as much of the juniper as possible, and place the tin over a medium-high heat. Add the gin and stir, scraping the base of the tin and bring to the boil. Cook until the liquid has almost evaporated, then add the stock and boil to reduce by half. Add the cream and boil for 2 minutes more, or until the sauce thickens slightly. Strain into a small saucepan and keep warm.

5 Carve the legs from the duck and separate the thigh from the drumstick. Remove the breasts and arrange the duck in a warmed serving dish. Pour a little sauce over, sprinkle with the reserved juniper berries and garnish with watercress.

COOK'S TIP

If you do not serve the legs, use the legs and duck carcass to make a duck stock for other game dishes.

Duck Stew with Olives

Ragoût de Canard aux Olives

This method of preparing duck has its roots in Provence. The sweetness of the onions, which are not typical in all regional versions, balances the saltiness of the olives.

Serves 6–8

2 ducks (about 1.4kg/3¼lb each), quartered, or 8 duck leg quarters
225g/½lb baby onions
30ml/2 tbsp plain flour
350ml/12fl oz/1½ cups dry red wine
500ml/16fl oz/2 cups duck or chicken stock
bouquet garni
100g/3½oz/1 cup stoned green or black olives, or a combination
salt, if needed, and freshly ground black pepper

1 Put the duck pieces, skin side down, in a large frying pan over a medium heat and cook for 10–12 minutes until well browned, turning to colour evenly and cooking in batches if necessary. Pour off the fat from the pan.

2 Heat 15ml/1 tbsp of the duck fat in a large flameproof casserole and cook the onions, covered, over a medium-low heat until evenly browned, stirring frequently. Sprinkle with flour and continue cooking, uncovered, for 2 minutes, stirring frequently.

3 ▲ Stir in the wine and bring to the boil, then add the duck pieces, stock and bouquet garni. Bring to the boil, then reduce the heat to very low and simmer, covered, for about 40 minutes, stirring occasionally.

4 ▼ Rinse the olives in several changes of cold water. If they are very salty, put in a saucepan, cover with water and bring to the boil, then drain and rinse. Add the olives to the casserole and continue cooking for a further 20 minutes until the duck is very tender.

5 Transfer the duck pieces, onions and olives to a plate. Strain the cooking liquid, skim off all the fat and return the liquid to the pan. Boil to reduce by about one-third, then adjust the seasoning and return the duck and vegetables to the casserole. Simmer gently for a few minutes to heat through.

Cook's tip

If you take the breasts from whole ducks for duck breast recipes, freeze the legs until you have enough for this stew, and make stock from the carcasses.

VENISON WITH ROQUEFORT BUTTER *Chevreuil au Roquefort*

Tender farmed venison is now widely available, but if venison is difficult to find, use beef instead.

SERVES 2

2 venison sirloin steaks, about 150–175g/5–6oz each
1 garlic clove, finely chopped
60ml/4 tbsp brandy
40g/1½oz/3 tbsp unsalted butter
40g/1½oz Roquefort cheese
freshly ground black pepper

1 ▲ Put the steaks in a small glass dish. Sprinkle with pepper and garlic and pour over the brandy.

2 Cover the dish and leave to marinate in a cool place, for up to 1 hour, or chill for up to 4 hours.

3 ▲ Using a fork, mash together 30g/1oz/2 tbsp of the butter and the cheese, or blend them in a food processor. Shape the mixture into a log, wrap and chill until needed.

4 Heat the remaining butter in a heavy frying pan over a medium-high heat. Drain the meat, reserving the marinade.

5 ▲ Add the steaks to the pan. Cook for about 5 minutes, turning once, until the meat is springy to the touch for medium-rare or firmer for more well done, then transfer the steaks to warmed plates.

6 Add the reserved marinade to the pan and bring to the boil, scraping the base of the pan. Pour over the meat, then top each steak with one or two slices of the Roquefort butter and serve.

DUCK WITH PEPPERCORNS *Magret de Canard aux Grains de Poivre*

Thick meaty duck breast, like steak, should be served medium-rare. Green peppercorn sauce is popular in modern French bistros, but you can also use somewhat milder pink peppercorns.

SERVES 2

5ml/1 tsp vegetable oil
2 duck breasts (about 225g/8oz each), skinned
60ml/4 tbsp chicken or duck stock
90ml/6 tbsp whipping cream
5ml/1 tsp Dijon mustard
15ml/1 tbsp green or pink peppercorns in vinegar, drained
salt
fresh parsley, to garnish

1 Heat the oil in a heavy frying pan. Add the duck breasts and cook over a medium-high heat for about 3 minutes on each side.

2 ▲ Transfer the duck breasts to a plate and cover to keep warm. Pour off any fat from the pan and stir in the stock, cream, mustard and peppercorns. Boil for 2–3 minutes until the sauce thickens slightly, then season with salt.

3 ▼ Pour any accumulated juices from the duck into the sauce, then slice the breasts diagonally. Arrange them on two warmed serving plates, pour over a little of the sauce and garnish with parsley.

ROAST LEG OF VENISON *Gigot de Chevreuil Rôti*

Although young venison does not need marinating to tenderize it, the marinade forms the base for a delicious, tangy yet slightly sweet sauce. You'll need to start this recipe two to three days ahead.

SERVES 6–8

1 onion, chopped
1 carrot chopped
1 celery stick, chopped
3 or 4 garlic cloves, crushed
4–6 fresh parsley sprigs
4–6 fresh thyme sprigs or 2.5ml/½ tsp dried thyme
2 bay leaves
15ml/1 tbsp black peppercorns, lightly crushed
750ml/1¼ pints/3 cups red wine
60ml/4 tbsp vegetable oil, plus more for brushing
1 young venison haunch (about 2.75kg/6lb), trimmed
30ml/2 tbsp plain flour
250ml/8fl oz/1 cup beef stock
1 unwaxed orange
1 unwaxed lemon
60ml/4 tbsp redcurrant or raspberry jelly
60ml/4 tbsp ruby port or Madeira
15ml/1 tbsp cornflour, blended with 30ml/2 tbsp of water
15ml/1 tbsp red wine vinegar
fresh herbs, to garnish
French Scalloped Potatoes, to serve

1 ▲ Place the onion, carrot, celery, garlic, parsley, thyme, bay leaves, peppercorns, wine and oil in a deep glass dish large enough to hold the venison, then add the venison and turn to coat. Cover the dish with clear film and leave to marinate in the fridge for 2–3 days, turning occasionally.

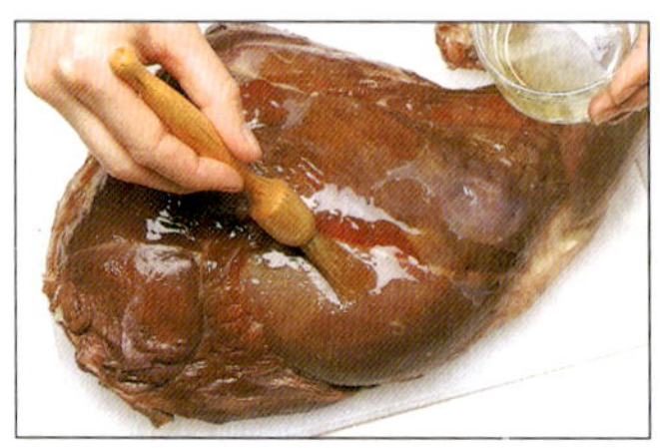

2 ▲ Preheat the oven to 180°C/350°F/Gas 4. Remove the meat from its marinade and pour the marinade into a saucepan. Pat the meat dry with kitchen paper, then brush the meat with a little oil on all sides and wrap tightly in foil.

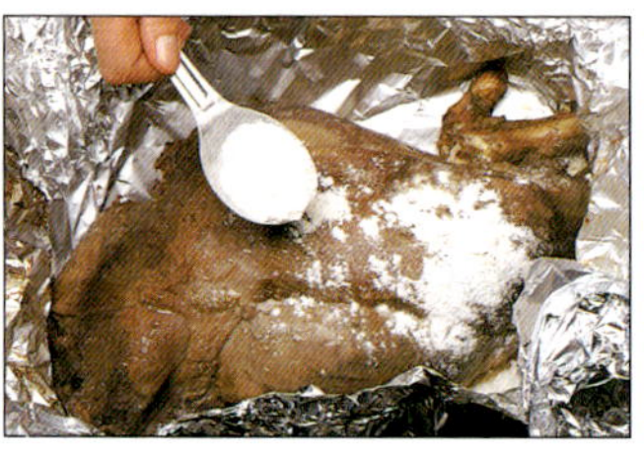

3 ▲ Roast the venison for 15–20 minutes per 450g/1lb for rare to medium meat. About 25 minutes before the end of the cooking time, remove the foil, sprinkle the venison with the flour and baste with the cooking juices.

4 Meanwhile, add the stock to the marinade and boil over a medium-high heat until reduced by half, then strain and set aside.

5 Using a vegetable peeler, remove the rind from the orange and half the lemon in long pieces. Cut the pieces into thin julienne strips. Bring a small saucepan of water to the boil over a high heat and add the orange and lemon strips. Simmer them for 5 minutes, then drain and rinse under cold running water.

6 ▲ Squeeze the juice of the orange into a medium saucepan. Add the jelly and cook over a low heat until melted, then stir in the port or Madeira and the reduced marinade and simmer gently for 10 minutes.

7 ▲ Stir the blended cornflour mixture into the marinade and cook, stirring frequently, until the sauce is slightly thickened. Add the vinegar and the orange and lemon strips and simmer for a further 2–3 minutes. Keep warm, stirring occasionally.

8 Transfer the meat to a board and stand, loosely covered with foil for 10 minutes before carving. Garnish with herbs and serve with the sauce and French Scalloped Potatoes.

CASSEROLED RABBIT WITH THYME *Fricassée de Lapin au Thym*

This is the sort of satisfying home cooking found in farmhouse kitchens and cosy neighbourhood restaurants in France, where rabbit is treated much like chicken and enjoyed frequently.

SERVES 4

1.2kg/2½lb rabbit
40g/1½oz/¼ cup plain flour
15g/½oz/1 tbsp butter
15ml/1 tbsp olive oil
250ml/8fl oz/1 cup red wine
350–500ml/12–16fl oz/1½–2 cups chicken stock
15ml/1 tbsp fresh thyme leaves, or 10ml/2 tsp dried thyme
1 bay leaf
2 garlic cloves, finely chopped
10–15ml/2–3 tsp Dijon mustard
salt and freshly ground black pepper

1 Cut the rabbit into eight serving pieces: chop the saddle in half and separate the back legs into two pieces each; leave the front legs whole.

2 ▼ Put the flour in a polythene bag and season with salt and pepper. One at a time, drop the rabbit pieces into the bag and shake to coat them with flour. Tap off the excess, then discard any remaining flour.

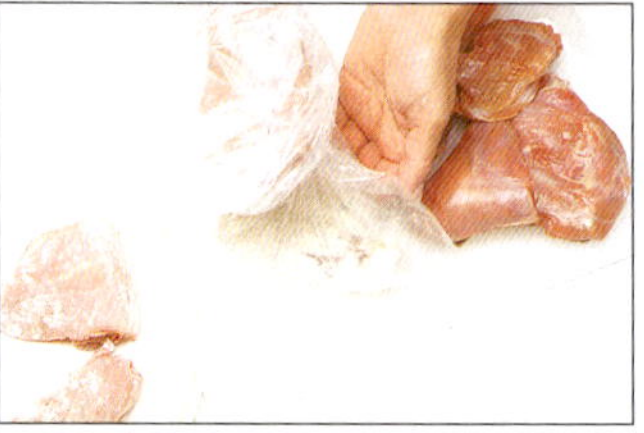

3 ▲ Melt the butter with the oil over a medium-high heat in a large flameproof casserole. Add the rabbit pieces and cook until golden, turning to colour evenly.

4 ▲ Add the wine and boil for 1 minute then add enough of the stock just to cover the meat. Add the herbs and garlic, then simmer gently, covered, for 1 hour, or until the rabbit is very tender and the juices run clear when the thickest part of the meat is pierced with a knife.

5 ▲ Stir in the mustard, adjust the seasoning and strain the sauce. Arrange the rabbit pieces on a warmed serving platter with some sauce and serve the rest separately.

Sautéed Foie Gras

Foie Gras Chaud

Even in France, fresh foie gras*, the liver of specially raised and fattened geese or ducks, is not too easy to come by. If you can find it, this quick recipe brings out its rich flavour.*

Serves 4

275g/10oz small baking potatoes, peeled
15g/½oz/1 tbsp butter
450g/1lb fresh foie gras*, cut into 8 × 2cm/¾in slices*
45–60ml/3–4 tbsp sherry vinegar or white wine vinegar
salt and freshly ground black pepper
fresh chives, to garnish

1 ▲ Cut the potatoes into 1.5mm/1/16in slices and cover with cold water if not using immediately.

2 ▲ Pat the potatoes dry. Melt the butter in a large frying pan over a medium heat. Make four 13cm/5in rounds of overlapping potato slices in the pan and press them down. Season with salt and pepper and cook for 6–8 minutes until the bases are well browned. Turn and brown the other side, for 5 minutes. Transfer to a baking sheet and keep warm in a low oven.

3 ▼ Season the *foie gras* with salt and pepper. Heat a large non-stick frying pan over a high heat and cook the slices, in one layer or in batches, for 3 minutes for 2cm/¾in slices, less for thinner slices, turning once.

4 ▲ Place the potato cakes on warmed plates and top with slices of *foie gras*. Pour the vinegar into the frying pan and boil briefly, scraping the base of the pan, then pour the sauce over the *foie gras*, dividing it evenly. Garnish with chives.

CHICKEN LIVER MOUSSE

Mousse de Foie de Volaille

This mousse makes an elegant yet easy first course. The onion marmalade makes a delicious accompaniment, along with a salad of chicory or other bitter leaves.

SERVES 6–8

450g/1lb chicken livers
175g/6oz/¾ cup butter, diced
1 small onion, finely chopped
1 garlic clove, finely chopped
2.5ml/½ tsp dried thyme
30–45ml/2–3 tbsp brandy
salt and freshly ground black pepper
green salad, to serve

FOR THE ONION MARMALADE

30g/1oz/2 tbsp butter
450g/1lb red onions, thinly sliced
1 garlic clove, finely chopped
2.5ml/½ tsp dried thyme
30–45ml/2–3 tbsp raspberry or red wine vinegar
15–30ml/1–2 tbsp clear honey
40g/1½oz/¼ cup sultanas

1 Trim the chicken livers, cutting off any green spots and removing any filaments or fat.

2 ▲ In a heavy frying pan, melt 30g/1oz/2 tbsp of the butter over a medium heat. Add the onion and cook for 5–7 minutes until soft and golden, then add the garlic and cook for 1 minute more. Increase the heat to medium-high and add the chicken livers, thyme, salt and pepper. Cook for 3–5 minutes until the livers are coloured, stirring frequently; the livers should remain pink inside, but not raw. Add the brandy and cook for a further minute.

3 ▲ Using a slotted spoon, transfer the livers to a food processor fitted with the metal blade. Pour in the cooking juices and process for 1 minute, or until smooth, scraping down the sides once. With the machine running, add the remaining butter, a few pieces at a time, until it is incorporated.

4 ▲ Press the mousse mixture through a fine sieve with a wooden spoon or rubber spatula.

COOK'S TIP

The mousse will keep for 3–4 days. If made ahead, cover and chill until ready to use. The onion marmalade can be made up to 2 days ahead and gently reheated over a low heat or in the microwave until just warm.

5 ▲ Line a 500ml/16fl oz/2 cup loaf tin with clear film, smoothing out as many wrinkles as possible. Pour the mousse mixture into the lined tin. Cool, then cover and chill until firm.

6 ▲ To make the onion marmalade, heat the butter in a heavy frying pan over a medium-low heat, add the onions and cook for 20 minutes until softened and just coloured, stirring frequently. Stir in the garlic, thyme, vinegar, honey and sultanas and cook, covered, for 10–15 minutes until the onions are completely soft and jam-like, stirring occasionally. Spoon into a bowl and cool to room temperature.

7 To serve, dip the loaf tin into hot water for 5 seconds, wipe dry and invert on to a board. Lift off the tin, peel off the clear film and smooth the surface with a knife. Serve sliced with a little of the onion marmalade and a green salad.

Meat Dishes

The produce displayed in a French butcher's shop is different from that in other countries. Meat is expensive, and butchers are expected to provide quality, choice and good service. The cuts, whether large or small, are always beautifully presented, and even stewing cuts, although they may be bony and gelatinous, are still carefully trimmed. There will be a wide choice of offal, too, as well as numerous kinds of sausages. Slow cooking methods like braising and casseroling are popular and meat is often marinated, while the more tender cuts are cooked quickly to keep the full flavour and succulence of the meat.

Steak with Anchovy Sauce *Entrecôte au Beurre d'Anchois*

This may sound like an unusual combination, but the anchovy adds flavour without tasting fishy.

Serves 2

40g/1½oz/3 tbsp butter
4 shallots, finely chopped
1 garlic clove, crushed
100ml/3½fl oz/6 tbsp whipping cream
25ml/1½ tbsp anchovy paste
15ml/1 tbsp chopped fresh tarragon
2 sirloin or fillet steaks, about 200–250g/7–9oz each
10ml/2 tsp vegetable oil
salt and freshly ground black pepper
parsley or tarragon sprigs, to garnish
sautéed potatoes, to serve

1 ▼ Melt 30g/1oz/2 tbsp of the butter in a small saucepan and fry the shallots and garlic until they are just soft. Stir in the cream, anchovy paste and tarragon, and simmer very gently for about 10 minutes.

2 ▲ Season the steaks. Heat the remaining butter with the oil in a heavy frying pan over a medium-high heat until it begins to brown.

3 Add the meat and cook for about 6–8 minutes, turning once, until done as preferred (medium-rare meat will still be slightly soft when pressed, medium meat will be springy and well-done firm.) Transfer the steaks to warmed serving plates and cover to keep warm.

4 ▲ Add 30ml/2 tbsp of water to the frying pan. Stir in the anchovy sauce and cook for 1–2 minutes, stirring and scraping the bottom of the pan. Adjust the seasoning and pour the sauce over the meat, then garnish with parsley or tarragon and serve with potatoes.

Variation

To make a tomato cream sauce to serve with the steak, substitute 5–10ml/1–2 tsp tomato purée for the anchovy paste.

Pepper steak

Steak au Poivre

There are many versions of this French bistro classic, some omit the cream, but it helps to balance the heat of the pepper. Use fairly thick steaks, such as fillet or lean sirloin.

Serves 2

30ml/2 tbsp black peppercorns
2 fillet or sirloin steaks, about 225g/8oz each
15g/½oz/1 tbsp butter
10ml/2 tsp vegetable oil
45ml/3 tbsp brandy
150ml/¼ pint/⅔ cup whipping cream
1 garlic clove, finely chopped
salt, if needed

1 ▲ Place the peppercorns in a sturdy polythene bag. Crush with a rolling pin until medium-coarse or, using the flat base of a small heavy saucepan, press down on the peppercorns, rocking the pan to crush them.

2 ▲ Put the steaks on a board and trim away any extra fat. Press the pepper on to both sides of the meat, coating it completely.

3 ▼ Melt the butter with the oil in a heavy frying pan over a medium-high heat. Add the meat and cook for 6–7 minutes, turning once, until done as preferred (medium-rare meat will still be slightly soft when pressed, medium will be springy and well-done firm). Transfer the steaks to a warmed platter or plates and cover to keep warm.

4 ▲ Pour in the brandy to deglaze the pan. Allow to boil until reduced by half, scraping the base of the pan, then add the cream and garlic. Boil gently over a medium heat for about 4 minutes until the cream has reduced by one-third. Stir any accumulated juices from the meat into the sauce, taste and add salt, if necessary, then serve the steaks with the sauce.

Beef Rib with Onion Sauce *Côte de Boeuf Compôte d'Oignon*

A rib of beef is a popular cut in France and a côte de boeuf, *serving two, is often found on bistro menus. The cooking technique of browning first, then finishing in the oven is typically French.*

Serves 2–4

1 beef rib with bone, about 1kg/2¼lb and about 4cm/1½in thick, well trimmed of fat
5ml/1 tsp "steak pepper" or lightly crushed black peppercorns
15ml/1 tbsp coarse sea salt, crushed
55g/2oz/4 tbsp unsalted butter

For the onion sauce

1 large red onion or 8–10 shallots, sliced
250ml/8fl oz/½ cup fruity red wine
250ml/8fl oz/½ cup beef or chicken stock
15–30ml/1–2 tbsp redcurrant jelly or seedless raspberry preserve
1.5ml/¼ tsp dried thyme
30–45ml/2–3 tbsp olive oil
salt and freshly ground black pepper

1 ▼ Wipe the beef with damp kitchen paper. Mix the "steak pepper" or crushed peppercorns with the crushed salt and press on to both sides of the meat, coating it completely. Leave to stand, loosely covered, for 30 minutes.

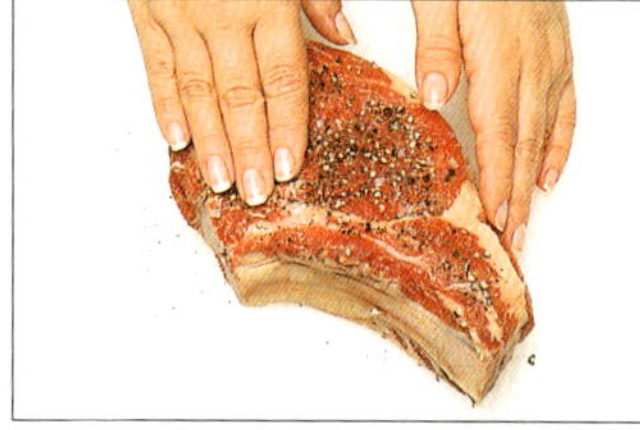

2 ▲ To make the sauce, melt 40g/1½oz/3 tbsp of the butter in a stainless steel saucepan over a medium heat. Add the onion or shallots and cook for 3–5 minutes until softened, then add the wine, stock, jelly or preserve and thyme and bring to the boil. Reduce the heat to low and simmer for 30–35 minutes until the liquid has evaporated and the sauce has thickened. Season with salt and pepper and keep warm.

3 ▲ Preheat the oven to 220°C/425°F/Gas 7. Melt the remaining butter with the oil in a heavy ovenproof frying pan or large flameproof casserole over a high heat. Add the meat and cook for 1–2 minutes until browned, turn and cook for 1–2 minutes on the other side. Immediately place the pan or casserole in the oven and roast for 8–10 minutes. Transfer the beef to a board, cover loosely and leave to stand for 10 minutes. With a knife, loosen the meat from the rib bone, and then carve into thick slices. Serve with the onion sauce.

CHÂTEAUBRIAND WITH BÉARNAISE *Châteaubriand Béarnaise*

Châteaubriand *is a lean and tender cut from the thick centre of the fillet that is pounded to give it its characteristic shape. It is usually served for two, but could easily stretch to three.*

SERVES 2

150g/5oz/⅔ cup butter, cut into pieces
25ml/1½ tbsp tarragon vinegar
25ml/1½ tbsp dry white wine
1 shallot, finely chopped
2 egg yolks
450g/1lb beef fillet, about 12.5–15cm/5–6in long, cut from the thickest part of the fillet
15ml/1 tbsp vegetable oil
salt and freshly ground black pepper
sautéed potatoes, to serve

1 Clarify the butter by melting in a saucepan over a low heat; do not boil. Skim off foam and set aside.

2 Put the vinegar, wine and shallot in a small heavy saucepan over a high heat and boil to reduce until the liquid has almost all evaporated. Remove from the heat and cool slightly. Add the egg yolks and whisk for 1 minute. Place the saucepan over a very low heat and whisk constantly until the yolk mixture begins to thicken and the whisk begins to leave tracks on the base of the pan, then remove the pan from the heat.

3 ▼ Whisk in the melted butter, drop by drop until the sauce begins to thicken, then pour in the butter a little more quickly, leaving behind the milky solids at the bottom of the pan. Season with salt and pepper and keep warm, stirring occasionally.

4 ▲ Place the meat between two sheets of greaseproof paper or clear film and pound with the flat side of a meat pounder or roll with a rolling pin to flatten to about 4cm/1½in thick. Season with salt and pepper.

5 Heat the oil in a heavy frying pan over a medium-high heat. Add the meat and cook for about 10–12 minutes, turning once, until done as preferred (medium-rare meat will be slightly soft when pressed, medium will be springy and well-done firm).

6 Transfer the steak to a board and carve in thin diagonal slices. Strain the sauce, if you prefer, and serve with the steak, accompanied by sautéed potatoes.

COOK'S TIP

Beef fillet is often cheaper when bought whole than when it has been divided into steaks. If you buy a whole fillet, you can cut a *Châteaubriand* from the thickest part, *filet mignon* steaks from less thick parts, *tournedos* from the thinner part and use the thinnest tail part for stir-frying or Stroganoff. If you wish, wrap tightly and freeze until needed.

FILET MIGNON WITH MUSHROOMS *Tournedos Rossini*

In the time of Escoffier, this haute cuisine *dish was made with truffle slices but large mushroom caps are more readily available and look attractive, especially when they are fluted.*

SERVES 4

4 thin slices white bread
120g/4oz pâté de foie gras *or* mousse de foie gras
70g/2½oz/5 tbsp butter
4 large mushroom caps
10ml/2 tsp vegetable oil
4 fillet steaks (about 2.5cm/1in thick)
45–60ml/3–4 tbsp Madeira or port
125ml/4fl oz/½ cup beef stock
watercress, to garnish

COOK'S TIP

If *pâté de foie gras* is difficult to find, you could substitute pork liver pâté.

1 ▼ Cut the bread into rounds about the same diameter as the steaks, using a large round cutter or by cutting into squares, then cutting off the corners. Toast the bread and spread with the *foie gras*, dividing it evenly. Place the croûtons on warmed plates.

2 ▲ Flute the mushroom caps using the edge of a knife blade, if you wish, for a decorative effect. Melt about 30g/1oz/2 tbsp of the butter over a medium heat and sauté the mushrooms until golden. Transfer to a plate and keep warm.

3 ▲ In the same pan, melt another 30g/1oz/2 tbsp of the butter with the oil over a medium-high heat, swirling to combine. When the butter begins to brown, add the steaks and cook for 6–8 minutes, turning once, until done as preferred (medium-rare meat will still be slightly soft when pressed, medium will be springy and well-done firm). Place the steaks on the croûtons and top with the mushroom caps.

4 Add the Madeira or port to the pan and boil for 20–30 seconds. Add the stock and boil over a high heat until reduced by three-quarters, then swirl in the remaining butter. Pour a little sauce over each steak, then garnish with watercress.

PROVENÇAL BEEF STEW *Daube de Boeuf à la Provençal*

This Provençal stew is named after the daubière, *the old earthenware container it was cooked in. Like most slow-cooked stews, it improves by cooking a day ahead and gently reheating.*

SERVES 6–8

30–60ml/2–4 tbsp olive oil
225g/8oz lean salt pork or thick cut rindless streaky bacon, diced
1.8kg/4lb chuck steak or other stewing beef cut into 7.5cm/3in pieces
750ml/1¼ pints/3 cups fruity red wine
4 carrots, thickly sliced
2 large onions, coarsely chopped
3 ripe tomatoes, peeled, seeded and coarsely chopped
15ml/1 tbsp tomato purée
2–4 garlic cloves, very finely chopped
bouquet garni
5ml/1 tsp black peppercorns
1 small onion, studded with 4 cloves
grated rind and juice of 1 unwaxed orange
30–45ml/2–3 tbsp chopped fresh parsley
salt and freshly ground black pepper

1 ▲ In a large heavy frying pan, heat 30ml/2 tbsp of the olive oil over a medium-high heat, add the salt pork or bacon and cook for 4–5 minutes, stirring frequently, until browned and the fat is rendered. Transfer with a slotted spoon to a large flameproof casserole.

2 Add enough meat to the pan to fit easily in one layer (do not overcrowd the pan or the meat will stew in its own juices and not brown). Cook for 6–8 minutes until browned, turning to colour all sides.

3 Transfer the meat to the casserole and continue browning the rest of the meat in batches, adding a little more oil if needed.

4 ▼ Set the casserole over a medium heat, pour in the wine and, if needed, add water to cover the beef and bacon. Bring to the boil, skimming off any foam that rises to the surface.

5 ▲ Stir in the carrots, onions, tomatoes, tomato purée, garlic, bouquet garni, peppercorns and clove-studded onion. Cover tightly and simmer over a low heat for about 3 hours, or until the meat and vegetables are very tender. Uncover the casserole and skim off any fat. Season with salt and pepper. Discard the bouquet garni and clove-studded onion and stir in the orange rind and juice and the parsley.

Burgundy Beef Stew

Boeuf Bourguignon

Tradition dictates that you should use the same wine in this stew that you plan to serve with it, but a less expensive full-bodied wine will do for cooking. The stew reheats very well.

Serves 6

1.5kg/3½lb lean stewing beef (chuck or shin)
175g/6oz lean salt pork or thick cut rindless streaky bacon
40g/1½oz/3 tbsp butter
350g/12oz baby onions
350g/12oz small button mushrooms
1 onion, finely chopped
1 carrot, finely chopped
2 or 3 garlic cloves, finely chopped
45ml/3 tbsp plain flour
750ml/1¼ pints/3 cups red wine, preferably Burgundy
25ml/1½ tbsp tomato purée
bouquet garni
600–750ml/1–1¼ pints/2½–3 cups beef stock
15ml/1 tbsp chopped fresh parsley
salt and freshly ground black pepper

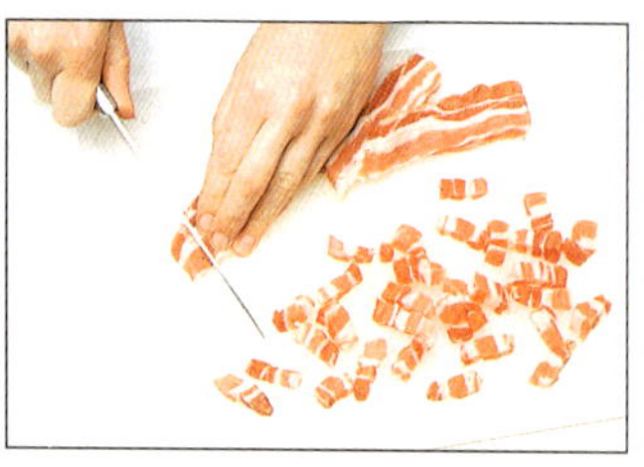

1 ▲ Cut the beef into 5cm/2in pieces and dice the salt pork or cut the bacon crossways into thin strips.

2 In a large heavy flameproof casserole, cook the pork or bacon over a medium heat until golden brown, then remove with a slotted spoon and drain. Pour off all but 30ml/2 tbsp of the fat.

3 ▲ Increase the heat to medium-high. Add enough meat to the pan to fit easily in one layer (do not crowd the pan or the meat will not brown) and cook, turning to colour all sides, until well browned. Transfer the beef to a plate and continue browning the meat in batches.

4 ▲ In a heavy frying pan, melt one-third of the butter over a medium heat, add the baby onions and cook, stirring frequently, until evenly golden. Set aside on a plate.

5 ▲ In the same pan, melt half of the remaining butter over a medium heat. Add the mushrooms and sauté, stirring frequently, until golden, then set aside with the baby onions.

6 ▲ When all the beef has been browned, pour off any fat from the casserole and add the remaining butter. When the butter has melted, add the onion, carrot and garlic and cook over a medium heat for 3–4 minutes until just softened, stirring frequently. Sprinkle over the flour and cook for 2 minutes, then add the wine, tomato purée and bouquet garni. Bring to the boil, scraping the base of the pan.

7 ▲ Return the beef and bacon to the casserole and pour on the stock, adding more if needed to cover the meat and vegetables when pressed down. Cover the casserole and simmer very gently over a low heat, stirring occasionally, for about 3 hours or until the meat is very tender. Add the sautéed mushrooms and baby onions and cook, covered, for a further 30 minutes. Discard the bouquet garni and stir in the parsley before serving.

Calves' liver with honey

Foie de Veau au Miel

Liver is prepared in many ways all over France – this is a quick and easy, slightly contemporary treatment. Cook the liver until it is browned on the outside but still rosy pink in the centre.

Serves 4

4 slices calves' liver (about 175g/6oz each and 1.2cm/½in thick)
plain flour, for dusting
30g/1oz/2 tbsp butter
30ml/2 tbsp vegetable oil
30ml/2 tbsp sherry vinegar or red wine vinegar
30–45ml/2–3 tbsp chicken stock
15ml/1 tbsp clear honey
salt and freshly ground black pepper
watercress sprigs, to garnish

1 ▼ Wipe the liver slices with damp kitchen paper, then season both sides with a little salt and pepper and dust the slices lightly with flour, shaking off any excess.

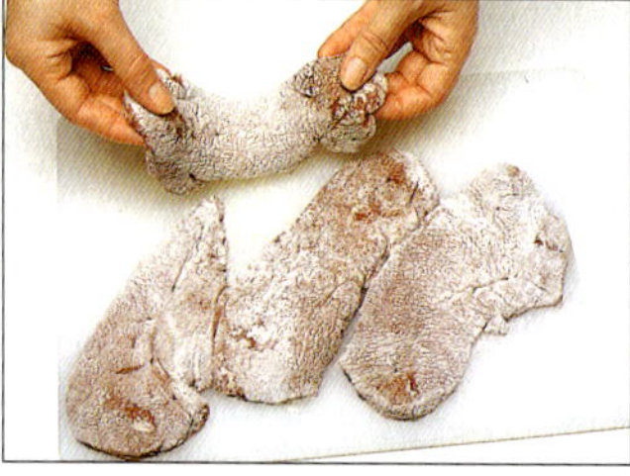

2 ▲ In a large heavy frying pan, melt half of the butter with the oil over a high heat and swirl to blend.

3 ▲ Add the liver slices to the pan and cook for 1–2 minutes until browned on one side, then turn and cook for a further 1 minute. Transfer to warmed plates and keep warm.

4 ▲ Stir the vinegar, stock and honey into the pan and boil for about 1 minute, stirring constantly, then add the remaining butter, stirring until melted and smooth. Spoon over the liver slices and garnish with watercress sprigs.

VEAL KIDNEYS WITH MUSTARD *Rognons de Veau à la Moutarde*

In France, veal kidneys are easily found, but this dish is equally delicious made with lamb's kidneys. Be sure not to cook the sauce too long once the mustard is added or it will lose its piquancy.

SERVES 4

2 veal kidneys or 8–10 lamb's kidneys, trimmed and membranes removed
30g/1oz/2 tbsp butter
15ml/1 tbsp vegetable oil
120g/4oz button mushrooms, quartered
60ml/4 tbsp chicken stock
30ml/2 tbsp brandy (optional)
175ml/6fl oz/¾ cup crème fraîche or double cream
30ml/2 tbsp Dijon mustard
salt and freshly ground black pepper
snipped fresh chives, to garnish

1 ▲ Cut the veal kidneys into pieces, discarding any fat. If using lamb's kidneys, remove the central core by cutting a V-shape from the middle of each kidney. Cut each kidney into three or four pieces.

2 ▲ In a large frying pan, melt the butter with the oil over a high heat and swirl to blend. Add the kidneys and sauté for about 3–4 minutes, stirring frequently, until well browned, then transfer them to a plate using a slotted spoon.

3 ▲ Add the mushrooms to the pan and sauté for 2–3 minutes until golden, stirring frequently. Pour in the chicken stock and brandy, if using, then bring to the boil and boil for 2 minutes.

4 ▼ Stir in the crème fraîche or double cream and cook for about 2–3 minutes until the sauce is slightly thickened. Stir in the mustard and season with salt and pepper, then add the kidneys and cook for 1 minute to reheat. Scatter over the chives before serving.

WHITE VEAL STEW *Blanquette de Veau*

A blanquette is a "white" stew traditionally enriched with cream and egg yolks. This bistro favourite is usually made with veal, but in the South of France it is often made with lamb.

SERVES 6

1.3kg/3lb boneless veal shoulder, cut into 5cm/2in pieces
1.5 litres/2½ pints/6¼ cups veal or chicken stock or water (or more if needed)
1 large onion, studded with 2 cloves
4 carrots, sliced
2 leeks, sliced
1 garlic clove, halved
bouquet garni
15ml/1 tbsp black peppercorns
70g/2½oz/5 tbsp butter
225g/½lb button mushrooms, quartered if large
225g/½lb baby onions
15ml/1 tbsp caster sugar
40g/1½oz/¼ cup plain flour
125ml/4fl oz/½ cup crème fraîche or double cream
pinch of freshly grated nutmeg
30–60ml/2–4 tbsp chopped fresh dill or parsley
salt and white pepper

1 Put the veal in a large flameproof casserole and cover with the stock or water. Bring to the boil over a medium heat, skimming off any foam that rises to the surface.

2 ▲ Add the studded onion, one of the sliced carrots, the leeks, garlic, bouquet garni and peppercorns, then cover and simmer over a medium-low heat for about 1 hour until the veal is just tender.

3 ▲ Meanwhile, in a frying pan, melt 15g/½oz/1 tbsp of the butter over a medium-high heat, add the mushrooms and sauté until lightly golden. Transfer to a large bowl using a slotted spoon.

4 ▲ Add another 15g/½oz/1 tbsp butter to the pan and add the baby onions. Sprinkle with the sugar and add about 90ml/6 tbsp of the veal cooking liquid, then cover and simmer for 10–12 minutes until the onions are tender and the liquid has evaporated. Transfer the onions to the bowl with the mushrooms.

COOK'S TIP

If you would like to use the traditional egg and cream *liaison*, stir the cream into two beaten egg yolks before whisking into the white sauce and proceed as above. Simmer until the sauce thickens, but do not allow the sauce to boil or it may curdle.

5 ▲ When the veal is tender, transfer it to the same bowl using a slotted spoon. Strain the cooking liquid and discard the cooked vegetables and bouquet garni, then wash the casserole and return it to the heat.

6 ▲ Melt the remaining butter, add the flour and cook for 1–2 minutes over a medium heat, but do not allow the mixture to brown. Slowly whisk in the reserved cooking liquid and bring to the boil, then simmer the sauce for 15–20 minutes until smooth and slightly thickened. Add the remaining carrots and cook for a further 10 minutes until tender.

7 Whisk the cream into the sauce and simmer until the sauce is slightly thickened. Return the reserved meat, mushrooms and onions to the sauce and simmer for 10–15 minutes until the veal is very tender, skimming and stirring occasionally. Season with salt and white pepper and a little nutmeg, then stir in the chopped dill or parsley and serve.

PAN-FRIED VEAL CHOPS *Côtes de Veau à la Poële*

Veal chops from the loin are an expensive cut and are best cooked quickly and simply. The flavour of basil goes well with veal, but other herbs can be used instead if you prefer.

SERVES 2

30g/1oz/2 tbsp butter, softened
15ml/1 tbsp Dijon mustard
15ml/1 tbsp chopped fresh basil
olive oil, for brushing
2 veal loin chops, 2.5cm/1in thick (about 225g/8oz each)
salt and freshly ground black pepper
basil sprigs, to garnish

COOK'S TIP

If you prefer, replace the basil in the herb butter with fresh thyme or marjoram, or use a mixture of both. Or, omit the herb butter and top the veal chops with Tapenade.

1 ▲ To make the basil butter, cream the butter with the mustard and chopped basil in a small bowl, then season with pepper.

2 Lightly oil a heavy frying pan or griddle. Set over a high heat until very hot but not smoking. Brush both sides of each chop with a little oil and season with a little salt.

3 ▼ Place the chops on the pan or griddle and reduce the heat to medium. Cook for 4–5 minutes, then turn and cook for a further 3–4 minutes until done as preferred (medium-rare meat will still be slightly soft when pressed, medium meat will be springy and well-done firm). Top each chop with half the basil butter and serve at once.

VEAL ESCALOPES WITH TARRAGON *Veau à l'Estragon*

These thin slices of veal need little cooking, and the sauce is made very quickly as well.

SERVES 4

4 veal escalopes (about 120–150g/4–5oz each)
15g/½oz/1 tbsp butter
30ml/2 tbsp brandy
250ml/8fl oz/1 cup chicken or beef stock
15ml/1 tbsp chopped fresh tarragon
salt and freshly ground black pepper
tarragon sprigs, to garnish

1 Place the veal escalopes between two sheets of greaseproof paper or clear film and pound with the flat side of a meat mallet or roll them with a rolling pin to flatten to about 6mm/¼in thickness. Season with salt and pepper.

2 ▼ Melt the butter in a large frying pan over a medium-high heat. Add enough meat to the pan to fit easily in one layer (do not overcrowd the pan, cook in batches if necessary) and cook for 1½–2 minutes, turning once. (It should be lightly browned, but must not be overcooked.) Transfer to a serving platter or plates and cover to keep warm.

3 ▲ Add the brandy to the pan, then pour in the stock and bring to the boil. Add the tarragon and continue boiling until the liquid is reduced by half.

4 Return the veal to the pan with any accumulated juices and heat through. Serve immediately, garnished with tarragon sprigs.

MOUTARDE
PREPAREE
DE DIJON
POUPON

VEAL STEW WITH TOMATOES *Sauté de Veau Marengo*

The combination of tomatoes and orange in this dish brings to mind Mediterranean sunshine.

SERVES 6

60ml/4 tbsp plain flour
1.3kg/3lb boneless veal shoulder, cut into 4cm/1½in pieces
30–45ml/2–3 tbsp olive oil
4 or 5 shallots, finely chopped
2 garlic cloves, very finely chopped
300ml/½ pint/1¼ cups dry white wine
450g/1lb tomatoes, peeled, seeded and chopped
grated rind and juice of 1 unwaxed orange
bouquet garni
15ml/1 tbsp tomato purée
15g/½oz/1 tbsp butter
350g/¾lb button mushrooms, quartered if large
salt and freshly ground black pepper
chopped fresh parsley, to garnish

1 ▼ Put the flour in a polythene bag and season with salt and pepper. Drop the pieces of meat into the bag a few at a time and shake to coat with flour, tapping off the excess. Discard the remaining flour.

2 ▲ Heat 30ml/2 tbsp of the oil in a flameproof casserole over a medium-high heat. Add enough meat to the pan to fit easily in one layer (do not overcrowd the pan or the meat will not brown). Cook, turning to colour all sides, until well browned, then transfer to a plate. Continue browning the meat in batches, adding more oil if needed.

3 ▲ In the same pan, cook the shallots and garlic over a medium heat, stirring, until just softened, then stir in the wine and bring to the boil. Return the meat to the pan and add the tomatoes, orange rind and juice, bouquet garni and tomato purée. Bring back to the boil, then reduce the heat to low, cover and simmer gently for 1 hour.

4 Melt the butter in a frying pan over a medium heat and sauté the mushrooms until golden. Add the mushrooms to the casserole and cook, covered, for 20–30 minutes, or until the meat is very tender. Adjust the seasoning and discard the bouquet garni before serving. Garnish the stew with parsley.

ROAST LEG OF LAMB WITH BEANS *Gigot d'Agneau*

Leg of lamb is the classic Sunday roast. In France, the shank bone is not removed, but it is cut through for easier handling. The roast is often served with haricot or flageolet beans.

SERVES 8–10

2.7–3kg/6–7lb leg of lamb
3 or 4 garlic cloves
olive oil
fresh or dried rosemary leaves
450g/1lb dried haricot or flageolet beans, soaked overnight in cold water
1 bay leaf
30ml/2 tbsp red wine
150ml/¼ pint/⅔ cup lamb or beef stock
30g/1oz/2 tbsp butter
salt and freshly ground black pepper
watercress, to garnish

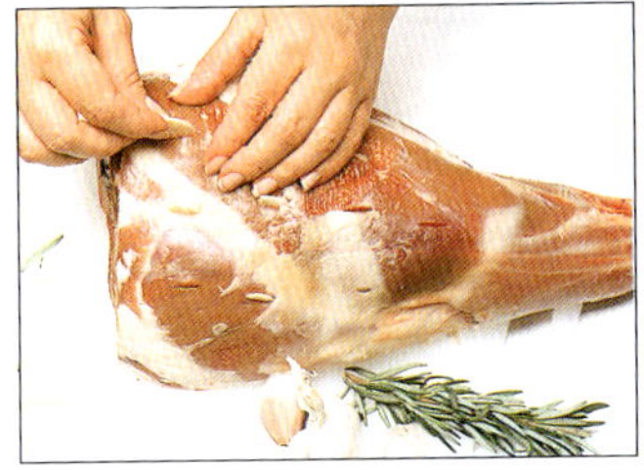

1 ▲ Preheat the oven to 220°C/425°F/Gas 7. Wipe the leg of lamb with damp kitchen paper and dry the fat covering well. Cut 2 or 3 of the garlic cloves into 10–12 slivers, then with the tip of a knife, cut 10–12 slits into the lamb and insert the garlic slivers into the slits. Rub with oil, season with salt and pepper and sprinkle with rosemary.

2 Set the lamb on a rack in a shallow roasting tin and put in the oven. After 15 minutes, reduce the heat to 180°C/350°F/Gas 4 and continue to roast for 1½–1¾ hours (about 18 minutes per 450g/1lb) or until a meat thermometer inserted into the thickest part of the meat registers 57–60°C/135–140°F for medium-rare to medium meat or 66°C/150°F for well-done.

3 Meanwhile, rinse the beans and put in a saucepan with enough fresh water to cover generously. Add the remaining garlic and the bay leaf, then bring to the boil. Reduce the heat and simmer for 45 minutes–1 hour, or until tender.

4 Transfer the roast to a board and stand, loosely covered, for 10–15 minutes. Skim off the fat from the cooking juices, then add the wine and stock to the roasting tin. Boil over a medium heat, stirring and scraping the base of the tin, until slightly reduced. Strain into a warmed gravy boat.

5 ▼ Drain the beans, discard the bay leaf, then toss the beans with the butter until it melts and season with salt and pepper. Garnish the lamb with watercress and serve with the beans and the sauce.

Roast Stuffed Lamb

Gigot Farcie

The lambs which graze in the salty marshes along the north coast of Brittany and Normandy are considered the best in France. The stuffing is suitable for either leg or shoulder joints.

Serves 6–8

1.8–2kg/4–4½lb boneless leg or shoulder of lamb (not tied)
30g/1oz/2 tbsp butter, softened
15–30ml/1–2 tbsp plain flour
125ml/4fl oz/½ cup white wine
250ml/8fl oz/1 cup chicken or beef stock
salt and freshly ground black pepper
watercress, to garnish
sautéed potatoes, to serve

For the stuffing
70g/2½oz/5 tbsp butter
1 small onion, finely chopped
1 garlic clove, finely chopped
55g/2oz/⅓ cup long grain rice
150ml/¼ pint/⅔ cup chicken stock
2.5ml/½ tsp dried thyme
4 lamb's kidneys, halved and cored
275g/10oz young spinach leaves, well washed
salt and freshly ground black pepper

1 ▲ To make the stuffing, melt 30g/1oz/2 tbsp of the butter in a saucepan over a medium heat. Add the onion and cook for 2–3 minutes until just softened, then add the garlic and rice and cook for about 1–2 minutes until the rice appears translucent, stirring constantly. Add the stock, salt and pepper and thyme and bring to the boil, stirring occasionally, then reduce the heat to low and cook for about 18 minutes, covered, until the rice is tender and the liquid is absorbed. Tip the rice into a bowl and fluff with a fork.

2 In a small frying pan, melt about 30g/1oz/2 tbsp of the remaining butter over a medium-high heat. Add the kidneys and cook for about 2–3 minutes, turning once, until lightly browned, but still pink inside, then transfer to a board and leave to cool. Cut the kidneys into pieces and add to the rice, season with salt and pepper and toss to combine.

3 In a frying pan, heat the remaining butter over a medium heat until foaming. Add the spinach leaves and cook for 1–2 minutes until wilted, drain off excess liquid, then transfer the leaves to a plate and leave to cool.

4 ▲ Preheat the oven to 190°C/375°F/Gas 5. Lay the meat skin-side down on a work surface and season with salt and pepper. Spread the spinach leaves in an even layer over the surface then spread the stuffing in an even layer over the spinach. Roll up the meat like a Swiss roll and use a skewer to close the seam.

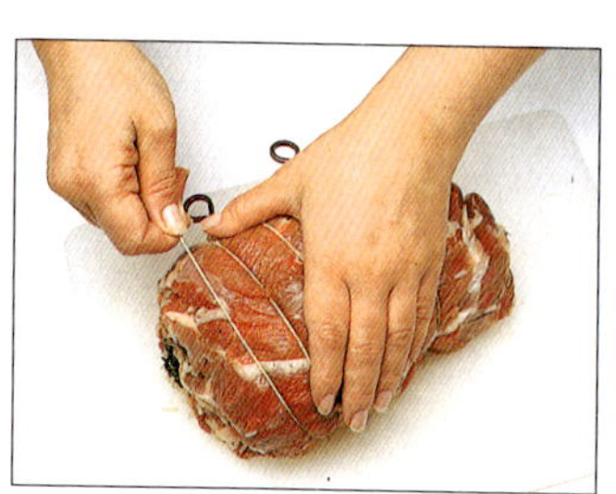

5 ▲ Tie the meat at 2.5cm/1in intervals to hold its shape, then place in a roasting tin, spread with the softened butter and season with salt and pepper. Roast for 1½–2 hours until the juices run slightly pink when pierced with a skewer, or until a meat thermometer inserted into the thickest part of the meat registers 57–60°C/135–140°F (for medium-rare to medium). Transfer the meat to a carving board, cover loosely with foil and leave to rest for about 20 minutes.

6 Skim off as much fat from the roasting tin as possible, then place the tin over a medium-high heat and bring to the boil. Sprinkle over the flour and cook for 2–3 minutes until browned, stirring and scraping the base of the tin. Whisk in the wine and stock and bring to the boil, then cook for 4–5 minutes until the sauce thickens. Season and strain into a gravy boat. Carve the meat into slices, garnish with watercress and serve with the gravy and potatoes.

Variation

If kidneys are difficult to obtain, substitute about 125g/¼lb mushrooms. Chop them coarsely and cook in the butter until tender. Don't use dark mushrooms – they will make the rice a murky colour.

RACK OF LAMB WITH MUSTARD *Carré d'Agneau à la Moutarde*

This recipe is perfect for entertaining. You can coat the lamb with the crust before your guests arrive, and put it in the oven when you sit down for the first course.

SERVES 6–8

3 racks of lamb (7–8 ribs each), trimmed of fat, bones "French" trimmed
2 or 3 garlic cloves
120g/4oz (about 4 slices) white or wholemeal bread, torn into pieces
25ml/1½ tbsp fresh thyme leaves or 15ml/1 tbsp rosemary leaves
25ml/1½ tbsp Dijon mustard
freshly ground black pepper
30ml/2 tbsp olive oil
fresh rosemary, to garnish
new potatoes, to serve

1 ▼ Preheat the oven to 220°C/425°F/Gas 7. Trim any remaining fat from the lamb, including the fat covering over the meat.

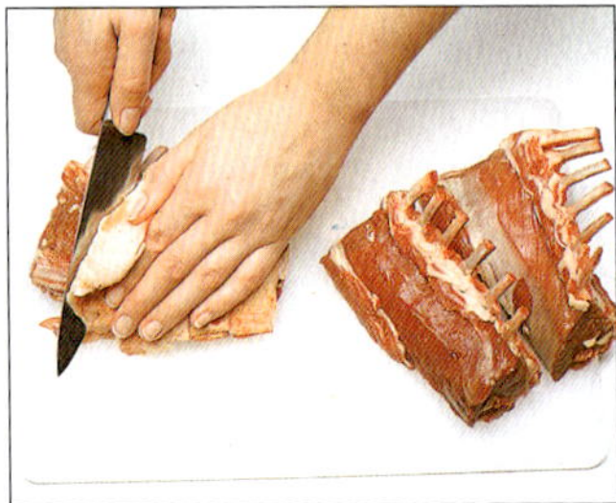

2 ▲ In a food processor fitted with the metal blade, with the machine running, drop the garlic through the feed tube and process until finely chopped. Add the bread, herbs, mustard and a little pepper and process until combined, then slowly pour in the oil.

3 ▲ Press the mixture on to the meaty side and ends of the racks, completely covering the surface.

4 Put the racks in a shallow roasting tin, and roast for about 25 minutes for medium-rare or 3–5 minutes more for medium (a meat thermometer inserted into the thickest part of the meat should register 57–60°C/135–140°F for medium-rare to medium). Transfer the meat to a carving board or warmed platter. Cut down between the bones to carve into chops. Serve garnished with rosemary and accompanied by new potatoes.

Lamb Chops with Mint *Côtes d'Agneau Vinaigrette à la Menthe*

Serving vinaigrette sauces with meat came in with nouvelle cuisine *and stayed. This one offers a classic combination – lamb and mint – in a new style.*

Serves 4

8 loin lamb chops or 4 double loin chops (about 2cm/¾in thick)
coarsely ground black pepper
fresh mint, to garnish
sautéed potatoes, to serve

For the mint vinaigrette

30ml/2 tbsp white wine vinegar
2.5ml/½ tsp clear honey
1 small garlic clove, very finely chopped
60ml/4 tbsp extra virgin olive oil
20g/¾oz/⅓ cup (packed) fresh mint leaves, finely chopped
1 ripe plum tomato, peeled, seeded and finely diced
salt and freshly ground black pepper

1 ▲ To make the vinaigrette, put the vinegar, honey, garlic, salt and pepper in a small bowl and whisk thoroughly to combine.

2 ▲ Slowly whisk in the oil, then stir in the mint and tomatoes and set aside for up to 1 hour.

3 ▼ Put the lamb chops on a board and trim off any excess fat. Sprinkle with the pepper and press on to both sides of the meat, coating it evenly.

Cook's tip

The chops may also be grilled under a preheated grill or barbecued over charcoal until done as you like.

4 ▲ Lightly oil a heavy cast iron griddle and set over a high heat until very hot but not smoking. Place the chops on the griddle and reduce the heat to medium. Cook the chops for 6–7 minutes, turning once, or until done as preferred (medium-rare meat will still be slightly soft when pressed, medium will be springy and well-done firm). Serve the chops with the vinaigrette and the sautéed potatoes, garnished with mint.

Lamb Stew with Vegetables *Navarin d'Agneau Printanier*

A navarin is a stew made with lamb and a selection of young tender spring vegetables such as carrots, new potatoes, baby onions, peas, French beans and especially turnips!

Serves 6

60ml/4 tbsp vegetable oil
1.3kg/3lb lamb shoulder or other stewing meat, well trimmed, cut into 5cm/2in pieces
45–60ml/3–4 tbsp plain flour
1 litre/1⅔ pints/4 cups beef or chicken stock
1 large bouquet garni
3 garlic cloves, lightly crushed
3 ripe tomatoes, peeled, seeded and chopped
5ml/1 tsp tomato purée
675g/1½lb small potatoes, peeled if wished
12 baby carrots, trimmed and scrubbed
120g/4oz French beans, cut into 5cm/2in pieces
30g/1oz/2 tbsp butter
12–18 baby onions, peeled
6 medium turnips, peeled and quartered
30ml/2 tbsp sugar
1.5ml/¼ tsp dried thyme
175g/6oz/1¼ cups peas
55g/2oz mange-tout
salt and freshly ground black pepper
45ml/3 tbsp chopped fresh parsley or coriander, to garnish

1 Heat 30ml/2 tbsp of the oil in a large heavy frying pan over a medium-high heat. Add enough of the lamb to fit easily in one layer (do not overcrowd the pan or the meat will not brown). Cook, turning to colour all sides, until well browned.

2 Transfer the meat to a large flameproof casserole and continue browning the rest of the meat in batches, adding a little more oil if needed. Add 45–60ml/3–4 tbsp of water to the pan and boil for about 1 minute, stirring and scraping the base of the pan, then pour the liquid into the casserole.

3 ▲ Sprinkle the flour over the browned meat in the casserole and set over a medium heat. Cook for 3–5 minutes until browned. Stir in the stock, the bouquet garni, garlic, tomatoes and tomato purée and season with salt and pepper.

4 ▲ Bring to the boil over a high heat, skimming off any foam that rises to the surface. Reduce the heat to low and simmer, stirring occasionally, for about 1 hour until the meat is tender. Cool the stew to room temperature, then chill, covered, overnight.

5 About 1½ hours before serving, take the casserole from the fridge and remove the fat from the surface, wiping the surface with kitchen paper to remove all traces of fat. Set the casserole over a medium heat and bring to a simmer.

6 Cook the potatoes in boiling salted water for 15–20 minutes until tender, then using a slotted spoon, transfer to a bowl and add the carrots to the same water. Cook for 4–5 minutes until just tender and transfer to the same bowl. Add the green beans and boil for 2–3 minutes until tender, yet crisp. Transfer to the bowl with the other vegetables.

7 ▲ Melt the butter in a heavy frying pan or saucepan over a medium-high heat. Add the onions and turnips with 45–60ml/3–4 tbsp water and cook, covered, for 4–5 minutes. Uncover the pan, stir in the sugar and thyme and cook, stirring and shaking the pan occasionally, until the onions and turnips are shiny and caramelized. Transfer them to the bowl of vegetables. Add 30–45ml/2–3 tbsp of water to the pan to deglaze and boil for 1 minute, scraping the base of the pan, then add this liquid to the lamb.

8 When the lamb and gravy are hot, add the reserved vegetables to the stew and stir gently to distribute. Stir in the peas and mange-touts and cook for 5 minutes until they turn a bright green, then stir in 30ml/2 tbsp of the parsley or coriander and pour into a large warmed serving dish. Scatter over the remaining parsley.

MOROCCAN LAMB STEW *Tagine d'Agneau aux Pois Chiches*

The colourful spicy cuisines of French colonial North Africa have left their mark on French cooking. Tagine, *named after the conical-shaped pottery dish in which it is cooked, is a favourite.*

SERVES 6–8

225g/8oz/1⅓ cups dried chick-peas soaked in cold water overnight
60ml/4 tbsp olive oil
10ml/2 tsp sugar
10ml/2 tsp ground cumin
5ml/1 tsp ground cinnamon
5ml/1 tsp ground ginger
2.5ml/½ tsp ground turmeric
2.5ml/½ tsp powdered saffron or paprika
1.3kg/3lb lamb shoulder, trimmed of all fat and cut into 5cm/2in pieces
2 onions, coarsely chopped
3 garlic cloves, finely chopped
2 tomatoes, peeled, seeded and chopped
75g/3oz/⅔ cup raisins, soaked in warm water
10–24 stoned black olives (such as Kalamata)
2 preserved lemons, thinly sliced, or grated rind of 1 unwaxed lemon
60–90ml/4–6 tbsp chopped fresh coriander
salt and freshly ground black pepper
450g/1lb couscous, to serve

1 Drain the chick-peas, rinse under cold running water and place in a large saucepan, then cover with water and boil vigorously for 10 minutes. Drain the chick-peas and return to a clean saucepan. Cover with fresh cold water and bring to the boil over a high heat, then reduce the heat and simmer, covered, for about 1–1½ hours until tender. Remove the pan from the heat, add a little salt and set aside.

2 In a large bowl, combine half the olive oil with the sugar, cumin, cinnamon, ginger, turmeric, saffron or paprika, pepper and 5ml/1tsp salt. Add the lamb, toss to coat well and set aside for 20 minutes.

3 ▲ In a large heavy frying pan, heat the remaining oil over a medium-high heat. Add enough lamb to fit easily in one layer (do not overcrowd the pan) and cook for 4–5 minutes, turning the pieces to colour all sides, until well browned. Transfer to a large flameproof casserole and continue browning the meat in batches, adding a little more oil if necessary.

4 ▲ Add the onions to the pan and stir constantly until well browned. Stir in the garlic and tomatoes with 250ml/8fl oz/1 cup water, stirring and scraping the base of the pan. Pour into the casserole and add enough water to just cover, then bring to the boil over a high heat, skimming any foam that rises to the surface. Reduce the heat to low and simmer for about 1 hour, or until the meat is tender when pierced with a knife.

5 ▲ Drain the chick-peas, reserving the liquid, and add to the lamb in the casserole with about 250ml/8fl oz/1 cup of the liquid. Stir in the raisins and their soaking liquid and simmer for 30 minutes more. Stir in the olives and sliced preserved lemons or lemon rind and simmer 20–30 minutes more, then add half the chopped coriander.

6 ▲ About ½ hour before serving, prepare the couscous according to the instructions on the packet. Spoon the couscous on to a warmed serving dish, spoon the lamb stew on top and sprinkle with the remaining fresh coriander.

COOK'S TIP

Preserved lemons are frequently used in Morrocan-style cooking. They are available in delicatessens and food halls but, if you can't find them, a little grated lemon rind makes an adequate substitute.

Pork with Camembert *Médaillons de Porc au Camembert*

Not surprisingly, most cheese-producing regions of France have a tradition of recipes using their own home-produced cheese. This recipe combines several of the fine products of Normandy.

Serves 3–4

350–450g/¾–1lb pork fillet
15g/½oz/1 tbsp butter
45ml/3 tbsp sparkling dry cider or dry white wine
125–175ml/4–6fl oz/½–¾ cup crème fraîche or whipping cream
15ml/1 tbsp chopped fresh mixed herbs, such as marjoram, thyme and sage
½ Camembert cheese (120g/4oz), rind removed (70g/2½oz without rind), sliced
7.5ml/1½ tsp Dijon mustard
freshly ground black pepper
fresh parsley, to garnish

1 ▼ Slice the pork fillet crossways into small steaks about 2cm/¾in thick. Place between two sheets of greaseproof paper or clear film and pound with the flat side of a meat mallet or roll with a rolling pin to flatten to a thickness of 1cm/½in. Sprinkle with pepper.

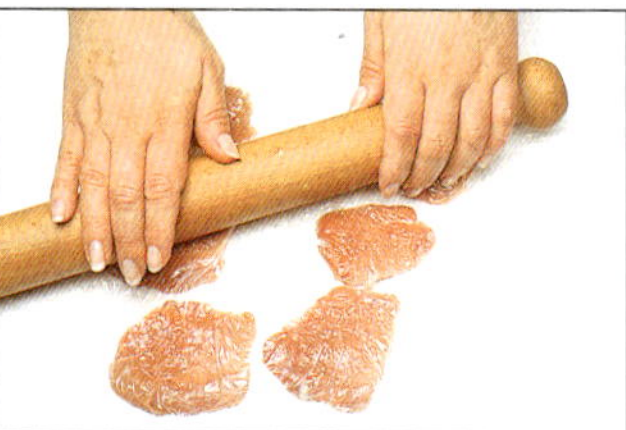

2 ▲ Melt the butter in a heavy frying pan over a medium-high heat until it begins to brown, then add the meat. Cook for 5 minutes, turning once, or until just cooked through and the meat is springy when pressed. Transfer to a warmed dish and cover to keep warm.

3 ▲ Add the cider or wine and bring to the boil, scraping the base of the pan. Stir in the cream and herbs and bring back to the boil.

4 ▲ Add the cheese and mustard and any accumulated juices from the meat. Add a little more cream if needed and adjust the seasoning. Serve the pork with the sauce and garnish with parsley.

Pork Fillet with Sage and Orange *Filet de Porc à la Sauge*

Sage is often partnered with pork – there seems to be a natural affinity. The addition of orange brings complexity and balances the sometimes overpowering flavour of sage.

Serves 4

2 pork fillets, about 350g/12oz each
15g/½oz/1 tbsp butter
125ml/4fl oz/½ cup dry sherry
175ml/6fl oz/¾ cup chicken stock
2 garlic cloves, very finely chopped
grated rind and juice of 1 unwaxed orange
3 or 4 sage leaves, finely chopped
10ml/2 tsp cornflour
salt and freshly ground black pepper
orange wedges and sage leaves, to garnish

1 ▼ Season the pork fillets lightly with salt and pepper. Melt the butter in a heavy flameproof casserole over a medium-high heat, then add the meat and cook for 5–6 minutes, turning to brown all sides evenly.

2 Add the sherry, boil for about 1 minute, then add the stock, garlic, orange rind and sage. Bring to the boil and reduce the heat to low, then cover and simmer for 20 minutes, turning once until the juices run clear when the meat is pierced with a knife or a meat thermometer inserted into the thickest part of the meat registers 66°C/150°F. Transfer the pork to a warmed platter and cover to keep warm.

3 ▲ Bring the sauce to the boil. Blend the cornflour and orange juice and stir into the sauce, then boil gently over a medium heat for a few minutes, stirring frequently, until the sauce is slightly thickened. Strain into a gravy boat or serving jug.

4 ▼ Slice the pork diagonally and pour the meat juices into the sauce. Spoon a little sauce over the pork and garnish with orange wedges and sage leaves. Serve the remaining sauce separately.

ROAST LOIN OF PORK WITH PRUNES *Rôti de Porc aux Pruneaux*

The combination of pork and prunes is often found in casseroles and stews from the Loire Valley, perhaps with one of the local wines. For the best flavour, soak the prunes overnight.

SERVES 6–8

18–24 prunes, stoned
750ml/1¼ pints/3 cups fruity white wine, preferably Vouvray
1.8kg/4lb centre cut pork loin (about 8 ribs), chined and skin removed
30ml/2 tbsp vegetable oil
1 large onion, coarsely chopped
1 large leek, sliced
2 carrots, chopped
1 celery stick, sliced
30ml/2 tbsp brandy (optional)
250ml/8fl oz/1 cup chicken stock
1 bouquet garni
30–45ml/2–3 tbsp cornflour, blended with 45ml/3 tbsp cold water
60ml/4 tbsp double cream
salt and freshly ground black pepper
watercress, to garnish
new potatoes, to serve

1 ▲ Put the prunes in a bowl, pour over the wine, then cover and leave to soak for several hours or overnight.

COOK'S TIP

It is important that the pork isn't overcooked – so for accurate timing, use a meat thermometer. Insert it into a fleshy part of the meat away from bones before roasting, or if using an instant-read thermometer, insert towards the end of cooking, following the manufacturer's instructions.

2 ▲ Preheat the oven to 200°C/400°F/Gas 6. Wipe the meat with damp kitchen paper, then dry the fat thoroughly. Score the surface of the fat with a sharp knife.

3 In a flameproof casserole or large heavy roasting tin, heat the oil over a high heat until hot. Add the onion, leek, carrot and celery and cook for 3–5 minutes until browned, stirring frequently. Add the brandy, if using, stock and bouquet garni and stir well.

4 ▲ Put the pork on top of the vegetables and place in the oven. Roast for about 1½ hours until the juices run clear when the meat is pierced with a skewer, or a meat thermometer inserted into the thickest part of the meat registers 66°C/150°F. (If the liquid in the casserole or roasting tin evaporates, add a little of the prune soaking liquid or water to prevent the vegetables from burning.) Transfer the meat to a warmed serving platter, cover loosely with foil and leave to stand for 15 minutes.

5 ▲ Using a slotted spoon, transfer the prunes to a medium saucepan. Skim off as much fat as possible from the casserole or roasting tin and place over a high heat. Add the prune liquid to the casserole or roasting tin and bring to the boil, stirring constantly and scraping the base. Boil for 3–4 minutes.

6 ▲ Stir the blended cornflour into the casserole or tin and cook, stirring frequently for 2–3 minutes until the sauce thickens, then strain the contents of the pan into the saucepan with the prunes, pressing the vegetables to extract all the juice. Return the saucepan to a medium heat, stir in the cream and simmer for 2 minutes, then season with salt and pepper. Reduce the heat to low and simmer gently, stirring frequently, until ready to serve.

7 Spoon the prunes on to the serving plate with a little of the sauce and pour the remaining sauce into a gravy boat or serving jug. Garnish with watercress before serving with new potatoes.

PARIS

PORK CHOPS WITH TOMATO SAUCE *Côtes de Porc Sauce Nénette*

Use the best pork chops for a tender result. This sauce is equally delicious with veal or chicken.

SERVES 4

15g/½oz/1 tbsp butter
15ml/1 tbsp vegetable oil
4 large centre loin pork chops, about 2.5cm/1in thick, trimmed
salt and freshly ground black pepper
60ml/4 tbsp white wine or chicken stock
2.5ml/½ tsp dried thyme
250ml/8fl oz/1 cup whipping cream
5ml/1 tsp tomato purée
15ml/1 tbsp Dijon mustard
1 tomato, peeled, seeded and chopped
15ml/1 tbsp chopped fresh tarragon, chervil or parsley
fresh tarragon or other herbs, to garnish
Straw Potato Cakes, to serve

1 ▼ Melt the butter with the oil in a large heavy frying pan over a high heat until sizzling. Season the pork chops with salt and pepper, then add to the pan and reduce the heat to medium-high. Cook for 2–3 minutes on each side until browned, then transfer the pork chops to a plate and pour off all the fat.

2 ▲ Add the wine or stock and thyme to the pan and bring to the boil. Cook for 2–3 minutes until the wine has almost evaporated.

3 ▲ Add the cream and tomato purée and simmer for 2 minutes, stirring frequently, then return the pork chops to the sauce and cook for 4–5 minutes over a medium-low heat until just firm to the touch. Take care not to overcook.

4 ▲ Add the mustard, chopped tomato and herbs, stirring and shaking the pan to distribute them, and cook for 1 minute to heat through. Serve the chops with the sauce, accompanied by Straw Potato Cakes and garnished with sprigs of tarragon or other fresh herbs.

BRAISED HAM WITH MADIERA SAUCE *Jambon Braisé au Madère*

The Morvan district of Burgundy is known for producing fine quality, mild cured hams. Accompanied by this rich Madeira sauce, a simple ham steak is transformed into an elegant dish.

SERVES 4

55g/2oz/4 tbsp unsalted butter
4 shallots, finely chopped
30g/1oz/2 tbsp plain flour
500ml/16fl oz/2 cups beef stock
15ml/1 tbsp tomato purée
90ml/6 tbsp Madeira
4 ham steaks (about 175–200g/ 6–7oz each)
salt and freshly ground black pepper
watercress, to garnish
creamed potatoes, to serve

1 ▲ Melt half the butter in a heavy medium-size saucepan, over a medium-high heat, then add the shallots and cook for 2–3 minutes until just softened, stirring frequently.

2 ▲ Sprinkle over the flour and cook for 3–4 minutes until well browned, stirring constantly, then whisk in the stock and tomato purée and season with pepper. Simmer over a low heat until the sauce is reduced by about half, stirring occasionally.

3 ▼ Taste the sauce and adjust the seasoning, then stir in the Madeira and cook for 2–3 minutes. Strain into a small serving bowl or gravy boat and keep warm. (The sauce can be made up to three days in advance and chilled. Reheat to serve.)

COOK'S TIP

To make the sauce a deeper, richer colour, add a few drops of gravy browning liquid to the stock.

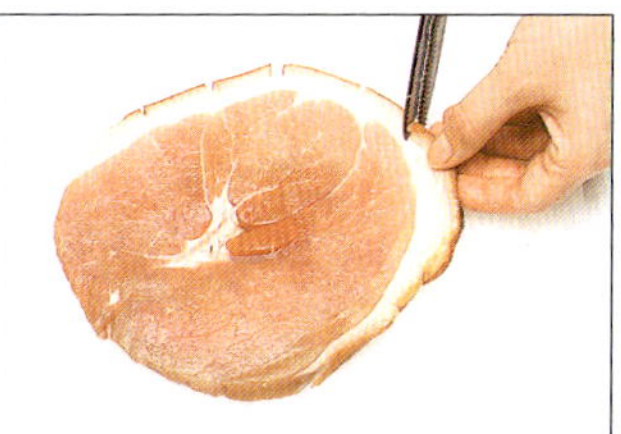

4 ▲ Snip the edges of the ham steaks to prevent them curling. Melt the remaining butter in a large heavy frying pan over a medium-high heat, then add the ham steaks and cook for 4–5 minutes, turning once, until the meat feels firm to the touch. Arrange the ham steaks on warmed plates and pour a little sauce over each. Garnish with watercress and serve the steaks with a little more of the sauce accompanied by creamed potatoes.

SAUERKRAUT WITH PORK AND SAUSAGES *Choucroûte Garnie*

This Alsatian speciality shows the German influence on the region's cuisine. Strasbourg is renowned for its pork and beef sausages – use them if you can.

SERVES 8

30ml/2 tbsp vegetable oil
1 onion, halved and sliced
120g/4oz smoked rindless streaky bacon rashers, chopped
900g/2lb bottled sauerkraut, well rinsed and drained
1 apple, peeled and sliced
1 or 2 bay leaves
2.5ml/½ tsp dried thyme
4–5 juniper berries
250ml/8fl oz/1 cup dry white wine
125ml/4fl oz/½ cup apple juice or water
6 Strasbourg sausages, knackwurst or frankfurters
6 spareribs
900g/2lb small potatoes, peeled
4 smoked gammon chops or steaks
salt and freshly ground black pepper

1 ▼ Preheat the oven to 150°C/300°F/Gas 2. Heat half the oil in a large flameproof casserole over a medium heat, then add the onion and bacon and cook, stirring occasionally for about 5 minutes until the onion is soft and the bacon just coloured.

2 ▲ Tilt the pan and spoon off as much fat as possible, then stir in the sauerkraut, apple, bay leaves, thyme, juniper, wine and apple juice or water. Cover the casserole, place in the oven and cook for 30 minutes.

3 In a second large flameproof casserole, heat the remaining oil over a medium-high heat and add the spareribs. Cook, turning frequently, until browned on all sides. Add the spareribs to the other casserole with the sausages and cook, covered, for 1½ hours, stirring occasionally.

4 ▲ Bring a large saucepan of lightly salted water to the boil over a medium-high heat. Add the potatoes and cook for 10 minutes. Drain and add to the casserole with the pork chops. Push them into the sauerkraut and continue cooking, covered, for 30–45 minutes more. Season with salt, if needed, and pepper before serving.

Toulouse Cassoulet

Cassoulet

There are as many versions of this regional speciality in Southwest France as there are towns.

Serves 6–8

450g/1lb dried white beans (haricot or cannellini), soaked overnight in cold water, then rinsed and drained
675g/1½lb Toulouse sausages
550g/1¼lb each boneless lamb and pork shoulder, cut into 5cm/2in pieces
1 large onion, finely chopped
3 or 4 garlic cloves, very finely chopped
4 tomatoes, peeled, seeded and chopped
300ml/½ pint/1¼ cups chicken stock
bouquet garni
60ml/4 tbsp fresh breadcrumbs
salt and freshly ground black pepper

1 Put the beans in a saucepan with water to cover. Boil vigorously for 10 minutes and drain, then return to a clean saucepan, cover with water and bring to the boil. Reduce the heat and simmer for 45 minutes, or until tender, then add a little salt and leave to soak in the cooking water.

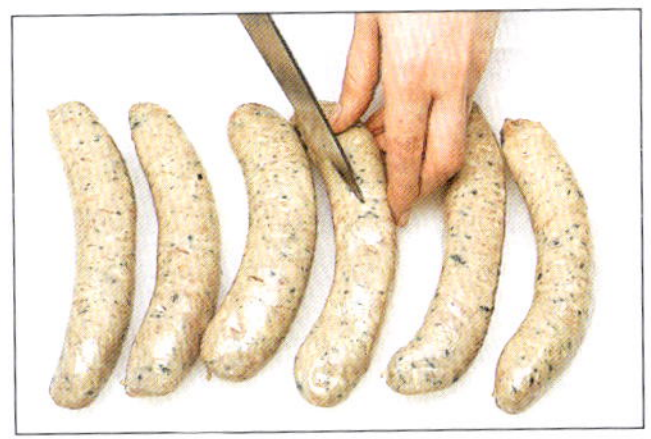

2 ▲ Preheat the oven to 180°C/350°F/Gas 4. Prick the sausages, place them in a large heavy frying pan over a medium heat and cook for 20–25 minutes until browned, turning occasionally. Drain on kitchen paper and pour off all but 15ml/1 tbsp of the fat from the pan.

3 Increase the heat to medium-high. Season the lamb and pork and add enough of the meat to the pan to fit easily in one layer. Cook until browned, then transfer to a large dish. Continue browning in batches.

4 Add the onion and garlic to the pan and cook for 3–4 minutes until just soft, stirring. Stir in the tomatoes and cook for 2–3 minutes, then transfer the vegetables to the meat dish. Add the stock and bring to the boil, then skim off the fat.

5 ▲ Spoon a quarter of the beans into a large casserole, and top with a third of the sausages, meat and vegetables.

6 Continue layering, ending with a layer of beans. Tuck in the bouquet garni, pour over the stock and top up with enough of the bean cooking liquid to just cover.

7 Cover the casserole and bake for 2 hours (check and add more bean cooking liquid if it seems dry). Uncover the casserole, sprinkle over the breadcrumbs and press with the back of a spoon to moisten them. Continue cooking the cassoulet, uncovered, for about 20 minutes more until browned.

Country-style Pâté with Leeks *Pâté de Porc aux Poireaux*

Traditionally this sort of pork pâté (or more correctly, terrine, since it has no crust) contains pork liver and egg to bind. This version uses leeks instead for a fresher flavour and a lighter result.

Serves 8–10

450g/1lb trimmed leeks (white and light green parts)
15g/½oz/1 tbsp butter
2 or 3 large garlic cloves, finely chopped
1kg/2¼lb lean pork leg or shoulder
150g/5oz smoked rindless streaky bacon rashers
7.5ml/1½ tsp chopped fresh thyme
3 sage leaves, finely chopped
1.5ml/¼ tsp quatre èpices *(a mix of ground cloves, cinnamon, nutmeg and pepper)*
1.5ml/¼ tsp ground cumin
pinch of freshly grated nutmeg
2.5ml/½ tsp salt
5ml/1 tsp freshly ground black pepper
1 bay leaf

1 ▲ Cut the leeks lengthways, wash well and slice thinly. Melt the butter in a large heavy saucepan, add the leeks, then cover and cook over a medium-low heat for 10 minutes, stirring occasionally. Add the garlic and continue cooking for about 10 minutes until the leeks are very soft, then set aside to cool.

Cook's tip

In France, *cornichons* (small dill pickles) and mustard are traditional accompaniments for pork terrines along with slices of crusty baguette.

2 ▲ Trim all the fat, tendons and connective tissue from the pork and cut the meat into 3.5cm/1¾in cubes. Working in two or three batches, put the meat into a food processor fitted with the metal blade; the bowl should be about half-full. Pulse to chop the meat to a coarse purée. Alternatively, pass the meat through the coarse blade of a meat mincer. Transfer the meat to a large mixing bowl and remove any white stringy bits.

3 Reserve two of the bacon rashers for garnishing, and chop or grind the remainder. Add the bacon to the pork in the bowl.

4 Preheat the oven to 180°C/350°F/Gas 4. Line the base and sides of a a 1.5 litre/2½ pint/6¼ cup terrine or loaf tin with greaseproof paper or non-stick baking paper.

5 ▲ Add the leeks, herbs, spices and salt and pepper to the bowl with the pork and bacon and, using a wooden spoon or your fingertips, mix until well combined.

6 ▲ Spoon the mixture into the terrine or loaf tin, pressing it into the corners and compacting it. Tap firmly to settle the mixture and smooth the top. Arrange the bay leaf and bacon rashers on top, then cover tightly with foil.

7 ▲ Place the terrine or loaf tin in a roasting tin and pour boiling water to come halfway up the sides. Bake for 1¼ hours.

8 Lift the terrine or tin out of the roasting tin and pour out the water. Put the terrine back in the roasting tin and place a baking sheet or board on top. If the pâté has not risen above the sides of the terrine, place a foil-covered board directly on the pâté. Weight with two or three large cans or other heavy objects while it cools. (Liquid will seep out which is why the terrine should stand inside a roasting tin.) Chill until cold, preferably overnight, before slicing.

Pommery
UTARDE DE MEAUX
POMMERY
AROMATISEE

PASTRY AND CAKES

Pastry is a mainstay of French cuisine, although not particularly of home cooking. Delectable pastries and elegant tarts have always been available in local *pâtisseries* and French cooks are much more likely to buy these than labour over them at home. However, they do enjoy making simple fruit tarts and cakes. Most home-made cakes are based on a sponge, or *génoise*, which doesn't use baking powder, but relies on air beaten into the eggs for lightness. In addition, almost every French housewife has a "secret" recipe for a rich chocolate cake, one which they love to discuss, although rarely share!

APPLE TART

Tarte aux Pommes

This easy-to-make apple tart has rustic charm – it is just as you might find in a French farmhouse. Cooking the apples before putting them on the pastry prevents a soggy crust.

SERVES 6

900g/2lb medium cooking apples, peeled, quartered and cored
15ml/1 tbsp lemon juice
55g/2oz/¼ cup caster sugar
40g/1½oz/4 tbsp butter
350g/¾lb shortcrust or sweet pastry
crème fraîche or lightly whipped cream, to serve

VARIATION

For Spiced Pear Tart, substitute pears for the apples, cooking them for about 10 minutes until golden. Sprinkle with 2.5ml/½ tsp ground cinnamon and a pinch of ground cloves and stir to combine before arranging on the pastry.

1 Cut each cooking apple quarter lengthways into two or three slices. Sprinkle with lemon juice and sugar and toss to combine.

2 ▲ Melt the butter in a large heavy frying pan over a medium heat and add the apples. Cook, stirring frequently, for about 12 minutes until the apples are just golden brown. Remove the frying pan from the heat and set aside. Preheat the oven to 190°C/375°F/Gas 5.

3 ▲ On a lightly floured surface, roll out the pastry to a 30cm/12in round and trim the edge if uneven. Carefully transfer the pastry round to a baking sheet.

4 ▲ Spoon the apple slices on to the pastry round, heaping them up, and leaving a 5cm/2in border all round the edge of the pastry.

5 ▲ Turn up the pastry border and gather it around the apples to enclose the outside apples. Bake the tart for 35–40 minutes until the pastry is crisp and browned. Serve warm, with crème fraîche or cream.

UPSIDE-DOWN APPLE TART *Tarte Tatin*

This tart was first made by two sisters who served it in their restaurant near Sologne in the Loire Valley. A special tarte tatin *tin is ideal, but an ovenproof frying pan will do very well.*

SERVES 8–10

225g/½lb puff or shortcrust pastry
10–12 large Golden Delicious apples
lemon juice
120g/4oz/½ cup butter, cut into pieces
120g/4oz/½ cup caster sugar
2.5ml/½ tsp ground cinnamon
crème fraîche or whipped cream, to serve

1 On a lightly floured surface, roll out the pastry into a 28cm/11in round less than 6mm/¼in thick. Transfer to a lightly floured baking sheet and chill.

2 Peel the apples, cut them in half lengthways and core. Sprinkle the apples generously with lemon juice.

3 ▲ In a 25cm/10in *tarte tatin* tin, cook the butter, sugar and cinnamon over a medium heat until the butter has melted and sugar dissolved, stirring occasionally. Continue cooking for 6–8 minutes, until the mixture turns a medium caramel colour, then remove the tin from the heat and arrange the apple halves, standing on their edges, in the tin, fitting them in tightly since they shrink during cooking.

4 Return the apple-filled tin to the heat and bring to a simmer over a medium heat for 20–25 minutes until the apples are tender and coloured. Remove the tin from the heat and cool slightly.

5 ▼ Preheat the oven to 230°C/450°F/Gas 8. Place the pastry on top of the apple-filled tin and tuck the edges of the pastry inside the edge of the tin around the apples. Pierce the pastry in two or three places, then bake for 25–30 minutes until the pastry is golden and the filling is bubbling. Leave to cool in the tin for 10–15 minutes.

6 To serve, run a sharp knife around edge of the tin to loosen the pastry. Cover with a serving plate and, holding them tightly, carefully invert the tin and plate together (do this carefully, preferably over the sink in case any caramel drips). Lift off the tin and loosen any apples that stick with a palette knife. Serve the tart warm with cream.

COOK'S TIP

If you do not have a heavy ovenproof tin, use a deep, straight-sided frying pan. If the handle is not ovenproof, wrap well in several layers of strong foil to protect from the heat.

LEMON TART

Tarte au Citron

This tart has a refreshing tangy flavour. You can find it in bistros and pâtisseries *all over France.*

SERVES 8–10

340g/12oz shortcrust or sweet shortcrust pastry
grated rind of 2 or 3 lemons
150ml/¼ pint/⅔ cup freshly squeezed lemon juice
100g/3½oz/½ cup caster sugar
60ml/4 tbsp crème fraîche or double cream
4 eggs, plus 3 egg yolks
icing sugar, for dusting

1 ▼ Preheat the oven to 190°C/375°F/Gas 5. Roll out the pastry thinly and use to line a 23cm/9in flan tin. Prick the base of the pastry.

2 ▲ Line the pastry case with foil and fill with baking beans. Bake for about 15 minutes until the edges are set and dry. Remove the foil and beans and continue baking for a further 5–7 minutes until golden.

3 ▲ Place the lemon rind, juice and sugar in a bowl. Beat until combined and then gradually add the crème fraîche or double cream and beat until well blended.

4 ▲ Beat in the eggs, one at a time, then beat in the egg yolks and pour the filling into the pastry case. Bake for 15–20 minutes, until the filling is set. If the pastry begins to brown too much, cover the edges with foil. Leave to cool. Dust with icing sugar before serving.

PEAR AND ALMOND CREAM TART *Tarte aux Poires Frangipane*

This tart is equally successful made with other kinds of fruit, and some variation can be seen in almost every good French pâtisserie. *Try making it with nectarines, peaches, apricots or apples.*

SERVES 6

3 firm pears
lemon juice
350g/¾lb shortcrust or sweet shortcrust pastry
15ml/1 tbsp peach brandy or water
60ml/4 tbsp peach preserve, strained

FOR THE ALMOND CREAM FILLING

100g/3½oz/¾ cup blanched whole almonds
55g/2oz/¼ cup caster sugar
70g/2½oz/5 tbsp butter
1 egg, plus 1 egg white
few drops almond essence

1 ▲ Roll out the pastry thinly and use to line a 23cm/9in flan tin. Chill the pastry case while you make the filling. Put the almonds and sugar in a food processor fitted with the metal blade and pulse until finely ground; they should not be pasty. Add the butter and process until creamy, then add the egg, egg white and almond essence and mix well.

2 Place a baking sheet in the oven and preheat to 190°C/375°F/Gas 5. Peel the pears, halve them, remove the cores and rub with lemon juice. Put the pear halves cut side down on a board and slice thinly crossways, keeping the slices together.

3 ▲ Pour the almond cream filling into the pastry case. Slide a palette knife under one pear half and press the top with your fingers to fan out the slices. Transfer to the tart, placing the fruit on the filling like spokes of a wheel. If you like, remove a few slices from each half before arranging and use to fill in any gaps in the centre.

4 Place the tart on the hot baking sheet and bake for 50–55 minutes, or until the filling is set and well browned. Cool on a wire rack.

5 ▼ Meanwhile, heat the brandy or water and the preserve in a small saucepan, then brush over the top of the hot tart to glaze. Serve the tart at room temperature.

Strawberry Tart

Tarte aux Fraises

This tart is best assembled just before serving, but you can bake the pastry case early in the day, make the filling ahead and put it together in a few minutes.

Serves 6

350g/¾lb rough-puff or puff pastry
225g/½lb cream cheese
grated rind of ½ orange
30ml/2 tbsp orange liqueur or orange juice
45–60ml/3–4 tbsp icing sugar, plus more for dusting (optional)
450g/1lb ripe strawberries, hulled

1 Roll out the pastry to about a 3mm/⅛in thickness and use to line a 28×10cm/11×4in rectangular flan tin. Trim the edges, neatly, then chill for 20–30 minutes. Preheat the oven to 200°C/400°F/Gas 6.

2 ▼ Prick the base of the pastry all over. Line the pastry case with foil, fill with baking beans and bake for 15 minutes. Remove the foil and beans and bake for 10 minutes until the pastry is browned. Gently press down on the pastry base to deflate, then leave to cool on a wire rack.

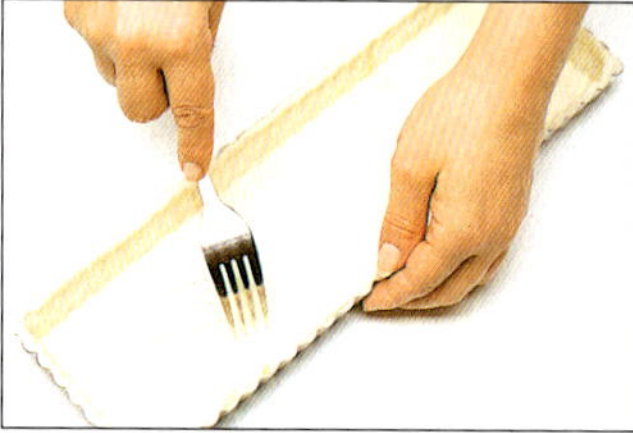

3 ▲ Using a hand mixer or food processor, beat together the cheese, orange rind, liqueur or orange juice and icing sugar to taste. Spread the cheese filling in the pastry case. Halve the strawberries and arrange them on top of the cheese filling. Dust with icing sugar, if you like.

Fresh Fruit Tartlets

Tartelettes aux Fruits

These tartlets are so pretty filled with colourful fruit. Use a selection of whatever soft fruit is in season – cut large fruits into pieces that will fit easily into the tartlet cases.

Serves 6

350g/¾lb shortcrust or sweet shortcrust pastry
60ml/4 tbsp apple jelly or raspberry jam
15–30ml/1–2 tbsp Kirsch or fruit juice
450g/1lb ripe small fruits (such as strawberries, raspberries, redcurrants, grapes, figs, kiwi fruit or apricots), hulled, stoned and sliced, as necessary

Variation

If you like spoon a little flavoured whipped cream into the pastry cases before filling with fruit. Whip about 125ml/4fl oz/½ cup whipping cream, sweeten to taste with icing sugar and flavour with a little brandy or a fruity liqueur.

1 Preheat the oven to 200°C/400°F/Gas 6. Lightly butter six 9cm/3½in tartlet tins.

2 ▲ Roll out the pastry to about a 3mm/⅛in thickness. Using a tartlet tin as a guide, cut out six rounds, re-rolling trimmings as necessary. Use the pastry rounds to line the tins, then roll the rolling pin over the top of the tins to cut off the excess pastry. Prick the bases with a fork.

3 Line the pastry cases with foil and add a layer of baking beans. Bake for 15 minutes until slightly dry and set, then remove the foil and beans and continue baking for a further 5 minutes. Cool on a wire rack.

4 ▲ Shortly before serving, melt the jam in a small saucepan over a low heat with the Kirsch or fruit juice until melted. Arrange the fruit in the tartlet shells and brush liberally with the glaze.

ALSATIAN PLUM TART

Tarte aux Prunes Alsacienne

Fruit and custard tarts, similar to a fruit quiche, are typical in Alsace. Sometimes they have a yeast dough base instead of pastry. You can use other seasonal fruits in this tart, or a mixture of fruit.

SERVES 6–8

450g/1lb ripe plums, halved and stoned
30ml/2 tbsp Kirsch or plum brandy
350g/¾lb shortcrust or sweet shortcrust pastry
30ml/2 tbsp seedless raspberry jam

FOR THE CUSTARD FILLING

2 eggs
55g/2oz/¼ cup caster sugar
175ml/6fl oz/¾ cup whipping cream
grated rind of ½ lemon
1.5ml/¼ tsp vanilla essence

COOK'S TIP

If you have time, chill the pastry case for 10–15 minutes before baking.

1 ▼ Preheat the oven to 200°C/400°F/Gas 6. Mix the plums with the Kirsch or plum brandy and set aside for about ½ hour.

2 Roll out the pastry thinly and use to line a 23cm/9in flan tin. Prick the base of the pastry case all over and line with foil. Add a layer of baking beans and bake for 15 minutes until slightly dry and set. Remove the foil and beans.

3 ▲ Brush the base of the pastry case with a thin layer of jam, then bake for a further 5 minutes. Transfer to a wire rack and reduce the oven temperature to 180°C/350°F/Gas 4.

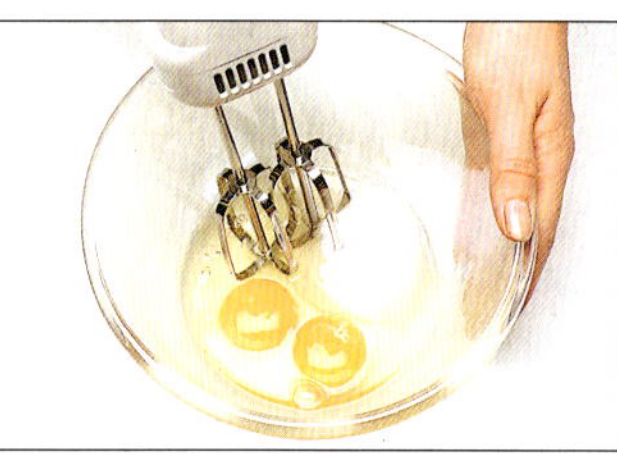

4 ▲ To make the custard filling, beat the eggs and sugar until well combined, then beat in the cream, lemon rind, vanilla essence and any juice from the plums.

5 ▲ Arrange the plums, cut side down, in the pastry case and pour over the custard mixture. Bake for about 30–35 minutes until a knife inserted in the centre comes out clean. Serve the tart warm or at room temperature.

NECTARINE PUFF PASTRY TARTS *Tartes Feuilletées aux Nectarines*

These simple fresh fruit pastries are easy to put together, but the puff pastry makes them seem very elegant. You could use peaches, apples or pears instead of nectarines.

SERVES 4

225g/½lb rough-puff or puff pastry
450g/1lb nectarines
15g/½oz/1 tbsp butter
30ml/2 tbsp caster sugar
freshly grated nutmeg
crème fraîche or lightly whipped cream, to serve (optional)

1 Lightly butter a large baking sheet and sprinkle very lightly with water.

2 ▲ On a lightly floured surface, roll out the puff pastry to a large rectangle, about 40×25cm/15×10in and cut into six smaller rectangles.

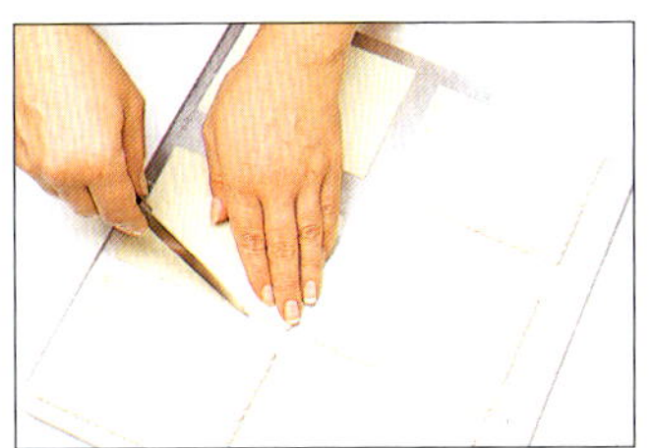

3 ▲ Transfer to the baking sheet. Using the back of a small knife, scallop the edges of the pastry. Then using the tip of the knife, score a line 1.2cm/½in from the edge of each rectangle to form a border. Chill for 30 minutes. Preheat the oven to 200°C/400°F/Gas 6.

4 ▼ Cut the nectarines in half and remove the stones, then slice the fruit thinly. Arrange the nectarine slices down the centre of the rectangles, leaving the border uncovered. Sprinkle the fruit with the sugar and a little nutmeg.

5 Bake for 12–15 minutes until the edges of the pastry are puffed and the fruit is tender.

6 Transfer the tarts to a wire rack to cool slightly. Serve warm with a little cream, if you like.

COOK'S TIP

These free-form puff pastry tarts can be made in other shapes, if you wish. Cut them in diamond shapes instead of rectangles, or cut into rounds, using a large cutter or a plate as a guide. Be sure to leave a border to allow the pastry to rise.

MINI MILLEFEUILLES

Petite Mille-Feuille

This pâtisserie classic is a delectable combination of tender puff pastry sandwiched with luscious pastry cream. As it is difficult to cut, making individual servings is a brilliant solution.

SERVES 8

450g/1lb rough-puff or puff pastry
6 egg yolks
70g/2½oz/⅓ cup caster sugar
45ml/3 tbsp plain flour
350ml/12fl oz milk
30ml/2 tbsp Kirsch or cherry liqueur (optional)
450g/1lb raspberries
icing sugar, for dusting
strawberry or raspberry coulis, to serve

1 Lightly butter two large baking sheets and sprinkle them very lightly with cold water.

2 ▼ On a lightly floured surface, roll out the pastry to a 3mm/⅛in thickness. Using a 10cm/4in cutter, or a saucer as a guide, cut out 12 rounds. Place on the baking sheets and prick each a few times with a fork. Chill for 30 minutes. Preheat the oven to 200°C/400°F/Gas 6.

3 Bake the pastry rounds for about 15–20 minutes until golden, then transfer to wire racks to cool.

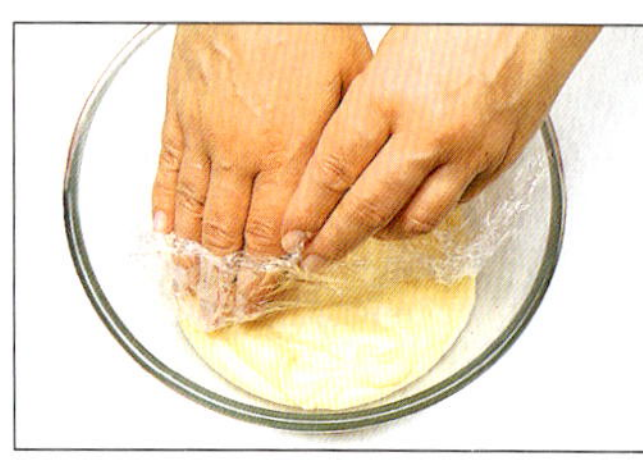

4 ▲ Whisk the egg yolks and sugar for 2 minutes until light and creamy, then whisk in the flour until just blended. Bring the milk to the boil over a medium heat and pour it over the egg mixture, whisking to blend. Return to the saucepan, bring to the boil and boil for 2 minutes, whisking constantly. Remove the pan from the heat and whisk in the Kirsch or liqueur, if using. Pour into a bowl and press clear film on to the surface to prevent a skin forming. Set aside to cool.

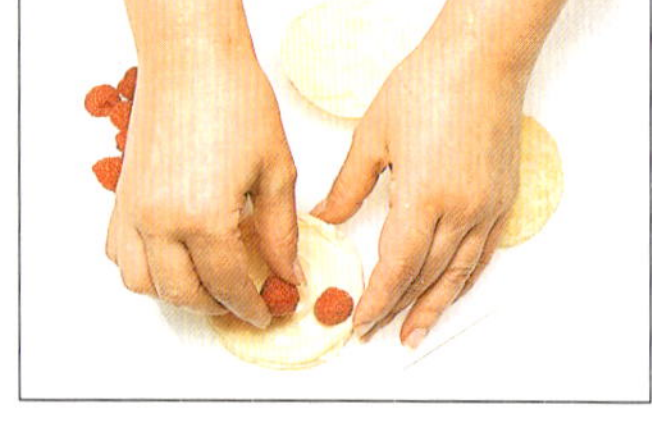

5 ▲ To assemble, carefully split the pastry rounds in half. Spread one round at a time with a little pastry cream. Arrange a layer of raspberries over the cream and top with a second pastry round. Spread with a little more cream and a few more raspberries. Top with a third pastry round flat side up. Dust with icing sugar and serve with the fruit *coulis*.

Chocolate Profiteroles *Profiteroles au Chocolat*

This mouth-watering dessert is served in cafés throughout France. Sometimes the profiteroles are filled with whipped cream instead of ice cream, but they are always drizzled with chocolate sauce.

Serves 4–6

275g/10oz plain chocolate
120ml/8 tbsp warm water
750ml/1¼ pints/3 cups vanilla ice cream
For the profiteroles
110g/3¾oz/¾ cup plain flour
1.5ml/¼ tsp salt
pinch of freshly grated nutmeg
175ml/6fl oz/¾ cup water
85g/3oz/6 tbsp unsalted butter, cut into 6 pieces
3 eggs

1 Preheat the oven to 200°C/400°F/Gas 6 and butter a baking sheet.

2 To make the profiteroles, sift together the flour, salt and nutmeg. In a medium saucepan, bring the water and butter to the boil. Remove from the heat and add the dry ingredients all at once. Beat with a wooden spoon for about 1 minute until well blended and the mixture starts to pull away from the sides of the pan, then set the pan over a low heat and cook the mixture for about 2 minutes, beating constantly. Remove from the heat.

3 ▲ Beat 1 egg in a small bowl and set aside. Add the remaining eggs, one at a time, to the flour mixture, beating well after each. Add the beaten egg by teaspoonfuls until the dough is smooth and shiny; it should pull away and fall slowly when dropped from a spoon.

4 ▼ Using a tablespoon, drop the dough on to the baking sheet in 12 mounds. Bake for 25–30 minutes until the pastry is well risen and browned. Turn off the oven and leave the puffs to cool with the oven door open.

5 To make the sauce, place the chocolate and water in a double-boiler or in a bowl placed over a pan of hot water and leave to melt, stirring occasionally. Keep warm until ready to serve, or reheat, over simmering water.

6 Split the profiteroles in half and put a small scoop of ice cream in each. Arrange on a serving platter or divide among individual plates. Pour the chocolate sauce over the top and serve at once.

SPONGE CAKE WITH FRUIT AND CREAM *Génoise aux Fruits*

Génoise *is the French cake used as the base for both simple and elaborate creations. You could simply dust it with icing sugar, or layer it with seasonal fruits to serve with tea.*

SERVES 6

120g/4oz/¾ cup plain flour
pinch of salt
4 eggs, at room temperature
120g/4oz/⅔ cup caster sugar
2.5ml/½ tsp vanilla essence
55g/2oz/4 tbsp butter, melted or clarified and cooled

FOR THE FILLING

450g/1lb fresh strawberries or raspberries
30–60ml/2–4 tbsp caster sugar
500ml/16fl oz/2 cups whipping cream
5ml/1 tsp vanilla essence

1 Preheat the oven to 180°C/350°F/Gas 4. Lightly butter a 23cm/9in springform tin or deep cake tin. Line the base with non-stick baking paper, and dust lightly with flour. Sift the flour and salt together twice.

2 ▲ Half-fill a medium saucepan with hot water and set over a low heat (do not allow the water to boil). Put the eggs in a heatproof bowl which just fits into the pan without touching the water. Using an electric mixer, beat the eggs at medium-high speed, gradually adding the sugar, for 8–10 minutes until the mixture is very thick and pale and leaves a ribbon trail when the beaters are lifted. Remove the bowl from the pan, add the vanilla essence and continue beating until the mixture is cool.

3 ▲ Fold in the flour mixture in three batches, using a balloon whisk or metal spoon. Before the third addition of flour, stir a large spoonful of the mixture into the melted or clarified butter to lighten it, then fold the butter into the remaining mixture with the last addition of flour. Work quickly, but gently, so the mixture does not deflate. Pour into the prepared tin, smoothing the top so the sides are slightly higher than the centre.

4 ▲ Bake in the oven for about 25–30 minutes until the top of the cake springs back when touched and the edge begins to shrink away from the sides of the tin. Place the cake in its tin on a wire rack to cool for 5–10 minutes, then invert the cake on to the rack to cool completely. Peel off the paper.

5 ▲ To make the filling, slice the strawberries, place in a bowl, sprinkle with 15–30ml/1–2 tbsp of the sugar and set aside. Beat the cream with 15–30ml/1–2 tbsp of sugar and the vanilla essence until it holds soft peaks.

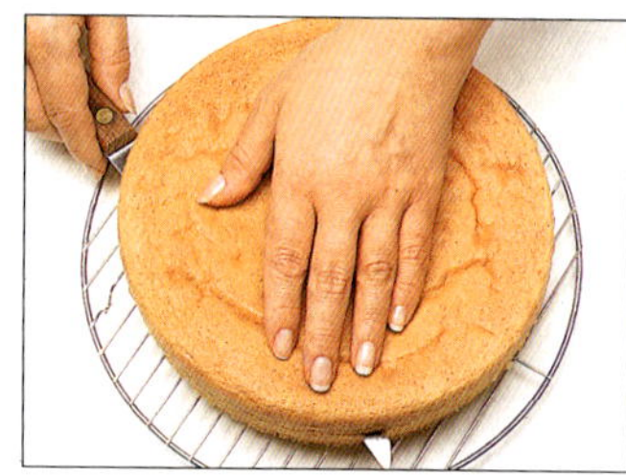

6 ▲ To assemble the cake (up to 4 hours before serving), split the cake horizontally, using a serrated knife. Place the top, cut side up, on a serving plate. Spread with a third of the cream and cover with an even layer of sliced strawberries.

7 Place the bottom half of the cake, cut side down, on top of the filling and press lightly. Spread the remaining cream over the top and sides of the cake. Chill the cake until ready to serve. Serve the remaining strawberries with the cake.

QUEEN OF SHEBA CAKE

Gâteau Reine de Saba

This rich chocolate and almond cake is so moist it needs no filling. It is wonderful for entertaining as it can be made in advance and stored, well wrapped, in the fridge for up to three days.

SERVES 8–10

100g/3½oz/⅔ cup whole blanched almonds, lightly toasted
120g/4oz/⅔ cup caster sugar
40g/1½oz/¼ cup plain flour
120g/4oz/½ cup unsalted butter, softened
150g/5oz plain chocolate, melted
3 eggs, separated
30ml/2 tbsp almond liqueur (optional)

FOR THE CHOCOLATE GLAZE

175ml/6fl oz/¾ cup whipping cream
225g/8oz plain chocolate, chopped
30g/1oz/2 tbsp unsalted butter
30ml/2 tbsp almond liqueur (optional)
chopped toasted almonds, to decorate

1 ▲ Preheat the oven to 180°C/350°F/Gas 4. Lightly butter a 20–23cm/8–9in springform tin or deep loose-based cake tin. Line the base with non-stick baking paper and dust the tin lightly with flour.

2 In the bowl of a food processor fitted with the metal blade, process the almonds and 30ml/2 tbsp of the sugar until very fine. Transfer to a bowl and sift over the flour. Stir to mix then set aside.

3 ▲ In a medium bowl, beat the butter with an electric mixer until creamy, then add half of the remaining sugar and beat for about 1–2 minutes until very light and creamy. Gradually beat in the melted chocolate until well blended, then add the egg yolks one at a time, beating well after each addition, and beat in the liqueur, if using.

4 ▲ In another bowl, beat the egg whites until soft peaks form. Add the remaining sugar and beat until the whites are stiff and glossy, but not dry. Fold a quarter of the whites into the chocolate mixture to lighten it, then alternately fold in the almond mixture and the remaining whites in three batches. Spoon the mixture into the prepared tin and spread evenly. Tap the tin gently to release any air bubbles.

5 Bake for 30–35 minutes until the edges are puffed but the centre is still soft and wobbly (a skewer inserted about 5cm/2in from the edge should come out clean). Transfer the cake in its tin to a wire rack to cool for about 15 minutes, then remove the sides of the cake tin and leave to cool completely. Invert the cake on to a 20cm/8in cake board and remove the base of the tin and the paper.

6 To make the chocolate glaze, bring the cream to the boil in a saucepan. Remove from the heat and add the chocolate. Stir gently until the chocolate has melted and is smooth, then beat in the butter and liqueur, if using. Cool for about 20–30 minutes until slightly thickened, stirring occasionally.

7 ▲ Place the cake on a wire rack over a baking sheet and pour over the warm chocolate glaze to cover the top completely. Using a palette knife, smooth the glaze around the sides of the cake. Spoon a little of the glaze into a piping bag fitted with a writing nozzle and use to write the name, if you like. Leave to stand for 5 minutes to set slightly, then carefully press the nuts on to the sides of the cake. Using two long palette knives transfer the cake to a serving plate and chill until ready to serve.

Reine de Saba

RICH CHOCOLATE CAKE *Torte au Chocolat*

This dark, fudgy cake is easy to make, stores well and is a chocolate lover's dream come true.

SERVES 14–16

250g/9oz plain chocolate, chopped
225g/8oz/1 cup unsalted butter, cut into pieces
5 eggs
100g/3½oz/½ cup caster sugar, plus 15ml/1 tbsp and some for sprinkling
15ml/1 tbsp cocoa powder
10ml/2 tsp vanilla essence
cocoa powder, for dusting
chocolate shavings, to decorate

1 Preheat the oven to 170°C/325°F/ Gas 3. Lightly butter a 23cm/9in springform tin and line the base with non-stick baking paper. Butter the paper and sprinkle with the a little sugar, then tip out the excess.

2 ▲ The cake is baked in a *bain-marie*, so carefully wrap the base and sides of the tin with a double thickness of foil to prevent water leaking into the cake.

3 Melt the chocolate and butter in a saucepan over a low heat until smooth, stirring frequently, then remove from the heat. Beat the eggs and 100g/3½oz/½ cup of the sugar with an electric mixer for 1 minute.

4 ▲ Mix together the cocoa and the remaining 15ml/1 tbsp sugar and beat into the egg mixture until well blended. Beat in the vanilla essence, then slowly beat in the melted chocolate until well blended. Pour the mixture into the prepared tin and tap gently to release any air bubbles.

5 ▲ Place the cake tin in a roasting tin and pour in boiling water to come 2cm/¾in up the sides of the wrapped tin. Bake for 45–50 minutes until the edge of the cake is set and the centre still soft (a skewer inserted 5cm/2in from the edge should come out clean). Lift the tin out of the water and remove the foil. Place the cake on a wire rack, remove the sides of the tin and leave the cake to cool completely (the cake will sink a little in the centre).

6 Invert the cake on to the wire rack. Remove the base of the tin and the paper. Dust the cake liberally with cocoa powder and arrange the chocolate shavings around the edge. Slide the cake on to a serving plate.

FRENCH CHOCOLATE CAKE *Gâteau au Chocolat*

This is typical of a French home-made cake – dense, dark and delicious. The texture is very different from a sponge cake and it is excellent served with cream or a fruit coulis.

SERVES 10–12

150g/5oz/¾ cup caster sugar, plus some for sprinkling
275g/10oz plain chocolate, chopped
175g/6oz/¾ cup unsalted butter, cut into pieces
10ml/2 tsp vanilla essence
5 eggs, separated
40g/1½oz/¼ cup plain flour, sifted
pinch of salt
icing sugar, for dusting
sweetened whipped cream, to serve

1 ▲ Preheat the oven to 170°C/325°F/Gas 3. Generously butter a 24cm/9½in springform tin, then sprinkle the tin with a little sugar and tap out the excess.

2 Set aside 45ml/3 tbsp of the sugar. Place the chocolate, butter and remaining sugar in a heavy saucepan and cook over a low heat until the chocolate and butter have melted and the sugar has dissolved. Remove the pan from the heat, stir in the vanilla essence and leave the mixture to cool slightly.

3 ▼ Beat the egg yolks into the chocolate mixture, beating each in well, then stir in the flour.

4 In a clean greasefree bowl, using an electric mixer, beat the egg whites slowly until they are frothy. Increase the speed, add the salt and continue beating until soft peaks form. Sprinkle over the reserved sugar and beat until the whites are stiff and glossy. Beat one third of the whites into the chocolate mixture, then fold in the remaining whites.

5 ▲ Carefully pour the mixture into the tin and tap the tin gently to release any air bubbles.

6 Bake the cake for about 35–45 minutes until well risen and the top springs back when touched lightly with a fingertip. (If the cake appears to rise unevenly, rotate after 20–25 minutes.) Transfer the cake to a wire rack, remove the sides of the tin and leave to cool completely. Remove the tin base. Dust the cake with icing sugar and transfer to a serving plate. Serve with whipped cream.

POUND CAKE WITH RED FRUIT *Quatre Quarts aux Fruits*

Quatre quarts *literally translates as "four quarters", in this case, the equal amounts of the four main ingredients. This orange-scented cake is good for tea or as a dessert with a fruit* coulis.

SERVES 6–8

450g/1lb fresh raspberries, strawberries or stoned cherries, or a combination of any of these
175g/6oz/⅞ cup caster sugar, plus 15–30ml/1–2 tbsp and some for sprinkling
15ml/1 tbsp lemon juice
175g/6oz/1⅓ cup plain flour
10ml/2 tsp baking powder
pinch of salt
175g/6oz/¾ cup unsalted butter, softened
3 eggs, at room temperature
grated rind of 1 orange
15ml/1 tbsp orange juice

1 Reserve a few whole fruits for decorating. In a food processor fitted with the metal blade, process the fruit until smooth.

2 ▼ Add 15–30ml/1–2 tbsp of the sugar and the lemon juice to the fruit purée, then process again to blend. Strain the sauce and chill.

3 Butter the base and sides of a 20×10cm/8×4in loaf tin or a 20cm/8in springform tin and line the base with non-stick baking paper. Butter the paper and the sides of the tin again, then sprinkle lightly with sugar and tip out any excess. Preheat the oven to 180°C/350°F/Gas 4.

4 ▲ Sift the flour, baking powder and a pinch of salt. In a medium bowl, beat the butter with an electric mixer for 1 minute until creamy. Add the sugar and beat for 4–5 minutes until very light and fluffy, then add the eggs, one at a time, beating well after each addition. Beat in the orange rind and juice.

5 ▲ Gently fold the flour mixture into the butter mixture in three batches, then spoon the mixture into the prepared tin and tap gently to release any air bubbles.

6 Bake the cake for 35–40 minutes until the top is golden and springs back when touched. Transfer the cake in its tin to a wire rack and leave to cool for 10 minutes. Remove the cake from the tin, then cool for about ½ hour. Remove the paper and serve slices or wedges of the warm cake with a little of the fruit sauce and decorate with the reserved fruit.

Individual Brioches

Petites Brioches

These buttery rolls with their distinctive little topknots are delicious with a spoonful or two of jam and a cup of café au lait *– or try them split and filled with scrambled eggs.*

Makes 8

7g/¼oz/scant 1 tbsp active dry yeast
15ml/1 tbsp caster sugar
30ml/2 tbsp warm milk
2 eggs
about 200g/7oz/1½ cups plain flour
2.5ml/½ tsp salt
85g/3oz/6 tbsp butter, cut into 6 pieces, at room temperature
1 egg yolk beaten with 10ml/2 tsp water, for glazing

1 ▲ Lightly butter eight individual brioche tins or muffin tins. Put the yeast and sugar in a small bowl, add the milk and stir until dissolved. Leave to stand for about 5 minutes until foamy, then beat in the egg.

2 ▲ Put the flour and salt into a food processor fitted with the metal blade, then with the machine running, slowly pour in the yeast mixture. Scrape down the sides and continue processing for about 2–3 minutes, or until the dough forms a ball. Add the butter and pulse about 10 times, or until the butter is incorporated.

3 Transfer the dough to a lightly buttered bowl and cover with a cloth. Set aside to rise in a warm place for about 1 hour until doubled in size, then punch down.

4 ▲ Set aside quarter of the dough. Shape the remaining dough into eight balls and put into the prepared tins. Shape the reserved dough into eight smaller balls, then make a depression in the top of each large ball and set a small ball into it.

5 Allow the brioches to rise in a warm place for about 30 minutes until doubled in size. Preheat the oven to 200°C/400°F/Gas 6.

6 Brush the brioches lightly with the egg glaze and bake them for 15–18 minutes until golden brown. Transfer to a wire rack and leave to cool before serving.

Cook's tip

The dough may also be baked in the characteristic large brioche tin with sloping fluted sides. Put about three-quarters of the dough into the tin and set the remainder in a depression in the top, cover and leave to rise for about 1 hour, then bake for 35–45 minutes.

SAVARIN WITH SUMMER FRUIT *Savarin aux Fruits*

This traditional dessert from Alsace-Lorraine is made from a rich yeast dough moistened with syrup and cherry liqueur. For babas au rhum, *the same dough can be baked in individual tins and soaked with rum syrup – either way it is quite delicious.*

SERVES 10–12

7g/¼oz/scant 1 tbsp active dry yeast
55g/2oz/¼ cup caster sugar
60ml/4 tbsp warm water
300g/10½oz/2¼ cups plain flour
4 eggs, beaten
5ml/1 tsp vanilla essence
100g/3½oz/7 tbsp unsalted butter, softened
450g/1lb fresh raspberries or strawberries
mint leaves, to decorate
300ml/½ pint/1¼ cups whipping cream, sweetened to taste and whipped, to serve

FOR THE SYRUP
225g/8oz/1¼ cup caster sugar
600ml/1 pint/2½ cups water
90ml/6 tbsp redcurrant jelly
45ml/3 tbsp Kirsch (optional)

1 ▲ Generously butter a 23cm/9in savarin or ring mould. Put the yeast and 15ml/1 tbsp of the sugar in a medium bowl, add the water and stir until dissolved, then leave the yeast mixture to stand for about 5 minutes until frothy.

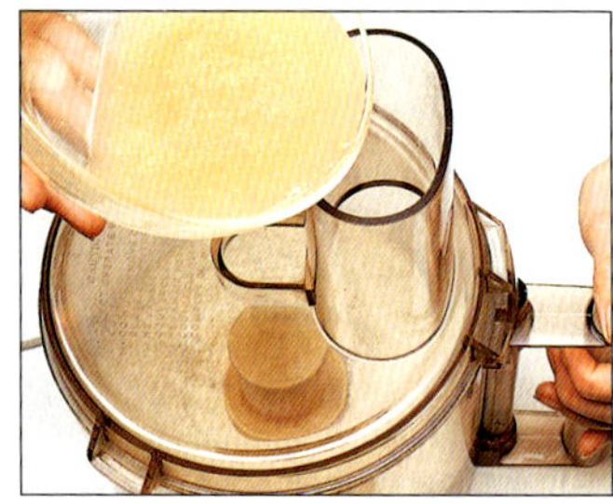

2 ▲ Put the flour and remaining sugar in a food processor fitted with the metal blade and pulse to combine. With the machine running, slowly pour in the yeast mixture, eggs and vanilla essence, then scrape down the sides and continue processing for 2–3 minutes, or until a soft dough forms. Add the butter and pulse about 10 times, until all the butter is incorporated.

3 ▲ Place the dough in spoonfuls into the mould, leaving a space between each mound of dough (this will fill in as the dough rises). Tap the mould gently to release any air bubbles, then cover with a tea towel and leave in a warm place to rise for about 1 hour. The dough should double in volume and come just to the top of the mould. Preheat the oven to 200°C/400°F/Gas 6.

4 Place the mould on a baking sheet in the oven and immediately reduce the temperature to 180°C/350°F/Gas 4. Bake for about 25 minutes until the top is a rich golden colour and springs back when touched. Turn out the cake on to a wire rack and cool slightly.

5 ▲ To make the syrup, blend the sugar, water and 60ml/4 tbsp of the redcurrant jelly in a saucepan. Bring to the boil over a medium-high heat, stirring until the sugar and jelly dissolve, and boil for 3 minutes. Remove from the heat and allow to cool slightly, then stir in the Kirsch, if using. In a small bowl, combine 30ml/2 tbsp of the hot syrup with the remaining redcurrant jelly and stir to dissolve. Set aside.

6 Place the rack with the cake, still warm, over a baking tray. Slowly spoon the syrup over the cake, catching any extra syrup in the tray and spooning it over the cake, until all the syrup has been absorbed. Carefully transfer the cake to a shallow serving dish (the cake will be very fragile) and pour over any remaining syrup. Brush the redcurrant glaze over the top, then fill the centre with raspberries or strawberries and decorate with mint leaves. Chill, then serve with cream.

Kirsch

Macaroons *Macarons*

Freshly ground almonds, lightly toasted beforehand to intensify the flavour, give these biscuits their rich taste and texture so, for best results, avoid using ready-ground almonds as a shortcut.

Makes 12

120g/4oz/1⅓ cup blanched almonds, toasted
160g/5½oz/⅞ cup caster sugar
2 egg whites
2.5ml/½ tsp almond or vanilla essence
icing sugar, for dusting

1 Preheat the oven to 180°C/350°F/Gas 5. Line a large baking sheet with non-stick baking paper. Reserve 12 almonds for decorating. In a food processor fitted with the metal blade, process the rest of the almonds and the sugar until finely ground.

2 With the machine running, slowly pour in enough of the egg whites to form a soft dough. Add the almond or vanilla essence and pulse to mix.

3 ▲ With moistened hands, shape the mixture into walnut-size balls and arrange on the baking sheet.

4 Press one of the reserved almonds on to each ball, flattening them slightly, and dust lightly with icing sugar. Bake the macaroons for about 10–12 minutes until the tops are golden and feel slightly firm. Transfer to a wire rack, cool slightly, then peel the biscuits off the paper and leave to cool completely.

Cook's tip

To toast the almonds, spread them on a baking sheet and bake in the preheated oven for 10–15 minutes until golden. Cool before grinding.

Madeleine Cakes *Madeleines*

These little tea cakes, baked in a special tin with shell-shaped cups, were made famous by Marcel Proust, who referred to them in his memoirs. They are best eaten on the day they are made.

Makes 12

165g/5½oz/1¼ cups plain flour
5ml/1 tsp baking powder
2 eggs
85g/3oz/¾ cup icing sugar, plus some for dusting
grated rind of 1 lemon or orange
15ml/1 tbsp lemon or orange juice
85g/3oz/6 tbsp unsalted butter, melted and slightly cooled

Cook's tip

If you don't have a special tin for making *madeleines*, you can use a bun tin, preferably with a non-stick coating. The cakes won't have the characteristic ridges and shellshape, but they are quite pretty dusted with a little icing sugar.

1 Preheat the oven to 190°C/375°F/Gas 5. Generously butter a 12 cup madeleine tin. Sift together the flour and baking powder.

2 ▲ Using an electric mixer, beat the eggs and icing sugar for 5–7 minutes until thick and creamy and the mixture forms a ribbon when the beaters are lifted. Gently fold in the lemon or orange rind and juice.

3 ▲ Beginning with the flour mixture, alternately fold in the flour and melted butter in four batches. Let the mixture stand for 10 minutes, then carefully spoon into the tin. Tap gently to release any air bubbles. Bake the *madeleines* for 12–15 minutes, rotating the tin halfway through cooking, until a skewer inserted in the centre comes out clean. Tip out on to a wire rack to cool completely and dust with icing sugar before serving.

PARIS

Almond Tile Biscuits *Tuiles d'Amandes*

These biscuits are named after the French roof tiles they so resemble. Making them is a little fiddly, so bake only four at a time until you get the knack. With a little practice you will find them easy.

Makes about 24

70g/2½oz/½ cup whole blanched almonds, lightly toasted
70g/2½oz/⅓ cup caster sugar
40g/1½oz/3 tbsp unsalted butter, softened
2 egg whites
2.5ml/½ tsp almond essence
35g/1¼oz/scant ¼ cup plain flour, sifted
55g/2oz/⅔ cup flaked almonds

1 Preheat oven to 200°C/400°F/Gas 6. Generously butter two heavy baking sheets.

Cook's tip

If the biscuits flatten or lose their crispness, reheat them on a baking sheet in a moderate oven, until completely flat, then reshape.

2 Place the almonds and about 30ml/2 tbsp of the sugar in a food processor fitted with the metal blade and pulse until finely ground; they should not be pasty.

3 ▼ With an electric mixer, beat the butter until creamy, then add the remaining sugar and beat for 1 minute until light and fluffy. Gradually beat in the egg whites until the mixture is well blended, then beat in the almond essence. Sift the flour over the butter mixture and fold in, then fold in the ground almond mixture.

4 ▲ Drop tablespoons of mixture on to the baking sheets about 15cm/6in apart. With the back of a wet spoon, spread each mound into a paper-thin 7.5cm/3in round. (Don't worry if holes appear, they will fill in.) Sprinkle each round with a few flaked almonds.

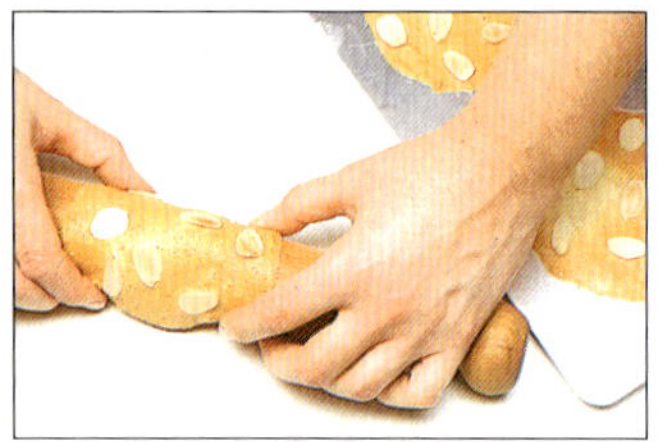

5 ▲ Bake the biscuits, one sheet at a time, for 5–6 minutes until the edges are golden and the centres still pale. Remove the baking sheet to a wire rack and, working quickly, use a thin palette knife to loosen the edges of one biscuit. Lift the biscuit on the palette knife and place over a rolling pin, then press down the sides of the biscuit to curve it.

6 Continue shaping the biscuits, transferring them to a wire rack as they cool and crisp. If the biscuits become too crisp to shape, return the baking sheet to the hot oven for 15–30 seconds to soften them, then continue as above. Store the biscuits in a single layer in airtight containers.

Spiced-Nut Palmiers

Palmiers

These delicate pastries, said to resemble palm trees, are popular throughout France. They are often simply rolled in sugar, but in this recipe the filling includes cinnamon and nuts.

Makes about 40

75g/2¾oz/½ cup chopped almonds, walnuts or hazelnuts
30ml/2 tbsp caster sugar, plus some for sprinkling
2.5ml/½ tsp ground cinnamon
225g/½lb rough-puff or puff pastry, defrosted if frozen
1 egg, lightly beaten

1 ▲ Lightly butter two large baking sheets, preferably non-stick. In a food processor fitted with a metal blade, process the nuts, sugar and cinnamon until finely ground. Transfer half to a small bowl.

2 ▲ Sprinkle the work surface and pastry with sugar and roll out the pastry to a 50×20cm/20×8in rectangle about 3mm/⅛in thick, sprinkling with more sugar as necessary. Brush the pastry lightly with beaten egg and sprinkle evenly with half of the nut mixture in the bowl.

3 ▼ Fold in the long edges of the pastry to meet in the centre and flatten with the rolling pin. Brush with egg and sprinkle with most of the nut mixture. Fold in the edges again to meet in the centre, brush with egg and sprinkle with the remaining nut mixture. Fold one side of the pastry over the other.

4 Using a sharp knife, cut the pastry crossways into 8mm/⅜in thick slices and place the pieces cut-side down about 2.5cm/1in apart on the baking sheets.

5 ▲ Spread the pastry edges apart to form a wedge shape. Chill the palmiers for at least 15 minutes. Preheat oven to 220°C/425°F/Gas 7.

6 Bake the palmiers for about 8–10 minutes until golden, carefully turning them over halfway through the cooking time. Watch carefully as the sugar can easily scorch. Transfer to a wire rack to cool.

BRITTANY BUTTER BISCUITS *Petites Gâteaux Bretons*

These little biscuits are similar to shortbread, but richer. Like most of the cakes and pastries from this province, they are made with the lightly salted butter, beurre demi-sel, *from around Nantes.*

MAKES 18–20

6 egg yolks, lightly beaten
15ml/1 tbsp milk
250g/9oz/2 cups plain flour
175g/6oz/⅞ cup caster sugar
200g/7oz/⅞ cup lightly salted butter, at room temperature, cut into small pieces

COOK'S TIP

To make one large Brittany Butter Cake, pat the dough with well floured hands into a 23cm/9in loose-based cake tin or springform tin. Brush with egg glaze and score the lattice pattern on top. Bake for 45 minutes–1 hour until firm to the touch and golden brown.

1 Preheat the oven to 180°C/350°F/Gas 4. Lightly butter a large heavy baking sheet. Mix 15ml/1 tbsp of the egg yolks with the milk to make a glaze and set aside.

2 ▲ Sift the flour into a large bowl and make a well in the centre. Add the egg yolks, sugar and butter and, using your fingertips, work them together until smooth and creamy.

3 ▲ Gradually bring in a little flour at a time from the edge of the well, working it to form a smooth, slightly sticky dough.

4 ▲ Using floured hands, pat out the dough to about a 8mm/¾in thickness and cut out rounds using a 7.5cm/3in cutter. Transfer the rounds to a baking sheet, brush each with a little egg glaze, then using the back of a knife, score with lines to create a lattice pattern.

5 Bake the biscuits for about 12–15 minutes until golden. Cool in the tin on a wire rack for 15 minutes, then carefully remove the biscuits and leave to cool completely on the rack. Store in an airtight container.

CHOCOLATE TRUFFLES *Truffes au Chocolat*

These truffles, like the prized fungi they resemble, are a Christmas speciality in France. They can be rolled in cocoa powder or nuts, or dipped in chocolate – use plain, milk or even white chocolate.

MAKES 20–30

175ml/6fl oz/¾ cup double cream
275g/10oz plain chocolate, chopped
30g/1oz/2 tbsp unsalted butter, cut into pieces
30–45ml/2–3 tbsp brandy (optional)
FOR THE COATING
cocoa powder
finely chopped pistachio nuts or hazelnuts
400g/14oz plain, milk or white chocolate or a mixture

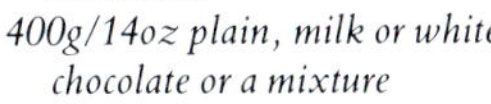

1 ▲ In a saucepan over a medium heat, bring the cream to the boil. Remove from the heat and add the chocolate, then stir until melted and smooth. Stir in the butter and the brandy, if using, then strain into a bowl and leave to cool. Cover and chill for 6–8 hours or overnight.

2 ▲ Line a large baking sheet with greaseproof paper. Using a small ice cream scoop or two teaspoons, form the chocolate mixture into 20–30 balls and place on the paper. Chill if the mixture becomes soft.

3 ▲ To coat the truffles with cocoa, sift the cocoa into a small bowl, drop in the truffles, one at a time, and roll to coat well, keeping the round shape. To coat with nuts, roll truffles in finely chopped nuts. Chill well wrapped, for up to 10 days.

4 To coat with chocolate, freeze the truffles for at least 1 hour. In a small bowl, melt the dark, milk or white chocolate over a pan of barely simmering water, stirring until melted and smooth, then allow to cool slightly.

5 Using a fork, dip the frozen truffles into the cooled chocolate, one at a time, tapping the fork on the edge of the bowl to shake off the excess. Place on a baking sheet lined with non-stick baking paper and chill at once. If the melted chocolate thickens, reheat until smooth. Wrap and store as for nut-coated truffles.

A L'OLIVIE

DESSERTS

In France a family meal usually ends with dessert. Though, since there may well have been two or three other courses, it is likely to be something light and refreshing – perhaps just a piece of fresh fruit, eaten with a knife and fork, or a simple fruit salad. In summer, fresh strawberries and raspberries are always welcome, either moistened with wine, or puréed for sorbets and mousses. In cooler weather, a compôte of winter fruits might be served, or, if the rest of the meal is light, a crusty apple charlotte or baked custard. Fancy desserts such as soufflés, crêpes and meringues are reserved for the weekends or special celebrations.

BAKED CARAMEL CUSTARD *Crème Caramel*

Also called crème renversée, *this is one of the most popular French desserts and is wonderful when freshly made. This is a slightly lighter version of the traditional recipe.*

SERVES 6–8

250g/9oz/1¼ cups granulated sugar
60ml/4 tbsp water
1 vanilla pod or 10ml/2 tsp vanilla essence
425ml/14fl oz/1¾ cups milk
250ml/8fl oz/1 cup whipping cream
5 large eggs
2 egg yolks

1 Put 175g/6oz/⅞ cup of the sugar in a small heavy saucepan with the water to moisten. Bring to the boil over a high heat, swirling the pan to dissolve the sugar. Boil, without stirring, until the syrup turns a dark caramel colour (this will take about 4–5 minutes).

2 ▼ Immediately pour the caramel into a 1 litre/1⅔ pint/4 cup soufflé dish. Holding the dish with oven gloves, quickly swirl the dish to coat the base and sides with the caramel and set aside. (The caramel will harden quickly as it cools.) Place the dish in a small roasting tin.

3 ▲ Preheat the oven to 170°C/325°F/Gas 3. With a small sharp knife, carefully split the vanilla pod lengthways and scrape the black seeds into a medium saucepan. Add the milk and cream and bring just to the boil over a medium-high heat, stirring frequently. Remove the pan from the heat, cover and set aside for 15–20 minutes.

4 In a bowl, whisk the eggs and egg yolks with the remaining sugar for 2–3 minutes until smooth and creamy. Whisk in the hot milk and carefully strain the mixture into the caramel-lined dish. Cover with foil.

5 Place the dish in a roasting tin and pour in enough boiling water to come halfway up the sides of the dish. Bake the custard for 40–45 minutes until a knife inserted about 5cm/2in from the edge comes out clean (the custard should be just set). Remove from the roasting tin and cool for at least ½ hour, then chill overnight.

6 To turn out, carefully run a sharp knife around the edge of the dish to loosen the custard. Cover the dish with a serving plate and, holding them tightly, invert the dish and plate together. Gently lift one edge of the dish, allowing the caramel to run over the sides, then slowly lift off the dish.

BAKED CUSTARD WITH BURNT SUGAR *Crème Brûlée*

This dessert actually originated in Cambridge, but has become associated with France and is widely eaten there. Add a little liqueur, if you like, but it is equally delicious without it.

SERVES 6

1 vanilla pod
1 litre/1⅔ pints/4 cups double cream
6 egg yolks
100g/3½oz/½ cup caster sugar
30ml/2 tbsp almond or orange liqueur
85g/3oz/⅓ cup soft light brown sugar

1 Preheat the oven to 150°C/300°F/Gas 2. Place six 125ml/4fl oz/½ cup ramekins in a roasting tin or ovenproof dish and set aside.

2 ▲ With a small sharp knife, split the vanilla pod lengthways and scrape the black seeds into a medium saucepan. Add the cream and bring just to the boil over a medium-high heat, stirring frequently. Remove from the heat and cover. Set aside to stand for 15–20 minutes.

3 ▲ In a bowl, whisk the egg yolks, caster sugar and liqueur until well blended. Whisk in the hot cream and strain into a large jug. Divide the custard equally among the ramekins.

4 ▲ Pour enough boiling water into the roasting tin to come halfway up the sides of the ramekins. Cover the tin with foil and bake for about 30 minutes until the custards are just set. Remove from the tin and leave to cool. Return to the dry roasting tin and chill.

5 Preheat the grill. Sprinkle the sugar evenly over the surface of each custard and grill for 30–60 seconds until the sugar melts and caramelizes. (Do not let the sugar burn or the custard curdle.) Place in the fridge to set the crust and chill completely before serving.

COOK'S TIP

To test whether the custards are ready, push the point of a knife into centre of one – if it comes out clean the custards are cooked.

FLOATING ISLANDS *Oeufs à la Neige*

Oeufs à la Neige *means "snow eggs", which is what these oval-shaped meringues look like. Originally they were poached in milk and this was then used to make the rich custard sauce.*

SERVES 4–6

1 vanilla pod
600ml/1 pint/2½ cups milk
8 egg yolks
55g/2oz/¼ cup granulated sugar
FOR THE MERINGUES
4 large egg whites
1.5ml/¼ tsp cream of tartar
225g/8oz/1¼ cup caster sugar
FOR THE CARAMEL
150g/5oz/¾ cup granulated sugar

1 Split the vanilla pod lengthways and scrape the tiny black seeds into a medium saucepan. Add the milk and bring just to the boil over a medium-high heat, stirring frequently. Remove the pan from the heat and cover. Set aside for 15–20 minutes.

2 In a medium bowl, whisk the egg yolks and sugar for 2–3 minutes until thick and creamy. Whisk in the hot milk and return the mixture to the saucepan. With a wooden spoon, stir over a medium-low heat until the sauce begins to thicken and coat the back of the spoon (do not allow the custard to boil or it may curdle). Immediately strain into a chilled bowl, allow to cool, stirring occasionally and then chill.

3 Half-fill a large wide frying pan or saucepan with water and bring just to simmering point. In a clean greasefree bowl, whisk the egg whites slowly until they are frothy. Add the cream of tartar, increase the speed and continue whisking until they form soft peaks. Gradually sprinkle over the caster sugar, about 30ml/2 tbsp at a time, and whisk until the whites are stiff and glossy.

4 ▲ Using two tablespoons, form egg-shaped meringues and slide them into the water (you may need to work in batches). Poach them for 2–3 minutes, turning once until the meringue is just firm. Using a large slotted spoon, transfer the cooked meringues to a baking sheet lined with kitchen paper to drain.

5 Pour the cold custard into individual serving dishes and arrange the meringues on top.

6 ▲ To make the caramel, put the sugar into a small saucepan with 45ml/3 tbsp of water to moisten. Bring to the boil over a high heat, swirling the pan to dissolve the sugar. Boil, without stirring, until the syrup turns a dark caramel colour. Immediately drizzle the caramel over the meringues and custard in a zig-zag pattern. Serve cold. (The caramel will soften if made too far ahead.)

MOCHA CREAM POTS

Petits Pots de Crème au Mocha

The name of this rich baked custard, a classic French dessert, comes from the baking cups, called pots de crème. *The addition of coffee gives the dessert an exotic touch.*

SERVES 8

15ml/1 tbsp instant coffee powder
500ml/16fl oz/2 cups milk
85g/3oz/⅓ cup caster sugar
225g/8oz plain chocolate, chopped
10ml/2 tsp vanilla essence
30ml/2 tbsp coffee liqueur (optional)
7 egg yolks
whipped cream and crystallized mimosa balls, to decorate

1 Preheat the oven to 170°C/325°F/Gas 3. Place eight 125ml/4fl oz/½ cup *pots de crème* cups or ramekins in a roasting tin.

2 ▲ Put the instant coffee into a saucepan and stir in the milk, then add the sugar and set the pan over a medium-high heat. Bring to the boil, stirring constantly, until the coffee and sugar have dissolved.

3 ▲ Remove the pan from the heat and add the chocolate. Stir until the chocolate has melted and the sauce is smooth. Stir in the vanilla essence and coffee liqueur, if using.

4 ▲ In a bowl, whisk the egg yolks to blend them lightly. Slowly whisk in the chocolate mixture until well blended, then strain the mixture into a large jug and divide equally among the cups or ramekins. Place them in a roasting tin and pour in enough boiling water to come halfway up the sides of the cups or ramekins.

5 ▼ Bake for 30–35 minutes until the custard is just set and a knife inserted into a custard comes out clean. Remove the cups or ramekins from the roasting tin and allow to cool. Place on a baking sheet, cover and chill completely. Decorate with whipped cream and crystallized mimosa balls, if you like.

Soft Cheese with Fruit Sauce

Coeur à la Crème

These elegant yet simple to prepare desserts get their French name, "hearts of cream", from the perforated heart-shaped moulds they are traditionally made in.

Serves 6–8

225g/8oz full-fat soft cheese (unsalted if possible), softened
250ml/8fl oz/1 cup soured cream
5ml/1 tsp vanilla essence
about 45ml/3 tbsp caster sugar, to taste
2 egg whites
pinch of cream of tartar
Cape gooseberries or other small fruit, to decorate

For the passion fruit sauce
6 ripe passion fruits
5ml/1 tsp cornflour blended with 5ml/1 tsp water
60ml/4 tbsp fresh orange juice
30–45ml/2–3 tbsp caster sugar, to taste
15–30ml/1–2 tbsp orange liqueur (optional)

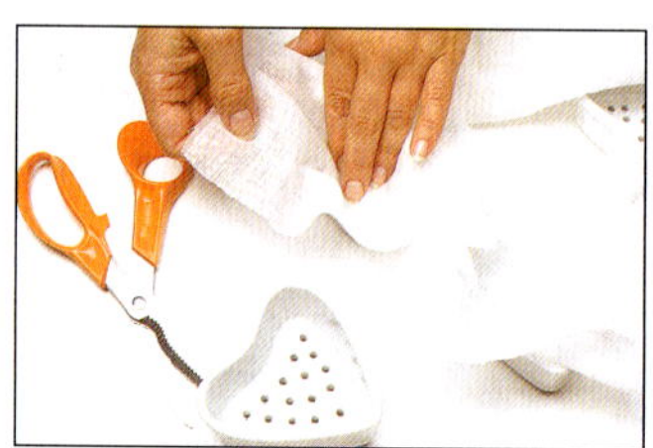

1 ▲ Line six to eight *coeur à la crème* moulds with muslin. In a large bowl, beat the soft cheese until smooth. Add the soured cream, vanilla essence and sugar, beating until smooth.

2 In a clean greasefree bowl, using an electric mixer, beat the egg whites slowly until they become frothy. Add the cream of tartar, increase the speed and continue beating until they form stiff peaks that just flop over a little at the top.

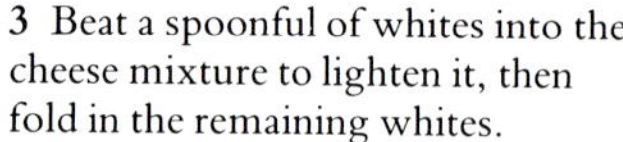

3 Beat a spoonful of whites into the cheese mixture to lighten it, then fold in the remaining whites.

4 ▲ Spoon the cheese mixture into the moulds, smooth the tops and place on a baking tray to catch any drips. Cover the tray with clear film and chill overnight.

5 ▲ To make the sauce, cut each passion fruit in half crossways and scoop the flesh and seeds into a medium saucepan. Add the blended cornflour and stir in the orange juice and sugar. Bring the sauce to the boil over a medium heat and simmer for 2–3 minutes until the sauce thickens, stirring frequently. Remove from the heat and cool slightly, then strain into a serving jug and stir in the orange liqueur, if using.

6 To serve, unmould the cheeses on to individual plates and remove the muslin. Pour round the fruit sauce and decorate with fruit.

CHOCOLATE LOAF WITH COFFEE SAUCE *Marquise au Chocolat*

This type of chocolate dessert is popular in many French restaurants. Sometimes the loaf is encased in sponge, but this version is easier and it can be served cold or frozen.

SERVES 6–8

175g/6oz plain chocolate, chopped
55g/2oz/4 tbsp butter, softened
4 large eggs, separated
30ml/2 tbsp rum or brandy (optional)
pinch of cream of tartar
chocolate curls and chocolate coffee beans, to decorate

FOR THE COFFEE SAUCE

600ml/1 pint/2½ cups milk
9 egg yolks
55g/2oz/¼ cup caster sugar
5ml/1 tsp vanilla essence
15ml/1 tbsp instant coffee powder, dissolved in 30ml/2 tbsp hot water

1 ▲ Line a 1.2 litre/2 pint/5 cup terrine or loaf tin with clear film, smoothing it evenly.

2 ▲ Put the chocolate in a bowl and set over hot water and set aside for 3–5 minutes, then stir until melted and smooth. Remove the bowl from the pan and quickly beat in the softened butter, egg yolks, one at a time, and rum or brandy, if using.

3 ▲ In a clean greasefree bowl, using an electric mixer, beat the egg whites slowly until frothy. Add the cream of tartar, increase the speed and continue beating until they form soft peaks, then stiffer peaks that just flop over a little. Stir one-third of the egg whites into the chocolate mixture, then fold in the remaining whites. Pour into the terrine or tin and smooth the top. Cover and freeze until ready to serve.

4 To make the coffee sauce, bring the milk to a simmer over a medium heat. Whisk the egg yolks and sugar for 2–3 minutes until thick and creamy, then whisk in the hot milk and return the mixture to the saucepan. With a wooden spoon, stir over a low heat until the sauce begins to thicken and coat the back of the spoon. Strain the custard into a chilled bowl, stir in the vanilla essence and coffee and set aside to cool, stirring occasionally. Chill.

5 To serve, uncover the terrine or tin and dip the base into hot water for 10 seconds. Invert the dessert on to a board and peel off the clear film. Cut the loaf into slices and serve with the coffee sauce. Decorate with the chocolate curls and chocolate coffee beans.

BITTER CHOCOLATE MOUSSE *Mousse au Chocolat Amer*

This is the quintessential French dessert – easy to prepare ahead, rich and extremely delicious. Use the darkest chocolate you can find for the best and most intense chocolate flavour.

SERVES 8

225g/8oz plain chocolate, chopped
60ml/4 tbsp water
30ml/2 tbsp orange liqueur or brandy
30g/1oz/2 tbsp unsalted butter, cut into small pieces
4 eggs, separated
90ml/6 tbsp whipping cream
1.5ml/¼ tsp cream of tartar
45ml/3 tbsp caster sugar
crème fraîche or soured cream and chocolate curls, to decorate

COOK'S TIP

As the flavour of this dessert depends on the quality of the chocolate used, it is worth searching in speciality shops for really good chocolate, such as Valrhona and Lindt Excellence.

1 Place the chocolate and water in a heavy saucepan. Melt over a low heat, stirring until smooth. Remove the pan from the heat and whisk in the liqueur and butter.

2 ▲ With an electric mixer, beat the egg yolks for 2–3 minutes until thick and creamy, then slowly beat into the melted chocolate until well blended. Set aside.

3 ▲ Whip the cream until soft peaks form and stir a spoonful into the chocolate mixture to lighten it. Fold in the remaining cream.

4 In a clean greasefree bowl, using an electric mixer, beat the egg whites slowly until frothy. Add the cream of tartar, increase the speed and continue beating until they form soft peaks. Gradually sprinkle over the sugar and continue beating until the whites are stiff and glossy.

5 ▲ Using a rubber spatula or large metal spoon, stir quarter of the egg whites into the chocolate mixture, then gently fold in the remaining whites, cutting down to the bottom, along the sides and up to the top in a semicircular motion until they are just combined. (Don't worry about a few white streaks.) Gently spoon into a 2 litre/3¼ pint/8 cup dish or into eight individual dishes. Chill for at least 2 hours until set and chilled.

6 Spoon a little crème fraîche or soured cream over the mousse and decorate with chocolate curls.

Chocolate Soufflés

Petits Soufflés au Chocolat

These soufflés are easy to make and can be prepared in advance – the filled dishes can wait for up to one hour before baking. For best results, use good quality Continental chocolate.

Serves 6

175g/6oz plain chocolate, chopped
150g/5oz/⅔ cup unsalted butter, cut in small pieces
4 large eggs, separated
30ml/2 tbsp orange liqueur (optional)
1.5ml/¼ tsp cream of tartar
45ml/3 tbsp caster sugar
icing sugar, for dusting

For the white chocolate sauce

90ml/6 tbsp whipping cream
75g/3oz white chocolate, chopped
15–30ml/1–2 tbsp orange liqueur
grated rind of ½ orange

1 Generously butter six 150ml/¼ pint/⅓ cup ramekins. Sprinkle each with a little caster sugar and tap out any excess. Place the ramekins on a baking sheet.

2 ▲ In a heavy saucepan over a very low heat, melt the chocolate and butter, stirring until smooth. Remove from the heat and cool slightly, then beat in the egg yolks and orange liqueur, if using. Set aside, stirring occasionally.

3 Preheat the oven to 220°C/425°F/Gas 7. In a clean greasefree bowl, whisk the egg whites slowly until frothy. Add the cream of tartar, increase the speed and whisk until they form soft peaks. Gradually sprinkle over the sugar, 15ml/1 tbsp at a time, whisking until the whites are stiff and glossy.

4 ▼ Stir a third of the whites into the cooled chocolate mixture to lighten it, then pour the chocolate mixture over the remaining whites. Using a rubber spatula or large metal spoon, gently fold the sauce into the whites, cutting down to the bottom, then along the sides and up to the top in a semicircular motion until they are just combined. (Don't worry about a few white streaks.) Spoon into the prepared dishes.

5 ▲ To make the white chocolate sauce, put the chopped white chocolate and the cream into a small saucepan. Place over a low heat and cook, stirring constantly until melted and smooth. Remove from the heat and stir in the liqueur and orange rind, then pour into a serving jug and keep warm.

6 Bake the soufflés for 10–12 minutes until risen and set, but still slightly wobbly in the centre. Dust with icing sugar and serve immediately with the sauce.

GINGER BAKED PEARS *Poires au Gingembre*

This simple dessert is the kind that would be served after Sunday lunch or a family supper. Try to find Comice or Anjou pears – the recipe is especially useful for slightly under-ripe fruit.

SERVES 4

4 large pears
300ml/½ pint/1¼ cups whipping cream
55g/2oz/¼ cup caster sugar
2.5ml/½ tsp vanilla essence
1.5ml/¼ tsp ground cinnamon
pinch of freshly grated nutmeg
5ml/1 tsp grated fresh root ginger

VARIATION

If preferred, you could substitute about 30ml/1 tbsp finely chopped stem ginger for the fresh root ginger and add a little of the ginger syrup to the cream.

1 Preheat the oven to 190°C/375°F/Gas 5. Lightly butter a large shallow baking dish.

2 ▼ Peel the pears, cut in half lengthways and remove the cores. Arrange, cut-sides down, in a single layer in the baking dish.

3 ▲ Mix together the cream, sugar, vanilla essence, cinnamon, nutmeg and ginger and pour over the pears.

4 Bake for 30–35 minutes, basting from time to time, until the pears are tender and browned on top and the cream is thick and bubbly. Cool slightly before serving.

PRUNES POACHED IN RED WINE *Compôte de Pruneaux Agennaise*

Serve this simple dessert on its own, or with crème fraîche or vanilla ice cream. The most delicious plump prunes come from the orchards around Agen in Southwest France.

SERVES 8–10

1 unwaxed orange
1 unwaxed lemon
750ml/1¼ pints/3 cups fruity red wine
500ml/16fl oz/2 cups water
55g/2oz/¼ cup caster sugar, or to taste
1 cinnamon stick
pinch of freshly grated nutmeg
2 or 3 cloves
5ml/1 tsp black peppercorns
1 bay leaf
900g/2lb large stoned prunes, soaked in cold water
strips of orange rind, to decorate

1 Using a vegetable peeler, peel two or three strips of rind from both the orange and lemon. Squeeze the juice from both and put in a large saucepan.

2 Add the wine, water, sugar, spices, peppercorns, bay leaf and strips of rind to the pan.

3 ▲ Bring to the boil over a medium heat, stirring occasionally to dissolve the sugar. Drain the prunes and add to the saucepan, reduce the heat to low and simmer, covered, for 10–15 minutes until the prunes are tender. Remove from the heat and set aside until cool.

4 ▼ Using a slotted spoon, transfer the prunes to a serving dish. Return the cooking liquid to a medium-high heat and bring to the boil. Boil for 5–10 minutes until slightly reduced and syrupy, then pour or strain over the prunes. Cool, then chill before serving, decorated with strips of orange rind, if you like.

CHERRY BATTER PUDDING *Clafoutis aux Cerises*

This dessert originated in the Limousin area of central France, where batters play an important role in the hearty cuisine. Similar fruit and custard desserts are found in Alsace.

SERVES 4

450g/1lb ripe cherries
30ml/2 tbsp Kirsch or fruit brandy or 15ml/1 tbsp lemon juice
15ml/1 tbsp icing sugar
30g/1oz/3 tbsp plain flour
45ml/3 tbsp granulated sugar
175ml/6fl oz/¾ cup milk or single cream
2 eggs
grated rind of ½ lemon
pinch of freshly grated nutmeg
1.5ml/¼ tsp vanilla essence

1 ▼ Stone the cherries if you like, then mix them with the Kirsch, fruit brandy or lemon juice and icing sugar and set aside for 1–2 hours.

2 ▲ Preheat the oven to 190°C/375°F/Gas 5. Generously butter a 28cm/11in oval gratin dish or other shallow ovenproof dish.

3 ▲ Sift the flour into a bowl, add the sugar and slowly whisk in the milk until smoothly blended. Add the eggs, lemon rind, nutmeg and vanilla essence and whisk until well combined and smooth.

4 ▲ Scatter the cherries evenly in the baking dish. Pour over the batter and bake for 45 minutes, or until set and puffed around the edges. A knife inserted in the centre should come out clean. Serve warm or at room temperature.

APPLE CHARLOTTE *Charlotte aux Pommes*

This classic dessert takes its name from the straight-sided tin with heart-shaped handles in which it is baked. The buttery bread crust encases a thick sweet, yet sharp apple purée.

SERVES 6

1.2kg/2½lb apples
30ml/2 tbsp water
120g/4oz/⅔ cup soft light brown sugar
2.5ml/½ tsp ground cinnamon
1.5ml/¼ tsp freshly grated nutmeg
7 slices firm textured sliced white bread
70–85g/2½–3oz/5–6 tbsp butter, melted
custard, to serve (optional)

1 ▲ Peel, quarter and core the apples. Cut into thick slices and put in a large heavy saucepan with the water. Cook, covered, over a medium-low heat for 5 minutes, and then uncover the pan and cook for 10 minutes until the apples are very soft. Add the sugar, cinnamon and nutmeg and continue cooking for 5–10 minutes, stirring frequently, until the apples are soft and thick. (There should be about 750ml/1¼ pints/3 cups of apple purée.)

COOK'S TIP

If preferred, microwave the apples without water in a large glass dish at High (100% power), tightly covered, for 15 minutes. Add the sugar and spices and microwave, uncovered, for about 15 minutes more until very thick, stirring once or twice.

2 ▼ Preheat the oven to 200°C/400°F/Gas 6. Trim the crusts from the bread and brush with melted butter on one side. Cut two slices into triangles and use as many as necessary to cover the base of a 1.4 litre/2¼ pint/6 cup charlotte tin or soufflé dish, placing them buttered-sides down and fitting them tightly. Cut fingers of bread the same height as the tin or dish and use them to completely line the sides, overlapping them slightly.

3 ▲ Pour the apple purée into the tin or dish. Cover the top with bread slices, buttered-side up, cutting them as necessary to fit.

4 Bake the charlotte for 20 minutes, then reduce the oven temperature to 180°C/350°F/Gas 4 and bake for 25 minutes until well browned and firm. Leave to stand for 15 minutes. To turn out, place a serving plate over the tin or dish, hold tightly, and invert, then lift off the tin or dish. Serve with custard if wished.

CRÊPES WITH ORANGE SAUCE

Crêpes Suzette

This is one of the best known French desserts and is easy to do at home. You can make the crêpes in advance, then you will be able to put the dish together quickly at the last minute.

SERVES 6

120g/4oz/⅔ cup plain flour
1.5ml/¼ tsp salt
30g/1oz/2 tbsp caster sugar
2 eggs, lightly beaten
250ml/8fl oz/1 cup milk
60ml/4 tbsp water
30ml/2 tbsp orange flower water or orange liqueur (optional)
30g/1oz/2 tbsp unsalted butter, melted, plus more for frying

FOR THE ORANGE SAUCE

85g/3oz/6 tbsp unsalted butter
55g/2oz/¼ cup caster sugar
grated rind and juice of 1 large unwaxed orange
grated rind and juice of 1 unwaxed lemon
150ml/¼ pint/⅔ cup fresh orange juice
60ml/4 tbsp orange liqueur, plus more for flaming (optional)
brandy, for flaming (optional)
orange segments, to decorate

1 ▲ In a medium bowl, sift together the flour, salt and sugar. Make a well in the centre and pour in the beaten eggs. Using an electric whisk, beat the eggs, bringing in a little flour until it is all incorporated. Slowly whisk in the milk and water to make a smooth batter. Whisk in the orange flower water or liqueur, if using, then strain the batter into a large jug and set aside for 20–30 minutes. If the batter thickens, add a little milk or water to thin.

2 ▲ Heat a 18–20cm/7–8in crêpe pan (preferably non-stick) over a medium heat. Stir the melted butter into the crêpe batter. Brush the hot pan with a little extra melted butter and pour in about 30ml/2 tbsp of batter. Quickly tilt and rotate the pan to cover the base with a thin layer of batter. Cook for about 1 minute until the top is set and the base is golden. With a palette knife, lift the edge to check the colour, then carefully turn over the crêpe and cook for 20–30 seconds, just to set. Tip out on to a plate.

3 ▲ Continue cooking the crêpes, stirring the batter occasionally and brushing the pan with a little melted butter as and when necessary. Place a sheet of clear film between each crêpe as they are stacked to prevent sticking. (Crêpes can be prepared ahead to this point – wrap and chill until ready to use.)

4 To make the sauce, melt the butter in a large frying pan over a medium-low heat, then stir in the sugar, orange and lemon rind and juice, the additional orange juice and the orange liqueur.

5 ▲ Place a crêpe in the pan browned-side down, swirling gently to coat with the sauce. Fold it in half, then in half again to form a triangle and push to the side of the pan. Continue heating and folding the crêpes until all are warm and covered with the sauce.

6 ▲ To flame the crêpes, heat 30–45ml/2–3 tbsp each of orange liqueur and brandy in a small saucepan over a medium heat. Remove the pan from the heat, carefully ignite the liquid with a match then gently pour over the crêpes. Scatter over the orange segments and serve at once.

SIMPLE FRUIT DESSERTS *Les Fruits Fraîches*

Weekday meals in a French home are likely to finish with fresh seasonal fruit – either a selection from the perpetually changing fruit bowl or an attractive yet simple-to-prepare fruit dessert.

Seasonal fruits can be made into lovely desserts quickly and easily. Each season produces its own special gems, strawberries in spring, peaches at the height of summer and apples, figs and citrus fruits in the run up to autumn.

Some fruits seem to go particularly well with each other, while others are perfect partners to certain herbs and spices. For a classic fruit dessert, try a plate of fresh peach slices sprinkled with fresh raspberries; or pan-fry apple slices in a little butter, then sprinkle them with a little sugar and cinnamon and serve with yogurt. Do the same with pear slices, but sprinkle with a little sugar and ginger, then top with a spoonful of diced stem ginger and a dash of its syrup.

Oranges go well with just about everything. Segment a few oranges, saving the juice, combine the segments with sliced kumquats and sprinkle with pomegranate seeds for a simple yet stunning dessert.

Strawberries, raspberries and blueberries are best just as they come. If you like, sprinkle them with a little sugar, more for the crunch than anything else, or with a splash of orange liqueur or just some good fresh cream. Try flavouring the cream with a few crushed bayleaves, cardamom seeds or fresh mint leaves, then just pour over the fruit, or whip and serve separately. For a quick elegant dessert, spoon sliced or quartered strawberries into pretty dessert *coupes* or Champagne glasses, sprinkle with a little sugar and a dash of raspberry liqueur. Just before serving, pour over a little pink Champagne.

Melon and kiwi slices look pretty together and are always refreshing. Serve ripe, aromatic mango slices on their own with a squeeze of lime juice or scatter over a few green or red grape halves to set off the colour.

Fresh figs go well with raspberries. For a more substantial dessert, cut a deep cross in the top of the figs and fill with a spoonful or two of soft cheese sweetened with honey and beaten with a little cream until fluffy. Sprinkle liberally with raspberries and douse with a little raspberry liqueur, if you like.

For fruit desserts, let the seasons, quality and a sense of colour be your guide. You will find that fruits which are ripe at the same time are usually good together.

Fresh Pineapple with Kirsch
Ananas au Kirsch

SERVES 6–8

1 large pineapple
30ml/2 tbsp caster sugar
10–20ml/2–4 tsp Kirsch or cherry brandy
mint sprigs, to decorate

Using a large sharp knife cut off the top and bottom of the pineapple. Stand the pineapple on a board. Cut off the peel from top to bottom using a small sharp knife, then lay the pineapple on its side and, following the direction of the eyes, use a sharp knife to remove them, cutting out a V-shaped wedge. You will end up with a spiral shape. Cut the pineapple into slices and use an apple corer or small round cutter to remove the tough central core, if you like. Arrange the slices on a large serving plate. Sprinkle evenly with sugar and Kirsch or cherry brandy. Chill until ready to serve, then decorate with mint sprigs.

Melon with Raspberries
Melons aux framboises

SERVES 2

2 tiny or 1 small ripe melon
120g/4oz/1 cup fresh raspberries
15–30ml/1–2 tbsp raspberry liqueur (optional)

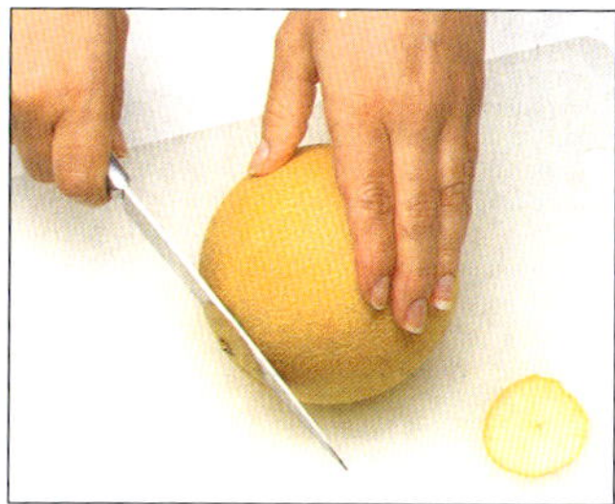

Cut off a thin slice from the bottom of each melon to create a stable base.

If the melons are tiny, cut off the top third and scoop out as much flesh as possible from each top. Cut the flesh into tiny dice. If a larger melon is used, cut off a thin slice from both the top and bottom to create two stable bases; then split melon in half. In either case, scoop out and discard seeds. Fill the centre of the melon halves with the raspberries and, if you like, sprinkle with a little liqueur. Chill before serving or serve on a bed of crushed ice.

Grilled Fruit Kebabs
Brochettes de fruits grillées

MAKES 4–6

4 or 5 kinds of firm ripe fruit, such as pineapple and mango cubes, nectarine and pear slices, grapes and tangerine segments
30g/1oz/2 tbsp unsalted butter, melted
grated rind and juice of 1 orange
sugar, to taste
pinch of ground cinnamon or nutmeg
yogurt, soured cream, crème fraîche or fruit coulis, *for serving*

Preheat the grill. Line a baking sheet with foil. Thread the fruit on to 4–6 skewers (dampened if wood), alternating fruits to create an attractive pattern. Arrange the skewers on foil, spoon over the melted butter, orange rind and juice and sprinkle with the sugar to taste, together with a pinch of cinnamon or nutmeg. Grill for 2–3 minutes until the sugar just begins to caramelize and serve the kebabs at once with yogurt, soured cream or crème fraîche.

POACHED PEACHES WITH RASPBERRY SAUCE *Pêche Melba*

The story goes that one of the great French chefs, Auguste Escoffier, created this dessert in honour of the opera singer Nellie Melba, now forever enshrined in culinary, if not musical, history.

SERVES 6

1 litre/1⅔ pints/4 cups water
55g/2oz/¼ cup caster sugar
1 vanilla pod, split lengthways
3 large peaches
FOR THE RASPBERRY SAUCE
450g/1lb fresh or frozen raspberries
15ml/1 tbsp lemon juice
30–40g/1–1½oz/2–3 tbsp caster sugar
30–45ml/2–3 tbsp raspberry liqueur (optional)
vanilla ice cream, to serve
mint leaves and fresh raspberries, to decorate (optional)

1 In a saucepan large enough to hold the peach halves in a single layer, combine the water, sugar and vanilla pod. Bring to the boil over a medium heat, stirring occasionally to dissolve the sugar.

2 ▼ Cut the peaches in half and twist the halves to separate them. Using a small teaspoon, remove the peach stones. Add the peach halves to the poaching syrup, cut-sides down, adding more water, if needed to cover the fruit. Press a piece of greaseproof paper against the surface, reduce the heat to medium-low, then cover and simmer for 12–15 minutes until tender – the time will depend on the ripeness of the fruit. Remove the pan from the heat and leave the peaches to cool in the syrup.

3 ▲ Remove the peaches from the syrup and peel off the skins. Place on several thicknesses of kitchen paper to drain (reserve the syrup for another use), then cover and chill.

4 ▲ Put the raspberries, lemon juice and sugar in a food processor fitted with the metal blade. Process for 1 minute, scraping down the sides once. Press though a fine sieve into a small bowl, then stir in the raspberry liqueur, if using, and chill.

5 To serve, place a peach half, cut-side up on a dessert plate, fill with a scoop of vanilla ice cream and spoon the raspberry sauce over the ice cream. Decorate with mint leaves and a few fresh raspberries, if using.

COOK'S TIP

Prepare the peaches and sauce up to one day in advance. Leave the peaches in the syrup and cover them and the sauce before chilling.

FRESH FRUIT WITH MANGO SAUCE *Fruits au Coulis de Mangue*

Fruit sauce, coulis, *became fashionable in the 1970s with* nouvelle cuisine. *This bright, flavourful sauce is easy to prepare and ideal to make a simple fruit salad seem special.*

SERVES 6

1 large ripe mango, peeled, stoned and chopped
rind of 1 unwaxed orange
juice of 3 oranges
caster sugar, to taste
2 peaches
2 nectarines
1 small mango, peeled
2 plums
1 pear or ½ small melon
30–55g/1–2oz/2 heaped tbsp wild strawberries (optional)
30–55g/1–2oz/2 heaped tbsp raspberries
30–55g/1–2oz/2 heaped tbsp blueberries
juice of 1 lemon
small mint sprigs, to decorate

1 ▲ In a food processor fitted with the metal blade, process the large mango until smooth. Add the orange rind, juice and sugar to taste and process again until very smooth. Press through a sieve into a bowl and chill the sauce.

2 Peel the peaches, if liked, then slice and stone the peaches, nectarines, small mango and plums. Quarter the pear and remove the core and seeds, or if using, slice the melon thinly and remove the peel.

3 ▼ Place the sliced fruits on a large plate, sprinkle the fruits with the lemon juice and chill, covered with clear film, for up to 3 hours before serving. (Some fruits may discolour if cut too far ahead of time.)

4 ▲ To serve, arrange the sliced fruits on serving plates, spoon the berries on top, drizzle with a little mango sauce and decorate with mint sprigs. Serve the remaining sauce separately.

ORANGES IN CARAMEL SAUCE

Oranges Caramelisés

The appeal of this refreshing dessert is the contrast between the sweetness of the caramel and the tangy tartness of the oranges. Made in advance, it is easy and convenient for entertaining.

SERVES 6

6 large unwaxed seedless oranges
100g/3½oz/½ cup granulated sugar

1 ▲ With a vegetable peeler, remove wide strips of rind from two of the oranges. Stack two or three strips at a time and cut into very thin julienne strips.

2 ▼ On a board, using a sharp knife, cut a slice from the top and the base of each orange. Cut off the peel in strips from the top to the base, following the contours of the fruit, then slice the peeled fruit crossways into rounds about 1cm/⅜in thick. Put the orange slices in a serving bowl and pour over any juice.

3 ▲ Half-fill a large bowl with cold water and set aside. Place the sugar and 45ml/3 tbsp water in a small heavy saucepan without a non-stick coating and bring to the boil over a high heat, swirling the pan to dissolve the sugar. Boil, without stirring, until the mixture turns a dark caramel colour. Remove the pan from the heat and, standing well back, dip the base of the pan into the cold water to stop the cooking.

4 ▲ Add 30ml/2 tbsp water to the caramel, pouring it down the sides of the pan, and swirl to combine. Add the strips of orange rind and return the pan to the heat. Simmer over a medium-low heat for 8–10 minutes until they are slightly translucent, stirring occasionally.

5 Pour the caramel and rind over the oranges, turn gently to mix and chill for at least 1 hour.

STRAWBERRIES WITH COINTREAU *Coupe de Fraises au Cointreau*

Strawberries at the height of their season are one of summer's greatest pleasures. Try this simple but unusual way to serve them. If you wish, use a mixture of fresh seasonal berries.

SERVES 4

1 unwaxed orange
40g/1½oz/3 tbsp granulated sugar
75ml/5 tbsp water
45ml/3 tbsp Cointreau or orange liqueur
450g/1lb/3 cups strawberries, hulled
250ml/8fl oz/1 cup whipping cream

1 ▲ With a vegetable peeler, remove wide strips of rind without the pith from the orange. Stack two or three strips at a time and cut into very thin julienne strips.

2 ▲ Combine the sugar and water in a small saucepan. Bring to the boil over a high heat, swirling the pan occasionally to dissolve the sugar. Add the julienne strips and simmer for 10 minutes. Remove the pan from the heat and leave the syrup to cool completely, then stir in the Cointreau or liqueur.

3 ▼ Reserve four strawberries for decoration and cut the rest lengthways in halves or quarters. Put them in a bowl and pour the syrup and orange rind over the top. Set aside for at least 30 minutes or for up to 2 hours.

4 ▲ Using an electric mixer or a whisk, whip the cream until it forms soft peaks. Sweeten to taste with a little of the syrup from the strawberries.

5 To serve, spoon the chopped strawberries into glass serving dishes and top with dollops of cream and the reserved strawberries.

CHOCOLATE MOUSSE CAKE

Gâteau Mousse au Chocolat

This special occasion dessert is a double batch of chocolate mousse, glazed with chocolate ganache *and decorated with long, slim chocolate curls – heaven for chocolate lovers!*

SERVES 8–10

275g/10oz plain chocolate, chopped
125g/4oz/½ cup unsalted butter, cut into pieces
8 eggs, separated
1.5ml/¼ tsp cream of tartar
45ml/3 tbsp brandy or rum (optional)
chocolate curls, to decorate
FOR THE CHOCOLATE GANACHE
250ml/8fl oz/1 cup double cream
225g/8oz plain chocolate, chopped
30ml/2 tbsp brandy or rum (optional)
30g/1oz/2 tbsp unsalted butter, softened

1 Preheat the oven to 180°C/350°F/Gas 4. Lightly butter two 20–25cm/8–9in springform tins or loose-based cake tins and line the bases with buttered greaseproof paper or non-stick baking paper.

2 ▲ In a saucepan, melt the chocolate and butter over a low heat until smooth, stirring frequently. Remove the pan from the heat and whisk in the egg yolks until completely blended. Beat in the brandy or rum, if using, and pour into a large bowl. Set aside, stirring occasionally.

3 In a clean greasefree bowl, using an electric mixer, beat the egg whites slowly until frothy. Add the cream of tartar, increase the speed and continue beating until they form soft peaks, then stiffer peaks that just flop over a little at the top.

4 Stir a large spoonful of whites into the chocolate mixture to lighten it, then fold in the remaining whites until they are just combined (a few white streaks do not matter).

5 ▲ Divide about two-thirds of the mousse between the two prepared tins, smoothing the tops evenly, and tap gently to release any air bubbles. Chill the remaining mousse.

6 Bake for 30–35 minutes until puffed; the cakes will fall slightly. Cool on a wire rack for 15 minutes, then remove the sides of the tins and leave to cool completely. Invert the cakes on to the rack, remove the cake tin bases and peel off the papers. Wash the cake tins.

7 ▲ To assemble the cake, place one layer, flat side down in one of the clean tins. Spread the remaining mousse over the surface, smoothing the top. Top with the second cake layer, flat side up. Press down gently so the mousse is evenly distributed. Chill for 2–4 hours or overnight.

8 ▲ To make the *ganache*, bring the cream to the boil in a heavy saucepan over a medium-high heat. Remove the pan from the heat and add the chocolate all at once, stirring until melted and smooth. Stir in the brandy or rum, if using, and beat in the softened butter. Set aside for about 5 minutes to thicken slightly (*ganache* should coat the back of a spoon in a thick smooth layer).

9 ▲ Run a knife around the edge of the assembled cake to loosen it, then remove the sides of the tin. Invert the cake on to a wire rack, remove the base and place the rack over a baking tray. Pour the warm *ganache* over the cake all at once, tilting gently to help spread it evenly on all surfaces. Use a palette knife to smooth the sides, decorate the top with chocolate curls, then leave to set.

Meringues with Chestnut Cream *Petits Mont Blancs*

This dessert takes its name from the famous peak in the French Alps, Mont Blanc, as the meringues piled high with chestnut purée and whipped cream resemble it.

Serves 6

2 egg whites
pinch of cream of tartar
100g/3½oz/½ cup caster sugar
2.5ml/½ tsp vanilla essence
chocolate shavings, to decorate

For the chestnut cream
60g/2oz/⅓ cup caster sugar
125ml/4fl oz/½ cup water
450g/1lb can unsweetened chestnut purée
5ml/1 tsp vanilla essence
350ml/12fl oz/1½ cups double cream

For the chocolate sauce
225g/8oz plain chocolate, chopped
175g/6oz/¾ cup whipping cream
30ml/2 tbsp rum or brandy (optional)

1 ▲ Preheat the oven to 140°C/275°F/Gas 1. Line a baking sheet with non-stick baking paper. Use a small plate to outline six 9cm/3½in circles and turn the paper over (so the meringue does not touch the pencil marks).

2 In a clean greasefree bowl, using an electric mixer, beat the egg whites slowly until frothy. Add the cream of tartar, then increase the speed and continue beating until they form soft peaks. Gradually sprinkle over the sugar, 30ml/2 tbsp at a time, and continue beating until the whites are stiff and glossy. Beat in the vanilla essence.

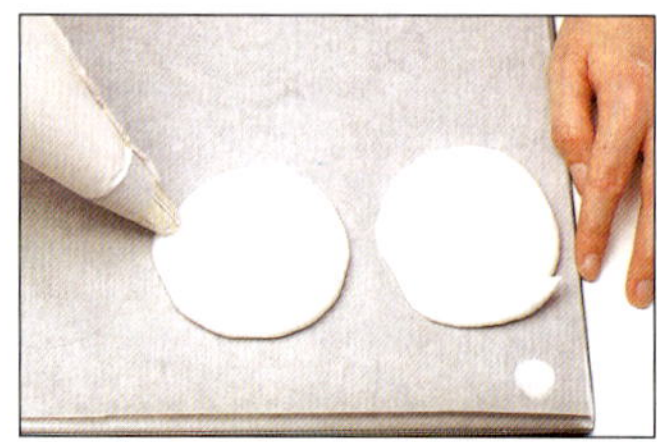

3 ▲ Spoon the whisked egg whites into a large piping bag fitted with a medium-size plain or star nozzle and pipe six spirals following the outlines on the marked paper. Bake for about 1 hour until the meringues feel firm and crisp, lowering the oven temperature if they begin to brown. Using a thin palette knife, transfer the meringues to a wire rack to cool completely.

4 ▲ To make the chestnut cream, place the sugar and water in a small saucepan over a medium-high heat and bring to the boil, stirring until the sugar dissolves. Boil for about 5 minutes, then remove the pan from the heat and set aside to cool. Put the chestnut purée in a food processor fitted with the metal blade and process until smooth. With the machine running, slowly add the sugar syrup in a thin stream until the chestnut purée is soft, but still holds its shape (you may not need all the syrup). Add the vanilla essence and process again then spoon into a medium bowl.

5 ▲ In another bowl, with an electric mixer, whisk the cream until soft peaks form, then add a spoonful to the chestnut cream and pulse to combine. Chill the remaining whipped cream.

6 ▲ Spoon the chestnut cream into a piping bag fitted with a large star nozzle. Pipe a mound of chestnut cream in a swirl on to each meringue then pipe or spoon the remaining cream on top of the chestnut cream to resemble a mountain peak. Chill until ready to serve.

7 To make the chocolate sauce, heat the chocolate and cream in a small saucepan over a medium-low heat stirring frequently. Remove the pan from the heat and stir in the rum or brandy, if using. Set aside to cool, stirring occasionally. (Do not chill or the sauce will set.)

8 To serve, place each meringue on a plate and sprinkle with chocolate shavings. Serve the chocolate sauce separately.

FROZEN RASPBERRY MOUSSE *Crème Glaçée aux Framboises*

This dessert is like a frozen soufflé. Freeze it in a ring mould, then you can fill the centre with fresh raspberries moistened with framboise *or raspberry liqueur or just a little orange juice.*

SERVES 6

350g/12oz/3 cups raspberries, plus more for serving
45ml/3 tbsp icing sugar
2 egg whites
1.5ml/¼ tsp cream of tartar
100g/3½oz/½ cup granulated sugar
25ml/1½ tbsp lemon juice
250ml/8fl oz/1 cup whipping cream
15ml/1 tbsp framboise *or Kirsch*
mint leaves, to decorate

1 Put the raspberries in a food processor fitted with the metal blade and process until smooth, then press through a sieve. Or, simply work the raspberries through the fine blade of a food mill.

2 Pour about a third of the purée into a small bowl, stir in the icing sugar, then cover and chill. Reserve the remaining purée for the mousse.

3 ▼ Half-fill a medium saucepan with hot water and set over a low heat (do not allow the water to boil). Combine the egg whites, cream of tartar, sugar and lemon juice in a heatproof bowl which just fits into the pan without touching the water. Using an electric mixer, beat at medium-high speed until the beaters leave tracks on the base of the bowl, then beat at high speed for about 7 minutes until the mixture is very thick and forms stiff peaks.

4 ▲ Remove the bowl from the pan and continue beating the egg white mixture for a further 2–3 minutes until it is cool. Fold in the reserved raspberry purée.

5 Whip the cream until it forms soft peaks and fold gently into the raspberry mixture with the liqueur. Spoon into a 1.4 litre/2½ pint/6 cup ring mould, then cover and freeze for at least 4 hours or overnight.

6 ▲ To unmould, dip the mould in warm water for about 5 seconds and wipe the base. Invert a serving plate over the mould and, holding it tightly against the mould, turn over together, then lift off the mould.

7 If you wish, fill the centre of the mousse with raspberries, decorate with mint leaves and serve with the sweetened raspberry purée.

ICED COFFEE AND NUT MERINGUE *Dacquoise Givrée*

This impressive frozen dessert may seem difficult, but it is actually very easy to prepare.

SERVES 8–10

100g/3½oz/1 cup hazelnuts, toasted
275g/10oz/1⅓ cups caster sugar
5 egg whites
pinch of cream of tartar
1 litre/1⅔ pints/4 cups coffee ice cream
FOR THE CHOCOLATE CREAM
500ml/16fl oz/2 cups whipping cream
275g/10oz plain chocolate, melted and cooled
30ml/2 tbsp coffee liqueur
white chocolate curls and fresh raspberries, to decorate

1 ▲ Preheat the oven to 180°C/350°F/Gas 4. Line three baking sheets with non-stick baking paper, then, using a plate as a guide, mark a 20cm/8in circle on each sheet and turn the paper over. In a food processor fitted with the metal blade, process the hazelnuts until chopped. Add a third of the sugar and process until finely ground.

2 In a clean greasefree bowl, whisk the egg whites until frothy, then add the cream of tartar and whisk until they form soft peaks.

out within the marked circles. Bake for 1 hour until firm and dry. Leave to cool in the turned-off oven, then peel off the paper.

3 ▼ Leave the ice cream to stand for 15–20 minutes in a large bowl and then beat with an electric mixer until smooth. Spread half of the ice cream over one meringue layer, top with a second meringue layer and spread with the remaining ice cream. Place the last meringue layer on top, press down gently, then wrap and freeze for at least 4 hours until firm.

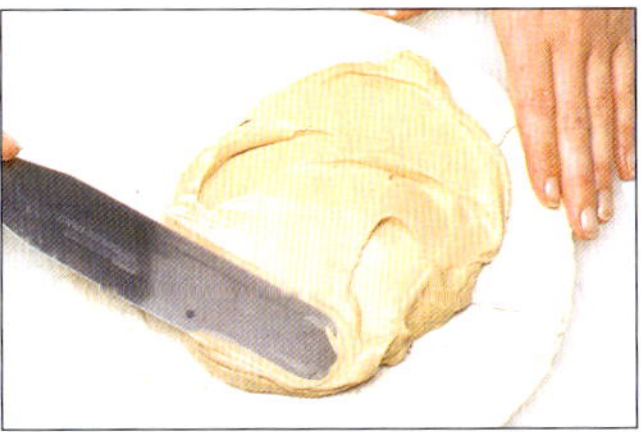

4 ▲ To make the chocolate cream, beat the whipping cream until soft peaks form. Quickly fold in the cooled melted chocolate and the liqueur. Take the meringue cake out of the freezer, unwrap and place on a serving plate. Spread the chocolate cream over the top and sides of the meringue and return to the freezer. Wrap when firm. To serve, leave the meringue to stand for 15 minutes at room temperature to soften slightly before cutting.

Blackcurrant Sorbet

Sorbet au Cassis

Blackcurrants, which are prolific in Burgundy, make a vibrant and intensely flavoured sorbet.

Serves 4–6

100g/3½oz/½ cup caster sugar
125ml/4fl oz/½ cup water
500g/1lb 2oz blackcurrants
juice of ½ lemon
15ml/1 tbsp egg white

1 In a small saucepan over a medium-high heat, bring the sugar and water to the boil, stirring until the sugar dissolves. Boil the syrup for 2 minutes, then remove the pan from the heat and set aside to cool.

2 ▼ Remove the blackcurrants from the stalks, by pulling them through the tines of a fork.

3 In a food processor fitted with the metal blade, process the blackcurrants and lemon juice until smooth. Alternatively, chop the blackcurrants coarsely, then add the lemon juice. Mix in the sugar syrup.

4 ▲ Press the purée through a sieve to remove the seeds.

5 ▲ Pour the blackcurrant purée into a non-metallic, freezerproof dish. Cover the dish with clear film or a lid and freeze until the sorbet is nearly firm, but still slushy.

6 ▲ Cut the sorbet into pieces and put into the food processor. Process until smooth, then with the machine running, add the egg white and process until well mixed. Tip the sorbet back into the dish and freeze until almost firm. Chop the sorbet again and process until smooth. Serve immediately or freeze, tightly covered, for up to 1 week. Allow to soften for 5–10 minutes at room temperature before serving.

CHOCOLATE SORBET *Sorbet au Chocolat*

This velvety smooth sorbet has long been popular in France. Bitter chocolate gives by far the richest flavour, but if you can't track this down, then use the very best quality dark Continental plain chocolate that you can find or the sorbet will be too sweet.

SERVES 6

150g/5oz bitter chocolate, chopped
120g/4oz plain chocolate, chopped
200g/7oz/1 cup caster sugar
500ml/16fl oz/2 cups water
chocolate curls, to decorate

1 ▲ Put all the chocolate in a food processor, fitted with the metal blade and process for 20–30 seconds until finely chopped.

2 ▲ In a saucepan over a medium-high heat, bring the sugar and water to the boil, stirring until the sugar dissolves. Boil for about 2 minutes, then remove from the heat.

3 ▼ With the machine running, pour the hot syrup over the chocolate. Allow the machine to continue running for 1–2 minutes until the chocolate is completely melted and the mixture is smooth, scraping down the bowl once.

4 ▲ Strain the chocolate mixture into a large measuring jug or bowl, and leave to cool, then chill, stirring occasionally. Freeze the mixture in an ice cream machine, following the manufacturer's instructions or see Cook's Tip (left). Allow the sorbet to soften for 5–10 minutes at room temperature and serve in scoops, decorated with chocolate curls.

COOK'S TIP

If you don't have an ice cream machine, freeze the sorbet until firm around the edges. Process until smooth, then freeze again.

PRALINE ICE CREAM IN BASKETS *Tulipes à la Glace Pralinée*

Praline, a delicious crunchy caramel and nut mixture, is a very popular flavouring in France – it can be made with almonds or hazelnuts or a mixture of the two, if you prefer.

SERVES 6–8

55g/2oz/½ cup blanched almonds or hazelnuts
175g/6oz/⅞ cup caster sugar
60ml/4 tbsp water
250ml/8fl oz/1 cup double cream
500ml/16fl oz/2 cups milk
6 egg yolks
FOR THE BISCUIT BASKETS
70g/2½oz/½ cup whole blanched almonds, lightly toasted
100g/3½oz/½ cup caster sugar
40g/1½oz/3 tbsp unsalted butter, softened
2 egg whites
2.5ml/½ tsp almond essence
35g/1¼oz/scant ¼ cup plain flour, sifted

1 ▲ Lightly brush a baking sheet with oil. Put the nuts in a saucepan with 75g/2½oz/⅓ cup of the sugar and the water. Bring to the boil over a high heat, swirling the pan to dissolve the sugar, then boil, without stirring, for 4–5 minutes until the syrup is a medium caramel colour and the nuts begin to pop. Immediately pour on to the baking sheet (do not touch the hot caramel). Set aside to cool completely.

2 Break the praline into small pieces. Put in a food processor fitted with the metal blade and process until finely ground. Or, put in a strong polythene bag and, crush with a rolling pin.

3 Pour the cream into a cold bowl and set aside. Bring the milk just to a simmer over a medium heat. In a medium bowl, whisk the egg yolks and remaining sugar for 2–3 minutes until thick and creamy, then whisk in the hot milk and return the mixture to the saucepan.

4 With a wooden spoon. stir over a low heat for 3–4 minutes until the sauce begins to thicken and coat the back of the spoon (do not boil or the custard may curdle). Immediately strain the custard into the bowl of cream to stop cooking further. Cool, then chill until cold. Stir in the praline and freeze in an ice cream maker, following the manufacturer's instructions.

5 Preheat the oven to 200°C/400°F/Gas 6. Generously butter two baking sheets. To make the biscuit baskets, put the almonds and about 30ml/2 tbsp of the sugar in a food processor fitted with the metal blade and process until finely ground. In a separate bowl, using an electric mixer, beat the butter until creamy.

6 ▲ Add the remaining sugar and beat for 1 minute until light and fluffy, then gradually beat in the egg whites until well blended; beat in the almond essence. Sift the flour over the butter mixture and fold in, then fold in the ground almond mixture.

7 ▲ Drop tablespoons of mixture about 20cm/8in apart on to the prepared baking sheets. With the back of a wet spoon, spread each mound into a paper-thin 10cm/4in round. (Do not worry if holes appear; they will fill in.)

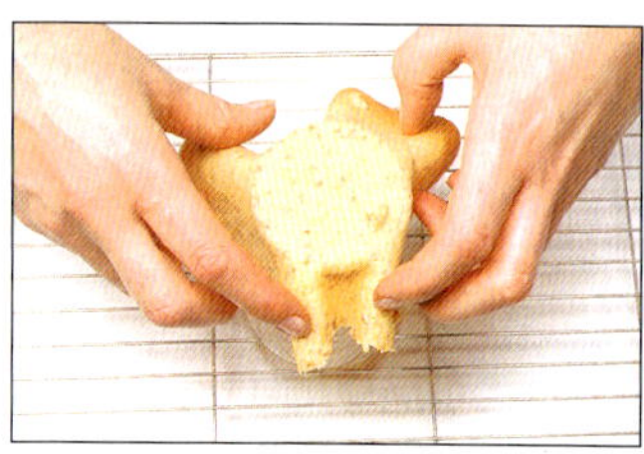

8 ▲ Bake the biscuits, one sheet at a time, for 4–5 minutes until the edges are golden and the centres are still pale. Transfer to a wire rack and, working quickly, loosen the edge of a hot biscuit and carefully transfer to an upturned drinking glass or ramekin, pressing gently over the base to form a fluted basket shape. Repeat with the remaining biscuits. If the biscuits become too crisp to shape, return them to the oven to soften for 15–30 seconds, then continue shaping. Set aside to cool completely before transferring to a wire rack.

9 To serve, leave the ice cream to soften at room temperature for 5–10 minutes. Place the baskets on dessert plates and fill with scoops of the ice cream.

BASIC RECIPES

This section includes essential basic recipes for French cooking – flavoursome stocks for soups and stews, classic savoury and sweet sauces and perfect pastries – all you need to get started.

HOME-MADE STOCKS

A sauce or stew is only as good as the stock, or *fond*, that it is made from. Stock is one of the easiest things to make as it requires almost no attention, after the first few minutes, and basically cooks itself.

Meat Stock
Fond de viande

MAKES 3 LITRES/5 PINTS/12 CUPS

3.6–4.5kg/8–10lb raw or cooked beef or veal bones and meat and/or poultry carcasses, clean trimmings and giblets
2 large unpeeled onions, halved and root end trimmed
2 medium carrots, scrubbed and cut in large pieces
1 large celery stick, cut in large pieces
2 leeks, cut in large pieces
1 or 2 parsnips, cut in large pieces
2–4 garlic cloves
1 large bouquet garni
15ml/1 tbsp black peppercorns

Place all the ingredients in a large stock pot and cover with cold water by at least 2.5cm/1in. Bring to the boil over a medium-high heat. As the liquid heats, foam will begin to appear on the surface. Begin skimming off the foam with a large spoon or ladle as soon as it appears, continuing until it stops surfacing; this will take at least 5 minutes and by then the stock will be boiling. Reduce the heat until the stock is just simmering and simmer very slowly, uncovered, for 4–5 hours, skimming occasionally. Do not allow the stock to boil again or cover it as this can cause the stock to sour or cloud.

Top up with boiling water during cooking if the liquid level falls below the bones and vegetables.
Ladle the stock into a large bowl; discard the bones and vegetables. Leave the stock to cool, then chill to allow any fat to solidify, then scrape off the fat. To remove any further traces of fat, "wipe" a piece of kitchen paper across the surface. The stock can be used as it is or, if you wish, reduced to concentrate the flavour and chilled or frozen.

Brown Stock
Fond brun

Brown stock has a rich flavour and deep colour, obtained by browning the meats and vegetables before cooking. Place the meat and vegetables in a large roasting tin and brown in the oven at 230°C/450°F/Gas 8 for 30–40 minutes, turning occasionally. Put ingredients in the stockpot with the bouquet garni and proceed as for Meat Stock.

Chicken Stock
Fond de volaille

MAKES 2 LITRES/3⅓ PINTS/8 CUPS

2kg/4½lb raw chicken carcasses, necks or feet or cooked carcasses
2 large onions, unpeeled, root end trimmed
3 carrots, scrubbed and cut in large pieces
1 celery stick, cut in large pieces
1 leek, cut in large pieces
2 garlic cloves, unpeeled and lightly smashed
1 large bouquet garni

Proceed as for Meat Stock, but simmer for 2 hours.

Brown Chicken Stock
Fond de volaille brun

Brown the chicken pieces in a frying pan, as roasting is too intense and the chicken could easily burn. Put the ingredients in the stockpot with the bouquet garni and proceed as for Chicken Stock.

Game Stock
Fond de gibier

Proceed as for Chicken Stock using game carcasses, with or without browning as described.

Fish Stock

Fumet de poisson

MAKES 2 LITRES/3⅓ PINTS/8 CUPS

900g/2lb heads and bones and trimmings from white flesh
1 onion, thinly sliced
1 carrot, thinly sliced
1 leek, thinly sliced
8 parsley stems
½ bay leaf
250ml/8fl oz/1 cup dry white wine
5ml/1 tsp black peppercorns

Put all the ingredients in a large non-reactive saucepan or flameproof casserole and add enough cold water to cover. Bring to the boil over a medium-high heat, skimming any foam which rises to the top. Simmer gently for 25 minutes; strain through a muslin-lined sieve. Cool, then chill. Reduce, if you wish, for storage or freezing.

COOK'S TIP

Make stock whenever you roast a piece of meat on the bone or a bird, or save bones and carcasses in the freezer until you have enough for a large pot of stock. After making stock, reduce it by at least half and freeze in an ice cube tray. Store the cubes in a strong freezer bag and add to soups and sauces without defrosting. Never add salt to the stock as it will be concentrated during reduction and always season sauces after adding the stock.

BASIC SAVOURY SAUCES

There is a huge repertoire of sauces in classic French cuisine, but many are variations of a few types which you can master with a little practice. Sauces are usually categorized by the way they are made.

REDUCTION SAUCES
These are simply the cooking juices, sometimes with additional liquid such as wine, stock and/or cream, boiled to concentrate the flavour and thicken by evaporation.

FLOUR-BASED SAUCES
This type of sauce is usually thickened with cooked butter and flour (*roux*) and they are among the most useful for the home cook. They can be made with milk for *béchamel* or stock for *velouté* sauce, are sometimes enriched with cream and may also be flavoured with other ingredients such as mushrooms, cheese, spices, mustard or tomato.

Sometimes the cooking liquid of soups and stews is thickened with flour, either by flouring the ingredients before browning them or by sprinkling over the flour during cooking. Alternatively, a flour and butter paste, known as *beurre manié*, may be stirred in at the end of cooking to thicken the liquid. Other flours, such as cornflour, potato flour or arrowroot, may also be used for thickening sauces.

EMULSIFIED SAUCES
Hollandaise, *Béarnaise* and butter sauces, are included in this group. These sauces are very quick to make, but can be tricky to prepare and keep warm. The most common cause of the sauce separating or curdling is overheating. Mayonnaise is also an emulsified sauce and all the ingredients should be at room temperature for best results.

FLAVOURED BUTTERS
These "hard" sauces, butter flavoured with herbs or garlic, are useful to have on hand to give a lift to plain vegetables or sautéed or grilled meat, poultry or fish. An even simpler flavoured butter, *beurre noisette*, is made by heating butter until it turns nutty brown before pouring over food.

VEGETABLE SAUCES
Sauces may also be thickened with vegetable purées, using, for instance, the aromatic vegetables cooked with a stew. Or a vegetable purée may be the sauce itself, for instance, fresh tomato sauce.

White Sauce

Béchamel

MAKES ABOUT 250ML/8FL OZ/1 CUP

30g/1oz/2 tbsp butter
30g/1oz/3 tbsp plain flour
250ml/8fl oz/1 cup milk
1 bay leaf
freshly grated nutmeg
salt and freshly ground black pepper

Melt the butter in a heavy saucepan over a medium heat, add the flour and cook until just golden, stirring occasionally. Pour in half the milk, stirring vigorously until smooth, then stir in the remaining milk and add the bay leaf. Season with salt, pepper and nutmeg, then reduce the heat to medium-low, cover and simmer gently for about 5 minutes, stirring occasionally.

Velouté Sauce

Proceed as for White Sauce above, using stock or cooking liquid instead of milk.

Hollandaise Sauce

SERVES 6

175g/6oz/¾ cup unsalted butter, cut into pieces
3 egg yolks
15ml/1 tbsp cold water
15–30ml/1–2 tbsp fresh lemon juice
2.5ml/½ tsp salt
cayenne pepper

Clarify the butter by melting it in a small saucepan over a low heat; do not boil. Skim off any foam.

In a small heavy saucepan or in the top of a double boiler, combine the egg yolks, water, 30ml/1 tbsp of the lemon juice, and salt and pepper and whisk for 1 minute. Place the saucepan over a very low heat or place the double boiler top over barely simmering water and whisk constantly until the egg yolk mixture begins to thicken and the whisk begins to leave tracks on the base of the pan; remove from heat.

Whisk in the clarified butter, drop by drop until the sauce begins to thicken, then pour in the butter a little more quickly, making sure the butter is absorbed before adding more. When you reach the milky solids at the bottom of the clarified butter, stop pouring. Season to taste with salt and cayenne and a little more lemon juice if wished.

Béarnaise Sauce

Combine 30ml/2 tbsp each tarragon vinegar and dry white wine with 1 finely chopped shallot in a small heavy saucepan, set over a high heat and boil to reduce until the liquid has almost evaporated. Remove from the heat and leave to cool slightly. Proceed as for Hollandaise Sauce, but omit the lemon juice and add the egg yolks to the shallot mixture. Strain before serving if you prefer.

Butter Sauce
Beurre blanc

SERVES 4–6

2 shallots, finely chopped
90ml/6 tbsp white wine vinegar
15ml/1 tbsp single cream
176g/6oz/¾ cup unsalted butter, cut into 12 pieces
salt and white pepper

Put the shallots and vinegar in a small heavy saucepan. Boil over a high heat until the liquid has almost evaporated, leaving only about 15ml/1 tbsp. Stir in the cream. Reduce the heat to medium and add the butter, one piece at a time, whisking constantly until it melts before adding the next (lift the pan from the heat if the butter melts faster than it can be incorporated). Strain the sauce and adjust the seasoning before serving.

COOK'S TIP

Delicate sauces, such as Béarnaise, Hollandaise and Butter Sauce, are easy to keep warm in a wide-mouthed vacuum flask.

Mayonnaise

MAKES ABOUT 225ML/8FL OZ/1 CUP

2 egg yolks
15ml/1 tbsp Dijon mustard
250ml/8fl oz/1 cup extra virgin olive oil
lemon juice or white wine vinegar
salt and white pepper

Combine the egg yolks and mustard in a small bowl. Beat for 30 seconds until creamy. Beat in the olive oil drop by drop until the mixture begins to thicken, then add the remaining oil in a thin stream until the mixture is thick. Thin the mayonnaise with a little lemon juice or vinegar, and season to taste. Store in the fridge for up to 2 days.

BASIC SWEET SAUCES

Custard Sauce
Crème Anglaise

SERVES 4–6

1 vanilla pod
600ml/1 pint/2½ cups milk
8 egg yolks
50g/1¾oz/¼ cup granulated sugar

Split the vanilla pod lengthways and scrape the tiny black seeds into a saucepan. Add the milk and bring just to the boil, stirring frequently. Remove from the heat, cover and leave to stand for 15–20 mintues.

Whisk the egg yolks and sugar for 2–3 minutes until thick. Whisk in the hot milk and return the mixture to the saucepan.

With a wooden spoon, stir over a medium-low heat until the sauce begins to thicken and coat the back of the spoon (do not allow to boil or the custard may curdle). Immediately strain the sauce into a chilled bowl and leave to cool, stirring occasionally, then chill.

Fruit Sauce
Coulis de Fruit

Makes 300ml/½ pint/1¼ cups
450g/1lb fresh fruit, such as raspberries, strawberries, mangoes, peaches and kiwi fruit
15ml/1 tbsp lemon juice
30–45ml/2–3 tbsp caster sugar
30–45ml/2–3 tbsp fruit brandy or liqueur (optional)

Put the fruit, lemon juice and sugar in a food processor fitted with the metal blade. Process for 1 minute, scraping down the sides once. Press the fruit purée through a fine sieve into a small bowl, stir in the brandy or liqueur, if using, and chill for 1–2 hours until cold.

Chocolate Sauce
Sauce Chocolat

Makes 150ml/¼ pint/⅔ cup
75g/3oz plain chocolate, chopped
90ml/6 tbsp double or whipping cream
15–30ml/1–2 tbsp brandy or liqueur

In a small saucepan, bring the cream to the boil, then remove from the heat. Add the chocolate all at once and stir gently until melted and smooth. Stir in the brandy or liqueur, pour into a sauceboat and keep warm until ready to serve.

FRENCH PASTRY

French pastry has a firm, compact texture, much like shortbread, yet it is extremely light and crisp.

To make pastry the French use a special low-gluten flour. Plain flour produces good results, but better still, use a special cake and pastry flour, or use imported French flour which can be found in speciality shops, or look for low-gluten flour in health food shops.

Unsalted butter produces a crisp texture but, for a more tender result, substitute one part white vegetable cooking fat to three parts butter.

Pastry, especially *pâte sucrée*, can be flavoured with vanilla essence, ground cinnamon, brandy or a liqueur, and ground almonds or hazelnuts can be substituted for part of the flour.

When using a food processor, be careful not to overwork the pastry.

Shortcrust Pastry
Pâte Brisée

Pâte brisée, which means "broken dough", is a versatile basic shortcrust pastry. The ingredients are "broken together" or rubbed in. After the liquid is added, it is kneaded by a process called *fresage*, where the heel of one hand is used to blend the ingredients into a soft pliable dough.

Pâte brisée is suitable for pies, quiches, tarts and tartlets. For sweet recipes a little sugar may be added which gives the pastry extra colour and crispness.

For a 23–25cm/9–10in pie or tart or ten 7.5cm/3in tartlets
175g/6oz/1¼ cups plain flour, plus more if needed
2.5ml/½ tsp salt
5ml/1 tsp caster sugar (optional)
120g/4oz/½ cup unsalted butter, cut into small pieces
45–120ml/3–8 tbsp iced water

In a large bowl, sift together the flour, salt and sugar, if using. Add the butter and rub in using your fingertips, until fine crumbs form. Alternatively, whizz the ingredients in a food processor.

Slowly add the water, mixing until a crumbly dough begins to form; do not overwork the dough or it will be tough. Pinch a piece of dough: it should hold together. If the dough is crumbly add a little more water. If it is wet and sticky, sprinkle over a little more flour.

Turn the dough on to a piece of clear film. Hold the clear film with one hand and use your other hand to push the dough away from you until the dough is smooth and pliable. Flatten the dough to a round and wrap in the clear film. Chill for 2 hours or overnight. Leave to soften for 10 minutes at room temperature before rolling out.

To line a pie tin: lightly butter a 23–25cm/9–10in loose-based pie tin. On a lightly floured surface, roll out the dough to a thickness of about 3mm/⅛in. Gently roll the pastry loosely around the rolling pin, then unroll over the pie tin and gently ease the pastry into the tin, leaving a 2.5cm/1in overhang.

With floured fingers, press the overhang down slightly toward the base of the pan to reinforce the side; roll the rolling pin over the rim to cut off the excess. Press the pastry against the side of the tin to form a rim slightly higher than the side of the tin. If you like, crimp the edge. Prick the base with a fork and chill for at least 1 hour.

Rough-puff Pastry
Pâte demi-feuilletée

Puff pastry, *pâte feuilletée*, is tricky and time-consuming to make – this quick and easy pastry gives a similar feather-light result.

Makes 500g/1¼lb
200g/7oz/⅞ cup cold unsalted butter
200g/7oz/1½ cups superfine plain flour
1.5ml/¼ tsp salt
125ml/4fl oz/½ cup cold water

Cut the butter into 14 pieces and place in the freezer for 30 minutes, or until very firm.

Put the flour and salt into a food processor and pulse to combine. Add the butter and pulse three or four times; there should still be large lumps of butter. Run the machine for 5 seconds while pouring the water through the feed tube, then stop the machine. The dough should look curdy. Tip the mixture on to a lightly floured, cool work surface and gather into a flat ball – you should still be able to see pieces of butter. If the butter is soft, chill the dough for 30 minutes or longer.

Roll out the dough on a floured surface to a 40 × 15cm/16 × 6in rectangle. Fold in thirds, bringing one end down to cover the middle, then fold the other end over it, like folding a letter. Roll out again to a long rectangle and fold again the same way. Chill the dough for at least 30 minutes.

Roll and fold twice more, then chill and fold the dough, well wrapped, for at least 30 minutes, or for up to 3 days, before using.

Cook's tip

The richer the pastry dough, the harder it is to handle. However, if rolling the dough becomes too difficult, simply press it into the tin with your hands, patching any cracks or holes with extra dough.

Rich Shortcrust Pastry
Pâte Sucrée

Pâte sucré, sweet pastry, is a type of *pâte brisée* with sugar and egg yolks added. Sugar makes the dough more crumbly, or "sandy" and in fact it is often called *pâte sablée*, or "sandy pastry". It is somewhat difficult to handle, but is especially delicious for fruit tarts.

For a 23–25cm/9–10in tart or ten 7.5cm/3in tartlets
150g/5oz/1 cup plain flour, plus more if needed
2.5ml/½ tsp salt
45–60ml/3–4 tbsp icing sugar
120g/4oz/½ cup unsalted butter, cut into small pieces
2 egg yolks beaten with 30ml/2 tbsp iced water and 2.5ml/½ tsp vanilla essence (optional)

In a food processor fitted with the metal blade, process the flour, salt, sugar and butter for 15–20 seconds, until fine crumbs form. Remove the cover and pour in the beaten egg yolk and water mixture. Pulse the machine just until the dough begins to stick together. Do not allow the dough to form a ball or the pastry will be tough. If the dough appears dry, add a little water and pulse until the dough just holds together. Tip the dough onto a piece of clear film and, holding the film with one hand, use your other hand to push the dough away from you until it is smooth and pliable. Flatten the dough into a round and wrap in the film. Chill for at least 2 hours.

Glossary

The following terms are frequently used in French cooking. In the recipes we have tried to reduce the use of technical terms by describing the procedures, but understanding these words is helpful.

BAIN-MARIE: a baking tin or dish set in a roasting tin or saucepan of water. It allows the food to cook indirectly and protects delicate foods; a double boiler is also a kind of water bath, or *bain-marie*.

BAKE BLIND: to bake or partially bake a pastry case before adding a filling, usually done to prevent the filling making the pastry soggy.

BASTE: to moisten food with fat or cooking juices while it is cooking.

BEURRE MANIÉ: equal parts of butter and flour blended to a paste and whisked into simmering cooking liquid for thickening after cooking is completed.

BLANCH: to immerse vegetables and sometimes fruit in boiling water in order to loosen skin, remove bitterness or saltiness or preserve colour.

BOIL: to keep liquid at a temperature producing bubbles that break the surface.

BOUQUET GARNI: a bunch of herbs, usually including a bay leaf, thyme sprigs and parsley stalks, used to impart flavour during cooking, often tied for easy removal.

CLARIFY: to make an opaque liquid clear and remove impurities; stocks are clarified using egg white, butter by skimming.

COULIS: a purée, usually fruit or vegetable, sometimes sweetened or flavoured with herbs, but not thickened, used as a sauce.

CROÛTONS: small crisp pieces of fried or baked crustless bread.

DEGLAZE: to dissolve the sediment from the bottom of a cooking pan by adding liquid and bringing to the boil, stirring. This is then used as the basis for a sauce or gravy.

DEGREASE: to remove fat from cooking liquid, either by spooning off after it has risen to the top or by chilling until the fat is congealed and lifting it off.

DICE: to cut food into square uniform pieces about 5mm/¼in.

EMULSIFY: to combine two usually incompatible ingredients until smooth by mixing rapidly while slowly adding one to the other so they are held in suspension.

FOLD: to combine ingredients, using a large rubber spatula or metal spoon, by cutting down through the centre of the bowl, then along the side and up to the top in a semicircular motion; it is important not to deflate or over-work ingredients while folding.

FOOD MILL *(mouli-légumes)*: tool for puréeing found in most French kitchens which strains as it purées.

GLAZE: to coat food with a sweet or savoury mixture producing a shiny surface when set.

GRATINÉ: to give a browned, crisp surface to a baked dish.

HERBES DE PROVENCE: a mixture of aromatic dried herbs, which grow wild in Provence, usually thyme, marjoram, oregano and summer savory.

INFUSE: to extract flavour by steeping in hot liquid.

JULIENNE: thin matchstick pieces of vegetables, fruit or other food.

MACERATE: to bathe fruit in liquid to soften and flavour it.

PAPILLOTE: a greased non-stick baking paper or foil parcel, traditionally heart-shaped, enclosing food for cooking.

PAR-BOIL: to partially cook food by boiling.

POACH: to cook food, submerged in liquid, by gentle simmering.

REDUCE: to boil a liquid for the purpose of concentrating the flavour by evaporation.

ROUX: a cooked mixture of fat and flour used to thicken liquids such as soups, stews and sauces.

SAUTÉ: to fry quickly in a small amount of fat over a high heat.

SCALD: to heat liquid, usually milk, until bubbles begin to form around the edge.

SCORE: to make shallow incisions to aid penetration of heat or liquid or for decoration.

SIMMER: to keep a liquid at just below boiling point so the liquid just trembles.

SKIM: to remove froth or scum from the surface of stocks etc.

STEAM: moist heat cooking method by which vaporized liquid cooks food in a closed container.

SWEAT: to cook gently in fat, covered, so liquid in ingredients is rendered to steam them.

INDEX

H

I

J

K

L

M

N

O

P

T

U

V

W

Y

Notes

NOTES

Notes

Notes

Notes

Notes

NOTES

Notes